Death, Gender and Ethnicity

Death, Gender and Ethnicity examines the ways in which gender and ethnicity shape the experiences of dying and bereavement, taking as its focus the diversity of modes through which the universal event of death is encountered. As well as offering an extensive critical review of existing work on death, gender and ethnicity, the book addresses such topics as:

- stillbirth
- gendered parental bereavement through the death of a child
- gendered social construction of mourning and grief
- disruption of gender stereotypes at the time of death
- media treatment of the violent deaths of young women
- provision of palliative care for ethnic minorities
- issues facing immigrant ethnic minorities.

Finally it asks about the value of a postmodern approach to the diversity and indeed fragmentation of human experience which currently constitutes death and dying.

Drawing on a range of case studies, *Death, Gender and Ethnicity* seeks to develop a more sensitive theoretical approach which may not only inform future studies in this area but lead to the revision of some classic material.

David Field is Lecturer in Sociology at the University of Plymouth, **Jenny Hockey** is Lecturer in Health Studies at the University of Hull and **Neil Small** is Senior Research Fellow at the Trent Palliative Care Centre, Sheffield.

Death, Gender and Ethnicity

Edited by David Field,
Jenny Hockey and Neil Small

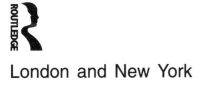

London and New York

First published 1997
by Routledge
11 New Fetter Lane, London EC4P 4EE

Simultaneously published in the USA and Canada
by Routledge
29 West 35th Street, New York, NY 10001

© 1997 David Field, Jenny Hockey and Neil Small, selection and
editorial matter; individual chapters, the contributors

Typeset in Times Ten by Florencetype Ltd, Stoodleigh, Devon

Printed and bound in Great Britain by
Redwood Books, Trowbridge, Wiltshire

British Library Cataloguing in Publication Data
A catalogue record for this book is available from the British Library

Library of Congress Cataloging in Publication Data
Death, gender and ethnicity / edited by David Field, Jenny Hockey,
and Neil Small.
    p. cm.
   Includes bibliographical references and index.
   1. Death–Social aspects–Great Britain. 2. Bereavement–Great
Britain. 3. Terminal care–Great Britain. 4. Sex role–Great Britain.
5. Ethnicity–Great Britain. 6. Minorities–Great Britain. 7. Great
Britain–Social conditions. I. Field, David. II. Hockey,
Jennifer Lorna. III Small, Neil.
HQ1073.5.G7D425 1997
306.9–dc20   96–33438
                                                                CIP

ISBN 0–415–14678–X (hbk)
       0–415–14679–8 (pbk)

Contents

Illustrations

FIGURES

TABLES

Notes on contributors

Pamela Dawson is Bromley Hospital's bereavement co-ordinator. She previously worked as a freelance bereavement consultant and is interested in the role of self-help in bereavement.

David Field is now Lecturer in Sociology at the University of Plymouth having previously been at the Universities of Ulster and Leicester. He has been working in the sociology of death and dying since 1979 and has written on nursing the dying, education for terminal care and various aspects of hospice care. He is the author of *Nursing the Dying* (Routledge, 1989).

Yasmin Gunaratnam is presently a research student at the London School of Economics. She has been involved in research and community development work around equal opportunities issues since 1986 and has published work for the King's Fund Centre on social care and health service development.

Elizabeth Hallam is an anthropologist lecturing in the Cultural History Group at the University of Aberdeen. Her research addresses historical anthropology, gender and cultural representations in Britain and Europe.

Jenny Hockey is an anthropologist lecturing in Health Studies in the Department of Social Policy at the University of Hull. She is author of *Experiences of Death: An Anthropological Account* (University of Edinburgh Press 1990) and, with A. James, *Growing Up and Growing Old. Ageing and Dependency in the Life Course* (Sage 1993).

Gerdien Jonker is a historian of religion at the University of Groningen, Holland, and is a stipendiate within the field of religious anthropology of the Berlin Science Council. She has published widely on the topic of burial. Her present research concentrates on burial practices and forms of social memory in migrant communities.

Jane Littlewood is Senior Lecturer in Social Policy and Politics at Goldsmiths' University of London. She is the author of *Aspects of Grief: Bereavement in Adult Life* (Routledge 1992). Her research interests include gender and death, widowhood and bereavement.

Alice Lovell is a Senior Lecturer in the Department of Education, Politics and Social Science at South Bank University, London. She has published work on maternity issues including pregnancy ending in miscarriage, stillbirth and early neo-natal death.

Mike Pickering is Lecturer in Communication and Media Studies at Loughborough University. He is the author of *Everyday Culture* (Open University Press 1987) and *Acts of Supremacy* (Manchester University Press 1991). His relevant research interests include the portrayal of death, dying and bereavement by the media and popular culture.

Gordon Riches is Senior Lecturer in Sociology and Counselling Research Methods at the University of Derby. His research interests lie in the field of critical life events and their impact on identity transformation.

Chris Smaje is a lecturer in sociology at the University of Surrey. Previously he was a health policy analyst at the King's Fund Institute in London. His current research interests are in health and health care of people from minority ethnic groups and in the sociology of race and ethnicity. He is the author of *Health, Race and Ethnicity: Making Sense of the Evidence* (King's Fund 1995).

Neil Small is a Senior Research Fellow at the Trent Palliative Care Centre, Sheffield. His current research interests include the history of hospices and AIDS. He is the author of *Politics and Planning in the NHS* (Open University Press 1989) and *AIDS: the Challenge* (Avebury 1993).

Neil Thompson is Professor of Social Work, Staffordshire University. He is the author of seven books, his most recent being *Age and Dignity: Working with Older People* (Arena 1995).

Tony Walter is Lecturer in Sociology at the University of Reading. He is the author of *Funerals and How to Improve Them* (Hodder 1990) and *The Revival of Death* (Routledge 1995).

Introduction

The themes addressed in this volume – death, gender and ethnicity – have until recently been pursued as largely separate areas of study. Yet, as the material presented indicates, gender and ethnicity are in no way set aside at the time of death or during bereavement. They remain salient features of social identity during the last stages of life, just as they do in its first moments. Indeed, if anything their significance intensifies, as evidenced in the case of shocked family mourners whose recently deceased grandmother, Olive, had her social identity radically transformed by a tiny slip of the minister's pen. This resulted in the entire congregation being invited to bid farewell to their dear departed *brother,* 'Clive'.

The contributors to this volume are sociologists and anthropologists with a shared research interest in death, dying and bereavement. Together, they provide a series of accounts of the interrelationship of death, gender and ethnicity. While death and dying have been a focus for research among theorists and practitioners from many fields, it is timely and indeed appropriate that social scientists for whom social differences are stock-in-trade should be questioning a tendency to treat death as if its universality somehow transcended rather than revealed such differences.

This book is the second to emerge from the annual symposia on Social Aspects of Death, Dying and Bereavement. With a strong sociological orientation, this volume is offered as a development of themes and issues raised in the first of these, *The Sociology of Death*, edited by David Clark. The majority of the chapters in this book were first presented as oral papers to the fourth and fifth annual symposia held in November 1994 and November 1995. The remaining chapters were specially commissioned for the book. Other papers from these symposia have been published elsewhere. We are grateful to the Medical Sociology Group of the British Sociological Association for giving financial support to these meetings.

In the opening chapter the editors provide an overview of the available material about death, gender and ethnicity in modern Britain, drawing particularly upon research in the sociology of health and illness. They also address the more general sociological and anthropological analyses of the place of gender and ethnicity in modern society. The aim of the chapter is to provide an empirical and theoretical context for the chapters which follow.

The next three chapters examine ways in which the experience of loss after a death is shaped by gender. Alice Lovell highlights the gendered nature of the institutions which frame the death of a baby, either *in utero* or around the time of a birth. Such losses tend to be undervalued and unattended to by others. When women struggle to come to terms with the loss of a child who might have been, they find the nature of their loss, and indeed of the child's identity, defined by the patriarchal frameworks of medicine and religion. Gordon Riches and Pam Dawson shift from the gendering of institutional contexts to the personal contexts of loss. They offer a critique of stereotypical models of gendered coping styles after the death of a child, arguing that not all men are strong and silent and that not all women are brought to an emotional and practical standstill. Moreover, individuals do not consistently adhere to the same 'coping style' at all times. Riches and Dawson explore the influence of socio-cultural factors upon couples' patterns of grieving and the wider structural relations within which discourses for the interpretation of their loss become available. Neil Thompson acknowledges death as an event which can throw gendered stereotypes into problematic relief. His chapter examines the social construction of mourning, maintaining that emotional responses which accord with traditional notions of masculinity, such as anger, are marginalised within conventional accounts of healthy grieving. Thompson argues both for a recognition of a broader range of emotional responses to loss and for a more balanced approach which allows both women and men access to a range of emotional and practical coping strategies.

The critique of a stereotypically gendered pattern of mourning is echoed in the next two chapters. Jenny Hockey compares the way women actually behave in public after a death with the ways in which their grieving is represented in paintings, photographs and written accounts. She argues that the predominance of representations of women grieving openly does not match the public behaviour required of modern women. Such representations provide members of a patriarchal society with a way of contemplating the possibility of death at the safe distance of a *woman's* body. Hockey concludes by asking how women themselves might read such images and narratives and how, as forms of representation, they might influence what women actually think and do. Elizabeth Hallam pursues this question in a chapter which examines the ways in which a life crisis event such as a mortal illness can open out personal and social relations to critical reflection. Bringing an anthropological perspective to bear on historical material from the early modern period in England, she examines another set of representations – engravings, household manuals and sermons – which affirm the subordination of women within 'orderly' household-based gender relations. These she then contrasts with women's own representations of themselves in the accounts of female witnesses from the Canturbury church courts, arguing that they constitute a renegotiation of existing gendered hierarchies.

In contrast to the focus on the gendered nature of mourning, Mike Pickering, Jane Littlewood and Tony Walter examine the way the gender of the deceased is depicted in the tabloid press. Like Jenny Hockey, they examine a set of representations – front-page reports of the violent deaths of young women. These are deaths which directly challenge the conventional moral order. Through presenting something of the disturbing style of the papers they are analysing, Pickering, Littlewood and Walter convey the alternation between initially sensationalist reporting using contra-intuitive depictions of gender and the subsequent use of 'moral tales' to reassert normal values.

Three chapters focus upon difference grounded in ethnicity. Chris Smaje and David Field address the perception that members of ethnic minority groups in modern Britain are under-using palliative care services. They provide a framework for examining this issue, discussing the need and demand for services, the knowledge of and attitudes towards services and the way services are provided. The tendency for service provision to be guided by the use of 'cultural checklists' is viewed with caution and they stress the need to think both structurally and culturally about the ways in which services may or may not be reaching different groups. Yasmin Gunaratnam develops the critique of the use of 'cultural checklists' or 'factfiles' to understand the needs of individuals from minority ethnic groups. The strong tendency to reify cultures and religious practices means that much of their fluidity or indeed unruliness is lost. Further, the needs of individuals can be overlooked in the attempt to observe cultural requirements. Such an approach also fails to address professional and structural power relations. Moreover, by taking ethnic minority culture as the focus rather than the dominant white culture it fails to address fundamental issues of racism and discrimination.

The dynamic and problematic nature of social change among migrant groups is central to the chapter by Gerdien Jonker. Social identity is at risk among migrant Greek and Turkish communities in Berlin, with the relevance of ethnic identity intensifying at the time of death. Her chapter details the issues faced by members of these communities when seeking to dispose of their dead in a way which allows for the re-membering of collective identity.

Neil Small concludes the collection with a review of theoretical approaches to understanding death and difference. Taking a critical stance to the longer established approaches he argues that a postmodern analysis has much to offer. The identification of broad historical periods or generally applicable stages of development does not adequately reflect the nature of the social and individual encounters with death. Further, separate consideration needs to be given to death, dying and the dead.

This book presents a range of theoretically informed substantive analyses of death and social difference which both reflect current directions in research and writing addressed to death and social difference and suggest further areas for investigation. It will, we hope, stimulate further work looking at these important aspects of modern British society.

David Field, Jenny Hockey, Neil Small

Chapter 1

Making sense of difference
Death, gender and ethnicity in modern Britain

David Field, Jenny Hockey and Neil Small

INTRODUCTION

Death has often been represented as the 'great leveller' who returns both monarch and beggar to a common dust. As such this image has been used both to diminish the political zeal of those who would reform earthly inequalities (Illich 1977) as well as to undermine the power and status of those who assume positions of authority. This volume demonstrates that while the image of death as the great leveller may have powerful political and religious overtones, it is a far from accurate representation. Worldly inequalities are in no way levelled at the time of death but persist, permeating every aspect of death and dying. The timing, place, manner and social implications of an individual's death are shaped by their social position in the society. Age, ethnicity, gender, social class and sexuality all profoundly affect the ways people experience death, dying and bereavement. Such forms of social differentiation should not be seen as fixed elements of a reified 'society' which bear down upon us in life and in death (West and Zimmerman 1991) for they are produced precisely through the ways in which we live our lives and encounter our deaths. Rather than being unaffected by them, differences and diversity in the manner and social implications of dying are both constituted by and constitutive of such social identities. This volume takes gender and ethnicity as its areas of interest but many of the chapters reveal the ways in which these are themselves cross-cut by other forms of social identity and social differentiation such as age and social class.

The ways in which a society deals with death reveal a great deal about that society, especially about the ways in which

Table 1.1 Selected causes of death in the United Kingdom: by sex and age, 1992

	Under 1	1–14	15–39	40–64	65–79	80 and over	All ages
Males (percentages)							
Infectious diseases	4.8	5.1	1.7	0.7	0.4	0.3	0.5
Cancer	1.0	17.3	13.5	34.3	31.6	20.9	28.0
Circulatory diseases*	4.0	4.0	10.7	43.8	48.2	47.3	45.5
Respiratory diseases	11.9	5.1	3.4	5.3	10.3	16.7	11.1
Injury and poisoning	17.6	34.2	52.7	6.6	1.3	1.2	4.2
All other causes	60.8	34.2	18.0	9.3	8.3	13.5	10.7
All males (=100%) (thousands)	1.1	1.3	10.2	58.4	140.9	94.9	306.6
Females (percentages)							
Infectious diseases	4.3	4.8	1.9	0.6	0.4	0.3	0.4
Cancer	1.5	18.0	33.3	51.8	30.6	14.2	24.3
Circulatory diseases*	5.6	4.4	10.7	26.7	46.6	52.3	46.6
Respiratory diseases	10.6	5.6	3.4	5.8	9.2	13.7	11.1
Injury and poisoning	16.8	25.8	28.9	4.0	1.4	1.4	2.2
All other causes	61.3	41.4	21.8	11.1	11.8	18.0	15.3
All females (=100%) (thousands)	0.7	0.9	4.8	36.4	111.5	169.9	324.2

Notes: *Includes heart attacks and strokes
Source: Social Trends, 1994. (Reproduced by permission of the Controller of HMSO and the Office for National Statistics.)

individuals are valued. In this introductory chapter we provide a selective overview of the place of gender and ethnicity in modern society in order to provide a context for the chapters which follow. We summarise the available material about mortality, gender and ethnicity, drawing particularly upon research in the sociology of health and illness. The relative absence of discussion and analysis of gender and ethnicity in the now extensive sociological literature about death, dying and bereavement in modern societies follows a similar pattern to the initial neglect and subsequent concern about these topics in sociology. We suggest that, with respect to gender, the insights of feminism have much to offer. We conclude our introduction with a brief consideration of the contribution of more general theoretical conceptualisations in sociology to the developing interest in the ways in which gender and ethnicity are related to death and dying in modern societies.

DEATH, ILLNESS AND GENDER

There are a number of striking differences in mortality and illness between men and women in Britain and other industrial societies. In all such societies at all ages the death rates of females are lower than those for males. The patterning of death is also different (Table 1.1). Men are more likely to experience and die from cardiovascular conditions (though these are important among women), cancers (except breast and cervix) and bronchitis. These are the major causes of death in our society. Especially large differences appear where individual acts are the cause of death. Males, especially young men, are more likely to die from suicide, homicide and accidents. Men are also much more likely to die in war, whereas women stand a greater risk of injury and death from domestic violence (Dobash and Dobash 1992). In terms of illness, women report more acute illness, make more physician visits, are more likely to be hospitalised (even when excluding childbirth and reproductive admissions) and consume more medicines than men (Blaxter 1990). The picture for chronic illness and disability is less clear cut, but again in the UK women generally have higher rates than men.

A number of empirical and conceptual explanations of the gender differences outlined above have been advanced (Clarke 1983, Nathanson 1977, Verbrugge 1985). There may be some influence from artefactual and definitional factors. There is some evidence that gender influences diagnosis and treatment, with doctors and nurses responding differentially to clients along gender lines. Two examples are the greater likelihood of women being diagnosed as mentally disordered and men being more likely to be candidates for heart surgery. However, it seems that clear differences exist between males and females with respect to mortality and physical morbidity.

Another source of explanation relates to biological differences in the susceptibility to death and disease (Waldron 1983). For example, genetic factors have been linked to higher rates of miscarriage and infant mortality of male babies and to the greater likelihood of women developing breast cancer. This latter is also linked to the female reproductive system. Differing hormonal balances between the sexes are thought to be linked to a variety of conditions, although outside the realm of reproduction there do not appear to be significant consequences for overall gender differences in mortality and illness. Where biological effects have been established they have mainly referred to within-sex differences rather than to between-sex differences.

A number of writers have argued that gender differences in death and illness are the product of differing behaviour patterns and styles of life between males and females. That is, that they are linked to gender roles within the society. Such explanations refer to two aspects – differential risks of illness between males and females and differences in the health and illness behaviour between the genders. The greater levels of fatal diseases among men do seem to be related to behaviour and environment, especially at work. It is suggested that male gender roles both expose men to greater risks and restrain men from 'giving in' to illness by restricting their activity and use of health services. By contrast, it is argued that female gender roles both expose women to less risk and permit (and possibly encourage) them to be more responsive to illness and to seek medical help. Help-seeking and 'emotionality' are part of conventional ideas about female roles, whereas males are expected to restrain their expression of emotion, to deny illness, and to be more reluctant to seek help from others. Thus, help-seeking (and help-giving) are congruent with idealised female gender roles in our society. It has been suggested that as females come to behave as males (note the assumption!) in their work and leisure activities, then their patterns and rates of mortality (and morbidity) will approximate the male patterns and rates. For example, the convergence in the levels of smoking between males and females is expected to result in increased levels of lung cancer among women, even though women rather than men are subject to pressure not to endanger the health of their children – born and unborn – through smoking.

The main weakness of these explanations is that it they tend to address the effects of gender largely in isolation from other social variables. For example, social class is known to be an important determinant of the likelihood of death and the prevalence of disease. Although females, as a category, live longer than males, males from the upper social classes will live longer than women from the lower social classes and are likely to experience less ill health. Social class influences illness-related gender behaviour in important ways which are still to be unravelled. Age is another important influence. The detailed analysis of gender and health status by Macintyre *et al.* (1996) confirms earlier reservations that it is misleading to assert that at all ages women are sicker than men (Clarke 1983). They conclude that both age and disease condition exert important influences on gender-specific levels of chronic illness.

A final set of explanations for gender differences in health and illness draws upon feminist analyses of the oppressive role of patriarchy in shaping the experiences of women in our society. Within the sociology of health and illness literature such work has largely focused upon relationships between female patients and male practitioners, especially within 'reproductive encounters' (e.g. Martin 1987; Scully 1980) and so does not bear as directly upon the issues of death, dying and bereavement which are our focus here. However, the broader issues raised by feminism provide an appropriate and useful way to begin our consideration of relationships between death and gender.

GENDER DIFFERENCES, DEATH, DYING AND BEREAVEMENT

Writings about death and dying have either generalised about broad trends (e.g. Ariès 1981, Blauner 1966) and recurring experiences (e.g. Glaser and Strauss 1965) or assumed that there are no significant gender differences. Observations that, for example, adult men of working age receive greater attention from hospital staff and are more likely to be told their terminal diagnosis than women, especially old women, were seldom integrated into wider theoretical explanations about gender differences in modern society. In short male deaths set the agenda for discussion and research, albeit in an unaware and unreflective manner. For example, the concern with the supposed fear of death in modern societies (Gorer 1965, Kellehear 1984, Sontag 1979) has been dominated by consideration of cancer, heart disease and latterly AIDS (Sontag 1989). For each of these, the research agendas have been dominated by male concerns. Although cancer affects significant numbers of women it is only in recent years that sustained research focusing on breast and cervical cancers has been apparent, and despite the growing number of women who are victims of heart disease there is still little research into the experiences of women suffering heart attack and heart failure.

A more striking contrast can be found in the discrepancy between the extensive literature about the 'fearful deaths' from cancer and AIDS with the relative neglect of miscarriage and stillbirths – fearful and feared deaths which affect many women. It is suggested that in the UK around 7,000 babies a year are born dead or die in the first week after birth (Rajan and Oakley 1993). In our society it appears to be women who bear the brunt of dealing with such 'tabooed deaths' both as victims and as carers of the victims. The attitudes of health staff may contribute to the difficulties some parents may experience in handling their sense of guilt, especially as some of the medical explanations for early deaths may reinforce individualistic explanations and victim-blaming tendencies (Lovell 1983 and in this volume).

Reactions to such early deaths are rooted in the ways in which societies value different categories of people. In pre-industrial societies there were high rates of death at the start of life, and such life was not highly valued. Entry to the social world was marked by survival until a ceremony of naming (e.g. baptism) took place, at which point the infant became socially recognised as a member of the community. Deaths prior to this time were scarcely recognised and infants and stillbirths did not receive full funeral rites (Hertz 1960). In modern society, where it can be presumed that infants will live and there are comparatively few births, early deaths are traumatic and potentially threatening; with most deaths occurring in old age it is now the deaths of the old which are undervalued. However, in modern society the ways in which the experiences of women with deaths at both the start and end of life are ignored and disregarded reflect the lower esteem placed upon women throughout the life course and in most areas of social life. The grief of women whose children have died either *in utero* or around the time of birth is made illegitimate through bureaucratic and ritual procedures which deny the social identity and meaning of the dead child or of 'failed' mothers.

The neglect of gender as an important substantive or explanatory category in the literature about modern death, dying and bereavement is similar to the general neglect of gender within academic circles prior to the 1960s. Second-wave feminism introduced the concept of gender into academic agendas. It highlighted and problematised gender issues, and particularly the subordinate social position of women, as reflected in research and writing within a whole range of academic disciplines. On the academic front feminism was a movement which called for more than just the inclusion of women in the academic community and in research studies. The political struggles of the late 1960s engendered not only activism oriented towards cultural and social change but also intellectual debate aimed at transforming the theoretical (masculinist) perspectives underpinning many academic disciplines. Thus the activists of the late 1960s fought around issues which, by the late 1970s, were being addressed by sociologists and a range of other social theorists and which demanded a reconceptualisation of the nature of knowledge itself. Core areas of attention were the documentation of gender-based social inequalities; the development of theories to explain women's subordination (focusing on aspects of society such as capitalism, patriarchy, the family, language, and women's 'natural' reproductive roles); the problematising of academic knowledge which rendered invisible the interests and experiences of women; and debates about the nature of gender itself.

Oakley (1972) defined gender as the social elaboration of biological sex differences. Thus sex referred to bodily difference and gender referred to social difference. This distinction underpinned research within anthropology and sociology which undermined naturalist arguments about women's place within society, and indeed gave such work its political edge. For example, naturalist arguments saw women's social position as wives and mothers and their 'nurturant' and emotionally expressive behaviour as based upon their distinctive biological capacity to bear children and to lactate. Once gender came to be clearly conceptualised as socially constructed rather than 'naturally' or 'biologically given', it was amenable to social change. Later theorists have problematised the straightforward distinction between the endowments of 'nature' and the constructions of 'society' (Grosz 1994). Instead, they argued, the body itself and the differences between women's and men's bodies, are 'mapped' and known through culturally specific gendered knowledges. This is a deeper critique of the accepted sexual order which claims that differences between 'men' and 'women' are produced within discourse, within the flow of daily thought and practice. An individual's gender is no mere cultural overlay which encompasses innate sexual differences; instead it is constituted through unfolding performances of femininity and masculinity which are predicated upon everyday taken-for-granted naturalist assumptions about the individual's 'sex'. Such assumptions, however, are profoundly cultural. Thus, the ways in which the body itself is perceived and experienced are gendered (Butler 1993). This includes, of course, the dying body.

One manifestation of gender differentiation within death, dying and bereavement concerns the area of care. Walter (1993) points out that the medicalisation of death in the eighteenth century saw a 'de-feminisation' of what had previously been an area of female control – the dying and dead body. In subordinate roles of informal carers and nurses, women nonetheless continued to undertake the more menial tasks of care. For example, the care of the dead body, which had come to be seen as distasteful by the end of the nineteenth century, constituted the one area of work remaining to the 'handywomen' who had acted as both layers-out and midwives in Coventry up until the 1920s (Adams 1993). Nurses (predominantly female) are the main group performing such bodily care in modern society although funeral directors (predominantly male) may also be involved. Women have continued to meet the need for care in more mundane ways both as unpaid 'lay' carers of the chronically ill and dying (Ungerson 1987) and as the main 'front-line' carers in the health service. In both roles the practical and emotional labour of women is central to the care of dying people, although the latter may be undervalued and overlooked.

Women are also central to the process of making sense of death. Cline (1995) argues that 'lifting the taboo' on death, dying and bereavement is something which women in particular can and should achieve. Indeed she argues that women rather than men suffer as a result of the 'taboo' in that they are charged with the tasks of nurturing and nursing, both of which make them vulnerable to suffering. In this volume Neil Thompson maintains that the grieving of males is hindered by negative views of masculine responses such as anger, and argues for a more flexible expression of emotion. Gordon Riches and Pam Dawson in their chapter challenge the conventional wisdom about gendered responses to grief in their examination of the ways fathers and mothers try to make sense of the death of their child.

Within the literature on death women have often represented the unacknowledged empirical basis of theorisation. The most obvious example of this is in the area of grief and bereavement where married women's grief following the death of a husband has been extensively documented. While women's grief has constituted core interview data, the gendered nature of this material becomes invisible when used as a basis for theorisation. The influential work of Parkes (1972) and Bowlby (1981) drew on studies of widows in order to develop models of bereavement which were then used to frame bereavement as a universal rather than culturally variable experience. It is plausible to argue that, as a result, while positing a general model which is equally applicable to men and women, their theories simply reflect the experiences of married women. For example, the notion that bereavement can be seen as a loss of the self most closely corresponds to the experiences of widows whose self-identity derived from the man they married, whose name they took, whose domestic life they serviced and upon whose income they depended.

More recently the deaths of women have come to attract considerable attention, as Bronfen (1992) and Pickering, Littlewood and Walter (this volume) indicate. Here again, however, they are highlighted according to their positioning within a patriarchal society. In Bronfen's view, it is the otherness or alterity of women which brings them, once dead, into view. She argues that within a patriarchal society which would deny death, its inevitable occurrence makes such repressions impossible to sustain. However, by localising what is a universal aspect of human life at the site of the woman's body, death can be acknowledged and indeed contemplated, but at a distance from the male self. Littlewood, Pickering and Walter show how the contemporary visibility of dead women, in the form of young victims of sexual attack, also serves to reinforce existing patriarchal structures through what they call 'moral'

Table 1.2   Place of death, England and Wales, 1992

Place of death	Male	Female	All
NHS Hospital	56%	53%	54.5%
Communal establishments*	13%	25%	18.5%
Own home	25%	19%	22%
Other	5%	3%	4%
Number of deaths	271,732	286,581	558,313

Note: *Includes hospice deaths, which account for approximately 4 per cent of all deaths
Percentages do not sum to 100 due to rounding
Source: Mortality Statistics, General: Review of the Registrar General on Death in England and Wales 1992, (1994) Office of Population Census and Surveys, London: HMSO, Table 7

tales. As Hockey's chapter in this volume argues, women have been made to stand for the Other, whether in grief or in death, and as such they provide a means of safely contemplating the ephemeral nature not only of human ties but also of human life itself. Hallam's chapter in this volume takes us further. Drawing on historical material she describes differences between representations of women and their own accounts to identify a means of examining personal and social relations in the context of life-crisis events.

Practically there are important differences between men and women in terms of how they die (i.e. the cause of death) and where they die (the place of death) (Field and James 1993, Seale and Cartwright 1994). We have already noted the relative lack of research interest about female causes of death. Table 1.2 shows that men are more likely to die in their own homes than are women and that women are almost twice as likely to die in 'communal institutions'. That is, they are more likely to die in nursing and residential homes. This is partly a product of the greater longevity of women in our society. Although there has been research into the experiences of dying in hospitals and hospices this has rarely paid much attention to gender differences. With respect to deaths in the home, it is well known that the gender differences in the patterns of care-giving which have been demonstrated elsewhere prevail. Female relatives (spouses and daughters) provide the bulk of the 'lay' care of the dying and where the husband is the main carer he is more likely to receive support in his caring from formal and lay sources. There is little research into the experience of dying in communal institutions, where the majority of women over the age of 85 will die. In one of the few such studies Hockey (1989) notes that women's 'self-identity' is put at greater risk than men's once they become dependent upon the care of other women.

While comparatively little research attention has been paid to women's experiences of death and dying, women have made a major contribution to the ways in which modern societies conceptualise and care for the dying and the bereaved. Despite the shift of the place of death from the domestic home where women played a central part to the hospital where medical men exercised direction and control, from the late 1950s onwards there has been a 're-feminisation' of the care of the dying and the bereaved. This has in part been a reaction against the 'medicalisation' of death (Blauner 1966, Illich 1977, Field 1994) and has been associated with the growth of the death-awareness movement in the USA (Lofland 1978) and in Britain with the growth of the modern hospice. In this context, women have not only been active but also found prominence as charismatic leaders (James and Field 1992). Elizabeth Kubler-Ross (1970) provided a seminal account of psychological reactions to dying which has had an international impact both on the ways in which the experience of dying is conceptualised and on the ways in which doctors, nurses and other health and social care staff are trained. Cicely Saunders has had a similarly powerful international impact with her emphasis upon meeting the needs of the dying in a holistic way and her practical demonstration of how this can be achieved through hospice care. Cruse – Bereavement Care, the British national organisation for bereaved people, provided initially for the social and emotional needs of widows and was founded in 1959 by a widow, Margaret Torrie.

DEATH, ILLNESS AND ETHNICITY

Discussion and debate about the nature, basis and meaning of ethnicity have been extensive and ongoing (Jenkins 1994, Lal 1983, Rex and Mason 1986, Smaje 1996). However, for our purposes it is sufficient to note that ethnicity is generally agreed to refer to a collective awareness of shared origins of descent and is a relational concept referring to a sense of identity as a member of a group and to difference from others. Although ethnicity is

Table 1.3   Patterns of mortality among minority ethnic groups

AFRICAN	*Higher death rates*: strokes, high blood pressure, violence/accidents, maternal deaths, tuberculosis
	Lower death rates: bronchitis
SOUTH ASIAN	*Higher death rates*: heart disease, diabetes, violence/accidents, tuberculosis
	Lower death rates: bronchitis, certain cancers
CARIBBEAN	*Higher death rates*: strokes, high blood pressure violence/accidents, diabetes, maternal deaths.
	Lower death rates: bronchitis

Source: Whitehead (Townsend, Davidson and Whitehead 1988)

often attributed on the basis of physical characteristics such as skin colour, it is not founded on any credible biologically differentiated 'races'. Ethnicity, like gender, is a socially constructed resource based upon religion, language and nationality.

In practice ethnicity in modern Britain is attributed upon the basis of 'country of origin'. Using this definition in the 1991 census 5.5 per cent of the population were defined as belonging to minority ethnic groups. The two largest aggregates were 'black' (1.6 per cent) from the West Indies or Africa, and 'Indian' (1.5 per cent) either directly or indirectly from the Indian sub-continent (more frequently referred to as 'South Asian'). Many members of minority ethnic groups were born in the UK (over 50 per cent of 'blacks' and 40 per cent of 'South Asians'). Indeed, 80 per cent of minority ethnic group members under the age of 25 were born in Britain, compared with 15 per cent of those over 25 (*General Household Survey* 1992).

The evidence about ethnic differences in health and health care in modern Britain is less extensive and well founded than that already discussed with respect to gender. Smaje (1995) provides an authoritative and detailed review of this evidence which informs our discussion here. One of the major difficulties is that much of the available evidence refers to migrants to Britain. Looking at overall mortality rates, Black and South Asian immigrants currently have overall mortality rates slightly higher than, but not dissimilar to, those of the British-born population, although immigrants from Ireland have much higher death rates. Within this pattern there are significant differences (Table 1.3). For example, while there has been an overall decline in infant mortality for all minority ethnic groups from the mid-1970s, these still have rates above the national average. Caribbean- and Pakistani-born mothers have particularly high rates of infant mortality whereas mothers born in Bangladesh and in East Africa now have infant mortality rates below those of UK-born mothers (Table 1.4).

A look at the major causes of death and illness in the UK shows that members of minority ethnic groups tend to have higher levels than the norm, although there are important exceptions to this and rates vary between different minority ethnic groups (Table 1.5). Circulatory diseases are a major source of morbidity and account for 40 per cent of all deaths in the UK. There are higher mortality rates from coronary heart disease than the national average among all males and females amongst minority ethnic groups, except for Caribbean males and females who have lower rates. In general women have lower levels than men. The particularly high rates among South Asian groups are likely to increase over time as these groups age. For strokes, rates are much higher than the national average and this is a major cause of death for all minority ethnic groups. The third highest cause of death among minority ethnic groups is cancer. Here the Irish have higher rates and blacks and South Asians lower. It is perhaps worth noting that there has been relatively little research on the risks for cancer in these groups, partly because ethnicity was not recorded on cancer registrations. Despite the lower death rates among people who are black and South Asian cancer is an important cause of death which is likely to increase as health-related behaviour, for example in terms of smoking and diet, has changed in these groups. Respiratory diseases are another major source of morbidity in the UK population. Here Irish migrants have the highest rates for all conditions. Black and South Asian groups have lower rates for bronchitis and asthma but have very high rates for TB. They also have higher rates for pneumonia, with the exception of African-Caribbean men. As Smaje and Field discuss in this volume, the younger demographic profile of most minority ethnic groups has important consequences for their patterns of mortality.

Some of the explanations for ethnic patterns of mortality and illness are similar to those given to explain gender differences. There are potentially serious artefactual effects relating to the difficulties in operationalising ethnicity, the reliance upon small-scale, local

Table 1.4 Infant mortality by mother's place of birth, England and Wales, 1982–5

Mother's place of birth	Infant Mortality Rate	Infant Mortality N*	Perinatal Mortality Rate	Perinatal Mortality N+	Neonatal Mortality Rate	Neonatal Mortality N*	Postneonatal Mortality Rate	Postneonatal Mortality N*
UK	9.7	21,515	10.1	22,503	5.6	12,438	4.1	9,077
Eire	10.1	269	10.4	279	5.9	158	4.1	111
India	10.1	459	12.5	576	6.1	278	3.9	181
Bangladesh	9.3	145	14.3	225	6.5	101	2.8	44
Pakistan	16.6	892	18.8	1,022	10.2	549	6.4	343
Caribbean	12.9	274	13.4	288	8.4	179	4.5	95
East Africa	9.3	255	12.8	351	6.3	172	3.0	83
West Africa	11.0	128	12.7	149	8.0	93	3.0	35

Notes: * Number of deaths
+ Number of deaths and stillbirths

Source: Balarajan and Raleigh (1990) (cited in Smaje 1995). (Reproduced by permission of the Controller of HMSO and the Office for National Statistics and the King's Fund Centre.)

Table 1.5   Mortality age 20–69 (Standardised Mortality Ratios),
England and Wales, 1979–83

Birthplace		All causes	Breast cancer	Lung cancer	Coronary heart disease	Cerebro-vascular disease
All Ireland	M	147		126	114	123
	F	123	100	139	120	117
Indian Sub-	M	111		47	136	153
Continent	F	94	71	38	146	125
Caribbean	M	90		35	45	176
Commonwealth	F	114	78	32	76	210
African	M	115		39	113	163
Commonwealth	F	127	77	75	97	139

(SMRs England and Wales = 100)

Source: Balarajan and Bulusu (1990) cited in Smaje (1995). (Reproduced by permission of the Controller of HMSO and the Office for National Statistics and the King's Fund Centre.)

studies, and the use of immigrant rather than British-born populations. In particular many studies are methodologically flawed. All of these difficulties apply to the limited number of studies looking at the provision of services to terminally ill minority ethnics group patients. As with sex, genetic factors are involved with a few conditions, such as sickle cell disease, to which members of Afro-Caribbean, Asian and other ethnic minorities are particularly vulnerable. However, the effects of such factors are insufficient to explain the broad sweep of ethnic differences. They certainly cannot explain the apparent lack of service use by many groups.

The effects of migration have been considered. Most 'first wave' immigrants were male, with younger, fitter and more wealthy individuals being most likely to have the energy and resources to cope with the difficulties of long-distance migration. It is sometimes argued that the poor health of Irish migrants reflects the relative ease of their migration to Britain. There are a number of negative consequences for health of migration associated with the disruption, stresses and losses it entails. Causal influences have been sought in the stresses of migration, the material deprivation of immigrant minority ethnic groups and the effects of racism and discrimination. The latter two factors are thought to persist as important influences upon the health and illness experiences of minority ethnic groups in modern Britain.

Cultural and behavioural differences are popular explanations for ethnic inequalities in health. Minority ethnic communities in Britain may maintain distinctive definitions of illness and traditions of health care (e.g. Bhopal 1986; Krause 1989) and their health beliefs and knowledge may be incongruent with that of the health services (Donovan 1986). It is known that knowledge of and attitudes towards services may affect use. Older American studies suggest that ways of experiencing pain, interpreting symptoms and relating to the medical profession vary between ethnic groups (Zborowski 1969, Zola 1966, Bates 1987) and there is anecdotal evidence to suggest a similar situation in Britain. Linguistic difficulties mainly affect older people, especially females, and may be an additional factor.

Language difficulties, religious differences and family customs may generate or exacerbate misunderstandings between minority group members and health workers. Ethnocentrism and insensitivity to cultural difference may mean that service delivery and provision may unthinkingly take the white middle-class pattern as normal. For example, taking the isolated nuclear family as the norm may lead to ignoring and excluding extended kin from participation in birth, death and chronic illness, especially in hospitals. Cultural and religious customs may not be adequately taken into account during physical examination, visiting the sick in hospital, diet, and dealing with death and dying. The recognition of such factors has led to the view that health workers need to be aware of, and show respect for, the values, beliefs and traditions of minority ethnic patients. However, attempts to use a 'cultural approach' are sometimes unrealistic, particularly when they lead to attempts to change a whole way of life. They can, therefore, become demeaning and unintentionally racist.

As with the well documented social class differences in mortality and illness (Townsend et al. 1988) material conditions can account for many of the health problems of minority communities. In this view, the poorer health status and higher levels of mortality of some minority ethnic groups are due to their material deprivation and disadvantage. This is widely accepted with respect to class inequalities in health but less often recognised in discussions about deprived minority ethnic communities. Factors which have been identified are that unemployment is higher among most minority ethnic groups, and that a disproportionate number of people from ethnic minorities are found in low-pay occupations and are more likely to experience poor working conditions such as outwork and unsafe work sites. It seems clear that material disadvantage does contribute to higher mortality rates among a number of minority ethnic populations (Andrews and Jewson 1993).

As noted, racism and discrimination are felt to have an important – though hard to specify – influence upon illness and the use of health services. One indication of the potential size of the problem is that 'official police figures' indicate that rates of racial violence in England and Wales more than doubled from 4,000 in 1988 to over 8,000 incidents in 1993 (Labour Party 1994). We need to distinguish between individual and institutional racism and between direct and indirect discrimination. On occasion, the lifestyles of minority ethnic communities have been portrayed as irrational, 'exotic' or inferior. The implication is that minority communities should solve their problems by adopting 'rational' and 'sensible western' modes of behaviour. Indeed, a number of health education campaigns have been launched along just these lines. This view fails to recognise the racist stereotypes sometimes incorporated in health services and neglects material deprivation as a source of health problems. Sometimes it seems as if such biological explanations are used as an excuse to do nothing or are used to 'blame the victims' – for example, high rates of congenital abnormalities among Pakistani mothers are blamed upon consanguinity despite the lack of firm evidence to support this interpretation (Smaje 1995: 42).

Another way in which indirect discrimination may work is by its effect upon the quality of and access to services for minority ethnic groups. Because their communities are often located in inner city areas, there are fewer services available to minority ethnic groups and they are more likely to encounter poorer quality NHS services and facilities. This may contribute to their poorer health and raised rates of mortality. For example, raised levels of infant mortality among South Asian babies may be linked to the poor quality of obstetric advice given to Asian mothers (Clarke and Clayton 1983). Lack of information, particularly written information in the language of choice, is another factor identified in local studies of use of breast and cervical screening, ante-natal and palliative care services. Failure to link and integrate services within community structures, for example by using religious and community centres to disseminate information or as places of service provision, is another perceived weakness. There is also concern about direct racism and discrimination in service delivery as it is clear that some health professionals discriminate against some minority ethnic group members which may contribute to the lower use of services.

ETHNICITY, DEATH AND BEREAVEMENT

The sociological and anthropological literature about death and ethnicity in modern societies is restricted in both its volume and scope. The most substantial study is that by Kalish and Reynolds (1976) who studied 'white', 'black', 'Japanese' and 'Mexican' American groups in Los Angeles. They found a number of differences between the groups. For example, black Americans had the lowest expressed preference to die at home and the least need to have family members spend time with them, as religious belief and church communities replaced the family for social support. They also had the highest overall life expectancy despite higher mortality from cancer, strokes and diabetes. White and Mexican Americans showed a greater reluctance to admit to pain than black Americans. Kalish and Reynolds also found differences between the groups in their wish to have someone told if they were dying. Three quarters of the white Americans, nearly two thirds of black Americans and one third of Mexican Americans said they would want someone to be told.

More common have been accounts of the death beliefs and funeral customs of different ethnic groups focusing upon ways of dealing with the body and with the 'spirit' or 'soul' of the deceased rather than upon the experience of death and dying in these groups. For example, in Britain there have been accounts of Jewish (Katz 1993), Hindu (Firth 1993a, 1996) and Sikh (Firth 1993a, Kalsi 1996) attitudes and practices. Such literature, reflecting its mainly anthropological origin, has focused upon 'cultural' rather than social structural factors and is little more than descriptions of various cultural beliefs and practices of disposal. Kalsi (1996) indicates that Sikh funeral practices in Britain exhibit both continuity and change, while retaining their important role of transmitting traditional values. However, a fundamental weakness of this literature is its insensitivity to the processes of change which occur as minority ethnic groups adapt to their new societies. Jonker (1996) describes such processes and the ambivalence surrounding them among Muslim immigrants in Berlin, highlighting the central roles of religious leaders and undertakers in mediating between competing religious, cultural and practical demands. Her chapter in this volume extends this analysis further.

In Britain a similar 'culturalist' approach has been adopted to address the perceived failings of the NHS to respond adequately to the needs of minority ethnic clients. Recognising that ignorance of ethnic beliefs, practices and values contributed significantly to service failures, a series of 'checklists' or 'cultural factfiles' was produced to inform health-care workers about cultural differences and sensitise them to the need to shape their care work to accommodate these (e.g. Henley 1987). Such information has been used by palliative care workers, often amplified to include detailed information about death, dying and bereavement (e.g. Firth 1993b, Neuberger 1993). Irish and colleagues (1993) have produced similar material exploring variations between selected ethnic groups in the USA, supplemented by the reflections of professional practitioners. Despite the good intentions and undoubted benefits of the use of such material there are also significant disadvantages resulting from the way such information is used, as Gunaratnam argues in this volume.

While ethnicity, like gender, is an important source of identity which must be recognised and respected by those working with dying people there is little consensus about how to carry this insight into practice. For example, Ajemian and Mount comment:

> Each person – health professional, volunteer, patient or family member – has a unique understanding of life and its meaning. This has been moulded by ethnic origins, social class and family expectations, as well as previous exposure to religion and philosophy. . . . To be effective, members of the helping professions must first understand themselves in relation to their own social mores, prejudices and world view – working out their own structure and meaning.
>
> (1981: 19–20)

Hardly a recipe for action! It is thus unsurprising that a special edition of the *Hospice Journal* (Infeld, Gordon and Harper 1995) concluded that 'while many people are individually knowledgeable and culturally sensitive . . . few hospices have systematically planned services to culturally diverse groups'. In part this reflects a lack of attention to the material conditions which shape the experiences of minority ethnic group members.

CONCEPTUALISING THE RELATIONSHIPS BETWEEN DEATH, GENDER AND ETHNICITY

There is now a substantial body of work assessing the effects of demographic changes such as changing expectations of life and migration, changing economic and material conditions, the transformation of family and household structures, changing gender relationships, increasing expectations of health care, secularisation and urbanisation upon patterns of death, dying and bereavement. In this chapter we have been mainly concerned with reviewing the evidence about differences in the patterns of illness and death between men and women and among ethnic groups in modern British society and possible explanations for these. However, while the applied nature of such work makes it accessible to health providers and purchasers, it is of only limited value for a wider understanding of the complex interrelationships which affect experiences of death, dying and bereavement. For a deeper appreciation and understanding of how gender and ethnicity relate to death, dying and bereavement in modern society we need to turn to broader sociological conceptualisations of gender and ethnicity. In the concluding chapter to this volume Small argues that 'post-modernist' approaches have much to offer. Here we briefly outline longer established sociological conceptualisations of the relationships between individuals and groups with the broader social structures which shape and influence their lives and suggest how these conceptualisations have contributed, or might contribute, to a broader understanding of our topic.

Any adequate account of the relationships between death, gender and ethnicity must be informed by a view of the nature of modern societies and how they 'work'. Typically such views remain implicit and unexamined. In sociology and anthropology the dominant explanatory framework is that of 'functionalism' or 'systems theory'. The theoretical assumptions behind this approach are that societies and social organisations have a social reality and 'facticity' of their own, independent of the individuals who comprise them. Thus they can, to use Durkheim's phrasing, be treated as 'social facts' in their own right (Durkheim 1950). It is further assumed that societies are made up of different but interrelated 'parts' – such as families and social institutions. These co-exist in some sort of stable balance, with the parts affecting each other in a reciprocal manner. Thus change in one part of the society, for example the occupational structure, will have consequences for other aspects of the society such as family and household structures and patterns of disease. These in turn will have consequences for the occupational structure. For example, changes in industrial technology lead to increasing use of part-time female labour, contributing to the enhanced economic status and independence of women, rising divorce rates and higher levels of stress-related illness.

Writers within the sociology of health and illness have drawn upon the full range of theoretical positions (Scambler 1987, Gerhardt 1989), but much of the empirical work we reviewed reflects the functionalist approach. Gender and ethnicity are largely treated as 'social facts' which represent real and significant dimensions of social experience with the intention being to establish interrelationships between these different aspects of social reality in order to explain differences in health status and health outcomes such as premature mortality. In such work causal relationships may be uncovered and unintended consequences of social action may be discovered. Thus, explanations of gender or ethnic differences in mortality and illness behaviour are largely concerned with explaining 'real differences', although discussions of artefactual explanations and the effects of social constructions of reality also figure. This can be very fruitful. For example, Smaje and Field in this book draw upon such literature to focus the growing concerns about the apparent absence of minority ethnic group members from palliative care services. However, at best such an approach is limited to the analysis of patterns of behaviour and the establishment of the broad social factors which shape or 'structure' individual behaviour. The functionalist approach has also been criticised for its conservative tendencies to place too much emphasis on consensus and shared values and to accept the 'status quo' as unproblematic and 'normal'.

The Marxist or political economy approach, while accepting the idea of societies as systems of interrelated parts, emphasises the unequal distribution of power and resources within societies and the conflictful nature of competing interests (Doyal and Pennell 1979). This approach gives explanatory priority to 'material' factors such as working conditions, income and housing when explaining differences in mortality and illness between different groups. For example, differences in the health of minority ethnic groups will be seen as resulting from their economic positions within society. Most women and most minority ethnic groups are economically disadvantaged within capitalist societies, are politically and socially disadvantaged and consequently have worse health than more advantaged males and the dominant ethnic group.

Political economy analyses draw attention to the consequences of power and resources for health and mortality. They further demonstrate the ways in which power is maintained through the actions and the 'ruling ideas' of social groups such as doctors. The biomedical model, with its emphasis upon individuals as the site of disease and upon medical (and social) intervention, functions to deflect attention away from the fundamental underlying economic and social inequalities which are the prime source of inequalities in health. In this analysis, medicine and the health system serve as important sources of social control in maintaining the structures of inequality in society. Such an approach informs some feminist analyses of the patriarchal nature of society. The insistence that material differences cross-cut and interact with those of gender and ethnicity is important, as insufficient attention has been given to such inter-relations. While gender and ethnicity are themselves important social divisions, they are not homogeneous but heterogeneous categories. However, as with functionalist explanations, this approach is limited to the analysis of the societal factors which shape or 'structure' individual behaviour.

Structuralist and post-structuralist frameworks have also been significant. For example, some anthropological accounts of death rituals reflect the influences of Lévi-Strauss (1968). The structuralist view is that social reality is experienced through sets of symbols or images which comprise an internally consistent system of meanings. Such work reveals the relationship between the beliefs and practices through which death is managed and those which pervade all aspects of the life within the culture. It also emphasises the need to examine death and dying within its wider social context by asking what death rituals reveal about the broader structuring of social life, for example, how the treatment of the dead body relates to the treatment of the living body. With its emphasis on elucidating the 'deep structures' which provide coherence to the management of both life and death, this approach does not fully address either the range of meanings and functions of ritual symbols or their mutability over time. The straightforward structuralist connection between an image or signifier (e.g. a black-coated figure with a scythe) and its meaning or signified (Death the reaper) has been questioned. Instead, poststructuralists argue, images or symbols can be read or interpreted in a variety of ways and their meanings can change over time. Signified and signifier carry no fixed relationship to each other and their meaning is a product of the social position of the reader. This seems to offer a fruitful line of approach to theorising gender- and ethnicity-based differences.

Interactionist sociology has made a major contribution to the understanding of how individuals make sense of their illness experiences, including dying and death (e.g. Roth and Conrad 1987). In contrast to the previous approaches it emphasises that the meaning of behaviour to the individual is crucial and that such meanings are both shaped by and define the social contexts of behaviour. In particular the approach stresses the roles of individuals in shaping and controlling behaviour. In this view social structures are not fixed and given 'social facts' but are continually being re-affirmed, maintained and changed in day-to-day interactions (both consensual and conflictful) between individuals. Particular emphasis is placed upon communication and meaning and how these affect the experiences of (dying) patients, their families, their relatives and others close to them, and those caring for them. There is now a substantial set of theoretically informed accounts of 'illness careers' which describe how people come to recognise themselves as ill (or dying), the critical 'turning points' or crises along the way to the management of the condition, and the negotiation and subsequent incorporation of altered identities and self-conceptions into new patterns of social life (Roth and Conrad 1987, Strauss 1994). Another body of work has looked at how the social contexts of organisations influence and shape individual behaviour and the provision of care. For example, how the social organisation of hospitals constrains and shapes medical and nursing work with dying patients (Glaser and Strauss 1965, Field 1989).

Interactionist work has provided rich, detailed and informative accounts of the experiences of illness and, to a lesser extent, of dying, which may be used to inform practice. However, such work is mainly limited to small-scale studies within organisations or to looking at disease conditions. Further, such studies rarely address the effect of broader social constraints upon individuals, such as political and economic structures. Thus, although valuable at the individual level, they can make only a limited contribution to our understanding of broader social and historical factors.

An alternative approach to understanding the meaning and experience of illness and, especially, of dying and grief, is the psychoanalytic or psychodynamic approach. In contrast to the interactionist approach which assumes that the way an individual behaves is continually open to change, this approach assumes that individual behaviour is based upon the early shaping of biologically given needs and drives which remain basically unaltered throughout a person's life. In this approach individuals are seen as 'closed' homeostatic entities with patterned and predetermined ways of responding to crises such as death and illness. Explanations of their reactions to illness, dying and the death of another are to be sought within the experiencing individual rather than in the social contexts and social relationships within which these experiences occur. For many anthropologists and sociologists this approach with its individualistic and deterministic model of interpretation is both misleading and unbelievable, even in its more social and less deterministic forms. Furthermore, its ethnocentric and masculinist framework raises questions about its adequacy for interpreting the behaviour of females (although some feminists have drawn upon this approach) and individuals from non-European cultures. Despite such misgivings, this approach has been very influential within the social sciences. Within our area of concern it has exerted significant influence upon the care of dying and bereaved people by health professionals. The impact of Kubler-Ross's psychodynamic conceptualisation of psychological reactions to dying (1970) and of Parkes's similar conceptualisation of the stages of grief (1972) upon the work of doctors, nurses, social workers, counsellors and other care workers cannot be underestimated.

This overview chapter has provided an empirical and theoretical introduction to the broadly defined topic area of this book. Drawing on work from the sociology of health and illness, it has tried to indicate how this material might be developed in order to refine current understandings of the relationships between gender, ethnicity and death. Some of the authors who follow are identifying new questions about the relationship between death and gender and between death and ethnicity while others are developing themes relating to specific aspects which they have been working on for some time. By locating their work within existing theoretical and substantive approaches to sickness and death and by drawing upon the insights of sociology and anthropology in the areas of gender and ethnicity, this chapter aims to provide a framework not only for their work but also for that which will follow.

REFERENCES

Adams, S. (1993) 'A gendered history of the social management of death and dying in Foleshill, Coventry, during the inter-war years', in D. Clark (ed.) *The Sociology of Death*, Oxford: Blackwell, pp. 149–68.

Ajemian, I. and Mount, B. M. (1981) 'The adult patients: cultural considerations in palliative care', in C. Saunders, D. H. Summers and N. Teller (eds) *Hospice: The Living Ideal*, London: Edward Arnold, pp. 19–30.

Andrews, A. and Jewson, N. (1993) 'Ethnicity and infant deaths: the implications of recent statistical evidence for materialist explanations', *Sociology of Health and Illness* 15: 137–56.

Ariès, P. (1981) *The Hour of our Death*, London: Penguin.

Balarajan, R. and Bulusu, L. (1990) 'Mortality among immigrants in England and Wales, 1979–83', in M. Britton (ed.) *Mortality and Geography: A Review in the Mid-1980s*, London: OPCS, pp. 103–21.

—— and Raleigh, V. (1990) 'Variations in perinatal, neonatal, postnatal and infant mortality by mother's country of birth, 1982–85', in M. Britton (ed.) *Mortality and Geography: A Review in the Mid-1980s*, London: OPCS, pp. 123–37.

Bates, M. (1987) 'Ethnicity and pain: a bio-cultural model', *Social Science and Medicine* 24: 47–50.

Bhopal, R. S. (1986) 'The interrelationship of folk, traditional and western medicine within an Asian community in Britain', *Social Science and Medicine* 22: 99–105.

Blauner, R. (1966) 'Death and social structure', *Psychiatry* 29: 378–94.

Blaxter, M. (1990) *Health and Lifestyles*, London: Routledge.

Bowlby, J. (1981) *Loss: Sadness and Depression*, Harmondsworth: Penguin.

Bronfen, E. (1992) *Over Her Dead Body: Death, Femininity and the Aesthetic*, Manchester: Manchester University Press.

Butler, J. (1993) *Bodies that Matter: on the Discursive Limits of Sex*, New York: Routledge.

Clarke, J. N. (1983) 'Sexism, feminism and medicalisation: a decade review of literature on gender and illness', *Sociology of Health and Illness* 5: 62–79.

Clarke, M. and Clayton, J. (1983) 'Quality of obstetric care provided for Asian immigrants in Leicestershire', *British Medical Journal* 286: 384–7.

Cline, S. (1995) *Lifting the Taboo. Women, Death and Dying*, London: Little, Brown & Co.

Dobash, R. E. and Dobash, R. B. (1992) *Women, Violence and Social Change*, London: Routledge.

Donovan, J. (1986) *We Don't Buy Sickness, It Just Comes*, London: Gower.

Doyal, L. with Pennell, I. (1979) *The Political Economy of Health*, London: Pluto.

Durkheim, E. [1893] (1950) *The Rules of Sociological Method*, Glencoe, Ill.: Free Press.

Field, D. (1989) *Nursing the Dying*, London: Tavistock/Routledge.

—— (1994) 'Palliative medicine and the medicalisation of death', *European Journal of Cancer Care* 3: 58–64.

—— and James, N. (1993) 'Where and how people die', in D. Clark (ed.) *The Future for Palliative Care: Issues of Policy and Practice*, Buckingham: Open University Press, pp. 16–29.

Firth, S. (1993a) 'Approaches to death in Hindu and Sikh communities in Britain', in D. Dickenson and M. Johnson (eds) *Death, Dying and Bereavement*, London: Sage, pp. 26–32.

—— (1993b) 'Cultural issues in terminal care', in D. Clark (ed.) *The Future of Palliative Care: Issues of Policy and Practice*, Buckingham: Open University Press, pp. 98–110.

—— (1996) 'The good death: attitudes of British Hindus', in G. Howarth and P. C. Jupp (eds) *Contemporary Issues in the Sociology of Death, Dying and Disposal*, Basingstoke: Macmillan, pp. 96–107.

General Household Survey (1992), London: HMSO.

Gerhardt, U. (1989) *Ideas about Illness: An Intellectual and Political History of Medical Sociology*, London: Macmillan.

Glaser, B. G. and Strauss, A. L. (1965) *Awareness of Dying*, Chicago: Aldine.

Gorer, G. (1965) *Death, Grief and Mourning in Contemporary Britain*, London: Cresset.

Grosz, E. (1994) *Volatile Bodies*, Bloomington: Indiana University Press.

Henley, A. (1987) *Caring in a Multiracial Society*, London: Bloomsbury Health Authority.

Hertz, R. [1907] (1960) *Death and the Right Hand*, New York: Free Press.

Hill, D. and Penso, D. (1995) *Opening Doors: Improving Access to Hospice and Specialist Care Services by Members of Black and Ethnic Minority Communities*, London: National Council for Hospice and Specialist Palliative Care Services, Occasional Paper 7.

Hockey, J. L. (1989) 'Residential care and the maintenance of social identity', in M. Jefferys (ed.) *Growing Old in the Twentieth Century*, London: Routledge, pp. 201–17.

Illich, I. (1977) *Limits to Medicine*, Harmondsworth: Penguin.

Infeld, D. L., Gordon, A. K. and Harper, B. C. (eds) (1995) *Hospice Care and Cultural Diversity*, New York: Haworth Press.

Irish, D., Lundquist, K. F. and Nelsen, V. J. (eds) (1993) *Ethnic Variations in Dying, Death and Grief: Diversity in Universality*, Washington: Taylor & Francis.

James, N. and Field, D. (1992) 'The routinization of hospice: charisma and bureaucratization', *Social Science and Medicine* 34: 1363–75.

Jenkins, R. (1994) 'Rethinking ethnicity: identity, categorization and power', *Ethnic and Racial Studies* 17:197–223.

Jonker, G. (1996) 'The knife's edge: Muslim burial in the diaspora', *Mortality* 1(1): 27–43.

Kalish, R. A. and Reynolds, D. K. (1976) *Death and Ethnicity: A Psychocultural Study*, Farmingdale, NY: Baywood.

Kalsi, S. (1996) 'Change and continuity in the funeral rituals of Sikhs in Britain', in G. Howarth and P. C. Jupp (eds) *Contemporary Issues in the Sociology of Death, Dying and Disposal*, Basingstoke: Macmillan, pp. 30–43.

Katz, J. (1993) 'Jewish perspectives on death, dying and bereavement', in D. Dickenson and M. Johnson (eds) *Death, Dying and Bereavement*, London: Sage, pp. 199–207.

Kellehear, A. (1984) 'Are we a "death denying" society? A sociological review', *Social Science and Medicine* 18: 713–23.

Krause, I. (1989) 'Sinking heart: a Punjabi communication of distress', *Social Science and Medicine* 29: 563–75.

Kubler-Ross, E. (1970) *On Death and Dying*, London: Tavistock.

Labour Party (1994) cited in *The Independent*, 18 March 1994.

Lal, B. (1983) 'Perspectives an ethnicity: old wine in new bottles', *Ethnic and Racial Studies* 6: 154–73.

Lévi-Strauss, C. (1968) *Structural Anthropology*, London: Allen Lane.

Littlewood, J. (1992) *Aspects of Grief: Bereavement in Adult Life*, London: Tavistock/Routledge.

Lofland, L. H. (1978) *The Craft of Dying: The Modern Face of Death*, London and Beverly Hills: Sage.

Lovell, A. (1983) 'Some questions of identity: late miscarriage, stillbirth and perinatal death', *Social Science and Medicine* 17: 755–61.

Macintyre, S., Hunt, K. and Sweeting, H. (1996) 'Gender differences in health: are things really as simple as they seem?', *Social Science and Medicine* 42: 617–24.

Martin, E. (1987) *The Woman in the Body: A Cultural Analysis of Reproduction*, Buckingham: Open University Press.

Nathanson, C. A. (1977) 'Sex, illness and medical care: a review of data, theory and method', *Social Science and Medicine* 11: 13–25.

Neuberger, J. (1993) 'Cultural issues in palliative care', in D. Doyle, G. Hanks and N. MacDonald (eds) *The Oxford Textbook of Palliative Medicine*, Oxford: Oxford University Press, pp. 507–13.

Oakley, A. (1972) *Sex, Gender and Society*, London: Temple Smith.

OPCS (1993) 'Ethnic group and country of birth: Great Britain', *1991 Census*, London: HMSO.

Parkes, C. M. (1972) *Bereavement: Studies of Grief in Adult Life*, Harmondsworth: Penguin.

Rajan, L. and Oakley, A. (1993) 'No pills for heartache: support in pregnancy loss', *Journal of Reproductive and Infant Psychology* 11: 75–87.

Rex, J. and Mason, D. (eds) (1986) *Theories of Race and Ethnic Relations*, Cambridge: Cambridge University Press.

Roth, J. and Conrad, P. (1987) *Research in the Sociology of Health Care: The Experience and Management of Chronic Disease*, Greenwich, Conn. and London: JAI Press.

Scambler, G. (1987) *Sociological Theory and Medical Sociology*, London: Tavistock.

Scully, D. (1980) *Men Who Control Women's Health: The Miseducation of the Obstetrician–Gynecologist*, Boston: Houghton-Mifflin.

Seale, C. and Cartwright, A. (1994) *The Year before Death*, Aldershot: Avebury.

Smaje, C. (1995) *Health, 'Race' and Ethnicity: Making Sense of the Evidence*, London: King's Fund.

—— (1996) 'The ethnic patterning of health: new directions for theory and research', *Sociology of Health and Illness* 18: 139–71.

Sontag, S. (1979) *Illness as Metaphor*, London: Allen Lane.

—— (1989) *AIDS and its Metaphors*, London: Allen Lane.

Strauss, A. L. (ed.) (1994) *Chronic Illness and the Quality of Life* (2nd edn), St Louis: C. V. Mosby.

Townsend, P., Davidson, N. and Whitehead, M. (1988) *Inequalities in Health: The Black Report/The Health Divide*, Penguin: Harmondsworth.

Ungerson, C. (1987) *Policy is Personal: Sex, Gender and Informal Care*, London: Tavistock.

Verbrugge, L. M. (1985) 'Gender and health: an update on hypotheses and evidence', *Journal of Health and Social Behaviour* 26: 156–82.

Waldron, I. (1983) 'Sex differences in illness incidence, prognosis and mortality: issues and evidence', *Social Science and Medicine* 17: 1107–23.

Walter, T. (1993) 'British sociology and death', in D. Clark (ed.) *The Sociology of Death*, Oxford: Blackwell, pp. 264–95.

West, C. and Zimmerman, D. H. (1991) 'Doing gender', in J. Lorber and Farrell, A. (eds) *The Social Construction of Gender*, London: Sage, pp. 13–37.

Zborowski, M. (1969) *People in Pain*, San Francisco: Jossey-Bass.

Zola, I. K. (1966) 'Culture and symptoms: an analysis of patients presenting complaints', *American Sociological Review* 31: 615–30.

Chapter 2

Death at the beginning of life

Alice Lovell

INTRODUCTION

This chapter addresses the experiences of losing a baby through miscarriage, stillbirth or early neonatal death. These losses, often not viewed as 'proper' bereavements, tend to be devalued because there appears to be no *person* to grieve for. Birth and death instead of being seen as two separate events are treated as though one cancelled out the other. Thus death at the beginning of life is a neglected area. This chapter will highlight some of the ways in which these losses have been ignored and consider reasons for this neglect.

After outlining problems of definition, birth and death will be set into the medical context. Death at the beginning of life will be viewed in the light of the bereavement literature and I shall then trace the emergence of miscarriage, stillbirth and perinatal loss as matters of social concern. 'Capturing the loss' is a section based on an empirical study (Lovell 1983) which illustrates some of the issues. This is followed by a section which focuses on miscarriage. It is argued that increasing attention is being paid to the mother's needs in respect of stillbirth and neonatal loss. These include ways to make the baby real by seeing the body, having a funeral and 'memorialising' the baby. However, there are conflicting interests which inhibit similar attention being paid to miscarriage. There are gaps in scriptures and other religious texts surrounding *all* these losses. These omissions mean that the needs of bereaved parents, from a range of religious backgrounds and cultures, are often overlooked. 'Religious professionals' is a section which takes up these issues using interview data from a recent study (Lovell 1995b). The findings have implications for practitioners in the 'caring' professions.

There are various ways of defining when a foetus becomes a baby but no definition is uniformly used. Miscarriage, stillbirth and early neonatal death are not Durkheimian 'social facts' but are socially constructed concepts and anything but fixed. As was noted in the *Perinatal Audit and Surveillance*

> A live birth is defined as a child who breathes or shows signs of life after complete expulsion from the mother regardless of the length of gestation. A stillbirth is currently defined as a child issuing from its mother after the 28th week of pregnancy which did not at any time after complete expulsion breathe or show any other signs of life. *Perinatal statistics are bedevilled by problems of definitions, for example, whether or not the infant was born alive, and, if not, what the period of gestation was. (Was the event to be classified as abortion or stillbirth?) ... Although the law places the onus of deciding whether a child was liveborn or stillborn on the parent (or other qualified informant) in practice the medical attendant usually decides.*
>
> (Chalmers and McIlwaine 1980: 18 – my emphasis)

There are definitions based on criteria of gestational size, weight and age. The definitions carry legal, social, ethical and religious consequences. Definition affects, for instance, the documentation, as well as assumptions about which are the 'lesser' losses. The definition of 'stillbirth' is based on the legal age of viability. In keeping with medical advances, in 1992, this cut-off was brought forward to twenty-four weeks (Stillbirth Definition Act 1992) and prior to this, on 1 January 1986, new stillbirth and neonatal death certificates were introduced in England and Wales (OPCS 1995, CESDI 1993). There are religious definitions – for instance, Roman Catholics consider that life begins at conception. There are cultural definitions. In some societies, babies are not regarded as possessing a full, independent existence apart from their mothers (MacLean 1971, Scheper-Hughes 1992).

As I have argued elsewhere (Lovell 1983), these losses are on a continuum of pregnancy and external definitions do not take into account women's perceptions about what has happened. Official definitions often bear little relation to women's feelings. Nevertheless, these definitions influence the ways in which women's experiences are defined and managed. They play their part in imposing a 'hierarchy of sadness' which assumes that the earlier the pregnancy fails, the 'lesser' the loss.

The hospital, as well as being the usual place of the 'deathbed', is also the usual place of birth. Birth and death have increasingly been removed from the home to hospital. Throughout history, and in most cultures, the management of reproduction has been a female concern. However, modern childbirth practices have been organised mainly for the convenience of the health professionals, particularly doctors. In industrialised societies health care in general, and childbirth in particular, have become the domain of male professionals (Hugman 1993, Witz 1992). Hospital confinement has drawn women both as providers and users of care into a relationship with medicine characterised by male dominance and female subjugation. For instance, midwives and many expectant mothers may think that home births are best but they have been opposed by the medical professionals who favour hospitals. The home birth issue also throws light on to the key to the power relations involved. Walter (1994) noted that power lies in the hands of those who have control over the body. Thus in the hospital context, on their own territory, at the beginning of life (childbirth) and the end of life, the professionals set the agenda.

Miscarriage, stillbirth and early neonatal deaths occur during or soon after pregnancy. Since most obstetricians are men and all users of maternity services are women, patriarchal structures contextualise the discourse of encounters. This chapter is concerned with the ways in which health professionals, religious functionaries (similarly male-dominated) and society in general put miscarriage, and particularly early miscarriage, at the 'bottom of the bereavement heap', trivialising women's experiences and needs. It is proposed that there is a socially constructed 'hierarchy of sadness' at work. However, this hierarchy, which follows gestational age as outlined above, does not necessarily reflect the feelings of the bereaved mother, or indeed of the often overlooked father. With the development of voluntary organisations and raised awareness, early neonatal death and stillbirth are now at least on the bereavement agenda but again, as with the home birth issue, the extent to which rhetoric is matched by practice is questionable.

TABOOED AND DEVALUED DEATHS

Gorer (1965) popularised the view that death is the taboo of the twentieth century. He argued that those who give in to outward signs of mourning are stigmatised as morbid. This position is losing ground to competing views. Anthropological and historical evidence indicates that most, if not all, human societies have developed some formal rituals for mourning. However, there has been a tendency to simplify and speed up procedures. Margaret Mead found that Manus funerals in 1953 (what she called the 'New Way') were very different from those in 1928 (the 'Old Way'):

> Short mourning is one of the tenets of the New Way ... the inconsolable parent or spouse may continue to wail ... but if the grief lasts more than two or three days, people become very much alarmed.
>
> (1956: 273)

Van Gennep developed the concept of *rite de passage* and identified patterns of ritual which accompany a passage from one situation to another. In his analysis of funerals, Van Gennep contrasted the customs of different societies, their beliefs about an after-life and the ways that rites of passage were marked. He suggested that the most widespread idea is that a world similar to, but pleasanter than, the earthly one exists and that everyone re-enters. However, he qualified 'everyone' as follows:

> Thus everyone re-enters again the categories of clan, age group, or occupation that he [*sic*] had on earth. It logically follows that the children who have not yet been incorporated into the society of the living cannot be classified in that of the dead. Thus, for Catholics, children who die without baptism forever remain in the transition zone, or limbo; the corpse of a semi-civilised infant not yet named, circumcised or otherwise ritually recognised, is buried without the usual ceremonies, thrown away, or burned – especially if the people in question think that he [*sic*] did not yet possess a soul.
>
> (1960: 152–3)

While women become invisible, swallowed up into a humankind described as 'he', exclusion of the unbaptised within Christianity is a recurring issue in the historical, contemporary and anthropological literature. Indeed, in virtually every religion, there are clearly set out rules, religious laws and procedures about what is to be done during the dying process and after the death of an 'adult'. The adult or 'person' is almost invariably defined with the male pronoun. On the whole, there is an almost blank page when it comes to babies. Miscarriage and stillbirth are virtually absent. These spaces in the Scriptures and religious texts, texts written by men, go some way to explaining why these losses have been, and continue to be, overlooked. In a later section of this chapter, examples drawn from a recent exploratory study (Lovell 1995b) will return to this theme.

Andersson Wretmark (1993) identified problems in ancient Nordic law in dealing with a dead unbaptised or stillborn infant. Those who had been blessed but not baptised had a 'between' position. They were not entitled to a church funeral but in some cases could be buried in the outskirts of the churchyard. She also noted that malformed infants constituted another problem, which was evident in my own research in the cases of babies with congenital abnormalities whose identities were 'spoiled' (see pp. 39–40 and Lovell 1983). MacLean (1971) noted that very young Yoruba children were not regarded as possessing an existence independent of their mothers and, partly for this reason and partly because their deaths were so common, she concluded that these infants were not mourned by the community or family apart from the mother who 'bewails their passing with wild abandoned weeping'. In her discussion of 'Funerals of the Unfortunate', Gittings explained that children who died in pre-industrial England, were given burials slightly less elaborate than those of adults but essentially similar. In the case of infants who died prior to their mothers being 'churched', grief was kept to a minimum but they were buried wearing their chrysoms, pieces of white cloth worn at the baptism:

> While the death of small babies was an expected occurrence in early Modern England and the loss felt either socially or personally was kept to a minimum, it is significant that their burial rituals still followed the traditional pattern, the customary decencies being rigorously carried out.
>
> (1988: 82)

Gittings contrasted these 'respectable' burials of children – together with various groups of unfortunates (who include executed criminals) – with the very different treatment accorded stillborn babies. The latter were barely considered to be human beings. The vital distinction between these and other children, or any of the groups of 'unfortunates' was again that they had not received baptism. Their bodies were sometimes left by the wayside in danger of being eaten by passing animals or simply to rot. In an attempt to avoid these indignities, a clause in the oath sworn by many seventeenth-century midwives included the instruction that any child stillborn should be buried:

> In such secret place as neither hog, dog nor any other beast may come unto it ... you shall not suffer any such child to be cast into the lanes or any other inconvenient place.
>
> (ibid.: 83)

Ariès (1974) traced changing attitudes towards death within western culture, with death accepted in terms of destiny up until the thirteenth century and becoming increasingly individualised and sometimes depicted in erotic terms between the fifteenth and eighteenth centuries. He proposed that the twentieth-century attitude is one of rejection. Ariès defined this as 'forbidden death': a technical phenomenon preferably occurring in hospital and stage-managed by medical professionals. The goal of the hospital team is an acceptable death without embarrassment to the survivors and devoid of uncontrolled emotional outbursts. Elias (1985) noted how death and dying tend to be hidden and Giddens (1991) took up the theme but referred to the phenomenon as 'sequestered' death which poses a threat to rationality and social management of modernity.

The received wisdom within sociology, professional literature and in general, proposed that in modern twentieth-century society, death, dying, bereavement and grief have become taboo topics. Those working in this area of research have long been aware of the paradox within this perspective. For a 'taboo' subject, there has been no shortage of literature on the topic! Walter (1994) is critical of theorising about the 'taboo-ness' and challenges the thesis that death in modern society is privately present but publicly absent. He also disputes the view that a new public discourse, that of medicine, has taken over from the old authority of religion (Walter et al. 1995). As well as suggesting that there has been a revival of death, and acting as something of an advocate of this revival, Walter (1994) argues that although death may be privately absent, it is publicly present. He pinpoints the mass media as the arena where it is very public and provides a series of examples in films and on television where death and dying are central themes. One of the difficulties with this position is that although films and television do present these themes, they are

depicted in 'media-bites'. For example, in a television documen-
tary, the viewer may see a real person dying, a process which may
take many months. For the purposes of the programme, it is
speeded up and compressed into forty minutes. The dramatisation
of a cot death may be presented as a 'social issue' in a soap opera.
However, such fleeting public representations of death, dying and
grief in the media arguably only reflect how our culture continues
to reject the issues. These depictions mirror the truncation of
emotional expression and serve as a metaphor for the ways our
society regards death and dying (see Pickering, Littlewood and
Walter in this book).

In contemporary, western Protestant culture there continues to
be token acknowledgement: a funeral, a letter or card of condo-
lence and a solemn expression when speaking of the departed.
Services celebrating the life of the deceased sometimes replace
traditional memorial rituals. But, as Walter correctly points out,
these are confined to people (usually men) of high status whose
lives are considered to have made a significant social contribution. Eventually though, and sooner rather than later, the
bereaved find that they are encouraged to return to 'business as
usual'. It may be claimed that death is a leveller but there are
inequalities in the ways in which a death is marked and the time
permitted for grief.

The losses considered in this chapter are those where life and
death appear to collide. In miscarriage, stillbirth and sometimes
early neonatal death, there is no obvious dying process. There
appears to be nobody to eulogise. These deaths, often without
bodies at all, are unusual deaths. Miscarriage, stillbirth and early
neonatal death continue to be relegated to a different class of
event. They are often seen as unfortunate experiences which
happened to the mother, couched in 'illness' terms and not
accorded the acknowledgement which accompanies the loss of a
person who left a mark on the world and occupied a place in the
memories of the people who knew him or her. These losses are
largely unrecognised and undervalued.

THE EMERGENCE OF STILLBIRTH AND
PERINATAL LOSS AS PUBLIC ISSUES

This section will first consider the work which contributed to the
emergence of stillbirth and perinatal loss as public issues. Second,

some of the ways in which these losses attracted attention in the media will be outlined. Third, the pioneering changes in management and the thinking behind them will be identified.

The lack of significance attached to stillbirth and perinatal death is evident in the literature. Armstrong (1986) traced the emergence of infant mortality as a socio-medical problem in Britain in the twentieth century. He noted that not until 1877 were the deaths of children under the age of one year specifically reported as the infant mortality rate (IMR). The creation of the IMR at that time suggests both an awareness of these young deaths and, more importantly, the social recognition of the infant as a discrete entity. In the nineteenth century, stillbirth seemed indistinguishable from miscarriages and abortions. By 1950, a new statistic emerged – 'perinatal mortality' – deaths in the first week of life plus stillbirths.

Until relatively recently, perinatal issues were studied clinically solely in relation to their aetiology and epidemiology. In the United States, Bruce (1962) and McLenahan (1962) were probably the first to look at the reactions of nurses to the mother who has a stillbirth. Bruce noted that nurses were disturbed by stillbirth and the mother's guilt and grief were mirrored in the nurse's feelings. She recommended that support be provided for nursing staff so that they in turn could help the mothers. She pointed out that nurses tended to overlook the most important gift they could give to the mother, namely themselves. This paper broke fresh ground in identifying the 'emotion' work involved in nursing. Furthermore, it is useful at this point to emphasise that much of the imperative for the provision of support for the bereaved mothers in clinical settings has arisen from the needs of *staff*.

In Sweden, Cullberg (1966) published what is probably the first paper on the psychiatric consequences of perinatal death. During his psychiatric training in 1958, Bourne treated two patients whom he described as 'capsized' by losing babies through stillbirth. Searching the journals and books, he was surprised to find nothing about the topic (Bourne, Lewis and Vallender 1992). His observation prompted one of the earliest studies in the area ten years later. Bourne (1968) identified a professional blind-spot characterised by the way that family doctors failed to know, notice or remember anything about their patients who had experienced a stillbirth. Giles (1970) in Australia examined women's reactions to perinatal death. In the United States, Kennell and Klaus (1971) called attention to the mourning process when a baby dies. In addition to her paper entitled 'Nothing was said sympathy-wise' (Lewis 1979), Hazelanne Lewis started the Stillbirth Association in 1978 which later became the Stillbirth and Neonatal Deaths Society (SANDS). The influence of this work grew slowly during the 1970s but was accelerated by attention in the national press. A journalist wrote a personal account of her experience of stillbirth (Mooney 1976) and a prominent paediatrician, the late Hugh Jolly, wrote articles in *The Times* (Jolly 1975a, 1975b) as well as in the medical press (Jolly 1976). In addition to pointing to the need to consider feelings of the family, particularly the father, he pressed for changes in the certification of stillbirth which was a 'Certificate of Disposal' without space for the baby's name. The Health Education Council (now the Health Education Authority) published a controversial leaflet (HEC 1979) which raised awareness in some health professionals and led to a degree of rethinking by a few individual consultants about the management of women who experience stillbirth and perinatal loss (miscarriage was still largely glossed over).

One of Stanford Bourne's colleagues, E. Lewis, examined the forces operating on the bereaved mother and her family, and on the professionals who care for her, to play down the tragedy (1972, 1976, Lewis and Page 1978). He argued that by whisking the dead baby out of sight and virtually ignoring the stillbirth, mourning can be inhibited which may result in psychiatrically defined depressive illness with somatic symptoms. Lewis stressed the importance of building up memories and 'bringing the stillborn baby back to death', suggesting ways in which this could be facilitated such as encouraging bereaved parents to see and hold their dead baby, give the child a name, and be involved in the arrangements for registration and burial. He emphasised the importance of a funeral and knowing where the baby is located, or, if cremated, knowing when and where this took place. These ideas differed markedly from usual theory and practice. He argued that these deaths were not merely 'just as sad' as any other death but that they were potentially *more* disturbing. Furthermore, he insisted that the way that they were managed made things worse. He opposed the usual practice, which he described as the 'rugger pass' designed to remove the dead baby quickly and close things over as if they had never occurred.

'CAPTURING' THE LOSS: AN EMPIRICAL STUDY

In 1974, when working in a pathology laboratory, I saw the backlog of stillbirth post mortem reports waiting to be typed. It was the evident lack of urgency combined with the sheer number which made me ask questions about (a) what became of the bodies and (b) what was done to help the bereaved parents. The staff were not entirely sure of the answer to the first question and answers ranged from 'they are buried with another body', 'they are incinerated' to 'the hospital takes care of them' (without being entirely sure *who* in the hospital dealt with this). In response to my second question about the parents, I was given an array of replies including 'nothing'. I was told that mothers were usually sent home as soon as possible and encouraged to 'try again'. Basically, there was no policy.

I noticed that childbirth and child-death – two distinct life events – were in temporal collision. One effect of this collision was that they often became bracketed together by health professionals, by lay people and even by the parents themselves creating a setting where acknowledgement that something significant had taken place was not fully accorded. The contradictory events of life and death were not simply conflated into one traumatic event but were treated *as if one cancelled out the other*.

The study that I undertook was based on interviews with thirty health professionals at four London hospitals and twenty-two bereaved mothers. Some of the factors examined were: seeing the dead baby, knowing what became of the baby, holding a funeral or other ritual, hospital management (length of stay and attitudes of staff), the role of counselling, information given, talking about what had happened and ways of memorialising the baby. I explored the relevance of these factors to a mother's acceptance or non-acceptance of the loss. The research was initially designed to investigate stillbirth and early neonatal death, the manifest reason for this being to limit the scope of the study (but there were probably latent reasons associated with my anxieties connected with the miscarriage/abortion issue). Early neonatal death was defined as death within a week and stillbirth, in keeping with the legal definition at that time, was defined as a baby of twenty-eight or more weeks' gestation who failed to live outside the uterus. I had no intention of including miscarriage, either early or 'late'. However, during the course of my first interview (referred to me by a GP as a stillbirth), the interviewee pointed out that 'technically it was a late miscarriage'. What this brought to light was the artificiality and anomalous status of these categories. Rather than exclude miscarriage altogether, the design was modified to include four women who had experienced 'late' miscarriages ('late' being defined as after twenty weeks).

One of my findings was that the mothers who seemed *least* able to make sense of their loss were those whose babies had been lost through late miscarriage and stillbirth. But these were perceived by health professionals as 'lesser' losses than early neonatal death. The mothers were less likely to have seen the baby and know what had become of him or her. They tended to describe themselves as being in an emotional limbo. There is nothing in law to prevent the interment of miscarried babies, but in practice it rarely happened. On the other hand, those mothers whose babies had lived and then died tended to be the mothers who had seen and held the baby, made arrangements for a funeral or other ritual, received explanations from health professionals and had an opportunity to talk about their experiences.

The professionals played a key part in defining the situation and the research highlighted attitudes and procedures which constructed and deconstructed the identities of the mother and the baby. Explanations from medical staff varied markedly according to social class differences with the higher socio-economic mothers being privileged. Cultural differences too played a part in the information communicated. The four Asian mothers were disadvantaged and given little in the way of explanation as to why their babies had died and not one of the four knew of the existence of support groups such as SANDS. Thus, gender, social class and ethnicity shaped these women's experiences of their loss.

A mother's decision about whether or not to see her dead baby was influenced by the attitudes of the hospital staff and my study emphasised the power relationships which shaped the social care. For instance, one mother who had not seen her dead baby recounted how her husband *had* been asked but in such a way that the expected answer was 'no'. A nurse, holding at arm's length what looked like a bedpan, asked him whether he wanted to see his hydrocephalic, stillborn son. When he shook his head, the nurse commented: 'Quite right, you wouldn't like it . . . it's an ugly little thing' – a remark which added to the parents' anguish by devaluing their child. The implication seemed to be that this was an object, unfit to be seen, unfit to be loved and not worthy of mourning. In contrast, another mother, who agreed to let the midwife decide whether her baby was 'fit to be seen', saw her baby when the midwife told her that the baby was 'perfect' and 'too beautiful for this world'. One baby was defined as beautiful and by implication, a tragic loss, someone the midwife might have loved. The other, the baby with hydrocephalus, was defined as 'ugly'.

MISCARRIAGE

It is estimated that as many as three quarters of all human conceptions do not result in the birth of a live baby but are lost at some point in pregnancy (Oakley, McPherson and Roberts 1990). At least half of pregnancies end in what is defined as 'miscarriage' or 'stillbirth'. The estimates of miscarriage are based on informed guesses. Pizer and Palinski (1980) put the rate at between 15 and 20 per cent (one in five) of all pregnancies but it may be much higher. Most occur within the first three months of pregnancy; late miscarriage is rarer and, again, exact figures are not available.

Around the time of my own study, and shortly afterwards, there was a growing body of research looking at the psychological effects of perinatal death (Peppers and Knapp 1980, Forrest 1982, Estok and Lehman 1983). Miscarriage continued to be neglected. But in the early 1980s, the Miscarriage Association was started in Bristol and local groups mushroomed until a National Committee was formed in 1990 although the organisation is still seriously underfunded. Texts were published giving explanations, practical advice, suggestions about coping and illustrated with personal accounts (Oakley, McPherson and Roberts 1984; Borg and Lasker 1981; Hey, Itzin, Saunders and Speakman 1989). Much as stillbirths had been downgraded and not viewed as proper bereavements, so too these books described how women who experienced a miscarriage felt this was dismissed by others – perhaps seen as a necessary loss rather than a significant emotional experience, in that the foetus was assumed not to have been viable. This literature offered a plea for more recognition of miscarriage.

In 1991, Bourne and Lewis, the influential medical pioneers who drew attention to stillbirth, took a different view, arguing:

> Parents of stillborn infants . . . should be encouraged to salvage everything they can from the experience . . . by contrast . . . people should not be pushed into magnifying miscarriage (common, one in three or four pregnancies) into tragedies.
>
> (1991: 1167–8)

While fully agreeing that nobody should be *pushed* and acknowledging that individuals react in differing ways to miscarriage, it is essential to allow people's experiences to be fully acknowledged. The frequency of the occurrence is not particularly comforting and this observation coming from male, medical professionals can feel insulting and irrelevant.

In her study of miscarriage, Moulder (1990) pointed out that many women complained about insensitive and neglectful treatment which made a bad experience worse. Rajan and Oakley (1991, 1993) found much unhappiness reported by bereaved mothers in their Social Support in Pregnancy study. Out of their sample of over 500 women, 217 (43 per cent) had one or more previous pregnancy losses (miscarriages, stillbirths, neonatal deaths and post-neonatal deaths). They wanted to discover whether women who had undergone pregnancy loss (20 per cent of which were miscarriages) benefited in their physical and emotional health from social support provided in subsequent pregnancies. Their data supported my findings that there is a need for the recognition of the dead baby as a person and for the legitimation of mourning. They emphasised the importance of the women's relationships with health professionals and acknowledgement that mourning is a healthy, albeit painful, process. They described it as a 'natural and healthy' process. The extent to which it is 'natural' is problematic and cannot be examined in detail here. There are no prescriptions. Perhaps 'miscarriage' and its repercussions offer a range of post-modern interpretations. It is salient, however, to refer to Nancy Scheper-Hughes' remarkable work on mother love and child-death in Brazil. She did not suggest that mother love in Alto do Cruzeiro is deficient or absent but that its expression is shaped by overwhelming economic and cultural constraints, and she identified 'a political economy' of the emotions (Scheper-Hughes 1992). Her analysis applies equally to interpretations of the meaning of miscarriage. As well as sociology illuminating these issues, it is for each bereaved person to define his or her own meanings.

WHERE ARE WE NOW? SOME IMPLICATIONS FOR CHANGING PRACTICE

A recent literature search produced over 200 recent articles on miscarriage, stillbirth and perinatal death. Should this should give cause for optimism? In recent years, many British hospitals have recognised the need to amend their policies and practice. In keeping with guidelines (SANDS 1995, Thomas 1990), some parents are now helped to see and hold their dead baby, and take time to say goodbye. In addition to giving mementoes, such as the wrist band, hospitals help organise a funeral or cremation, and perhaps entry in a book of remembrance. If the baby is lost prior to twenty-four weeks, a medical certificate may be given to acknowledge the baby's existence (Kohner 1992) even though this is not a legal requirement.

I suggest that there is still a long way to go. Bereaved parents, at a vulnerable time, are at the mercy of patchy services, dependent on individual professional styles. Genuine choices and control remain illusory. There is no single right answer about, for instance, what to do with the foetal remains. In the past, small embryos from abortions and foetal tissues were sometimes disposed of by giving them to researchers. The Polkinghorne Report (1989) stated that this should only be done with the parents' written consent. These concerns have been raised in the medical press where it has been noted that 'the abortus' has no status and that it is time for the law to become more sensitive and 'shed those artificial barriers of the classification of baby life' (e.g. *Lancet* editorials 1988, 1991). For many women, very early pregnancy loss may not be a tragedy, and dwelling upon the disposal of the remains is inappropriate, but for others, it *is* the loss of a baby needing to be mourned and acknowledged. Helen Davies' research into hospital policies has identified anomalies including the confusion between *incineration* and *cremation* (Davies 1995). There is evidence that women, *at the very least*, wish to be consulted about these matters (Jackman, McGee and Turner 1991, Bailes-Brown 1995).

RELIGIOUS PROFESSIONALS

In my early study, I noticed that as well as turning to midwives, doctors, nurses and other health professionals, bereaved mothers (often experiencing a bereavement for the first time) – even the irreligious – looked to religious professionals for help. Professionals and authority figures play a significant role in defining situations and shaping care. This observation led to my recent exploratory study based on in-depth interviews with functionaries of various religions and philosophies (Judaism, Islam, Methodism, Buddhism, Church of England, Roman Catholicism, Humanism and Hinduism).

Religion and belief systems leave their mark on official institutions through influence on public opinion which in turn influences public policy. Furthermore, religious and cultural rituals invest death with meaning. Rituals physicalise the spiritual and spiritualise the physical. The major belief systems teach that there is some form of continuity after death and provide comfort to the bereaved by helping them to make sense of loss although *very little is said about babies*. Humanism does not offer an after-life or deity but recognises the need for ceremonies, such as non-religious funerals, to mark important events.

In an earlier section, I emphasised how miscarriage, stillbirth and early neonatal loss are marginalised. This is exemplified at a superficial level by the way that the manufacturers of greetings cards, who now cover virtually every eventuality and are not usually slow to commercialise life events, have not, as yet, produced one to send after a pregnancy loss. At a more profound level, however, there is compounded neglect of *cultural* aspects of these losses. The few remembrance services for babies, including miscarried babies, are organised in conjunction with hospital chaplains. Although ostensibly non-denominational, they are almost invariably held in churches.

Furthermore, the practice at one London cemetery as described to me by a Humanist functionary is as follows:

> Once a month, a local hospital comes along with all the foetuses for a month. . . . They are given a Christian service. . . . parents are told this is going to happen. . . It's not an individual ceremony. . . The foetuses arrive in one coffin but individually wrapped with paperwork attached.

Although well-intentioned, it illustrates how the needs and wishes of non-Christians (and of the non-religious) are not taken into account.

In multi-cultural societies, bereaved mothers and bereaved fathers have wide-ranging needs. There is a growing literature addressing religious diversity, designed to educate health professionals about differing attitudes to illness and dying (Firth 1993, Katz 1993, Laungani 1996.) Gaining insights into a variety of religious beliefs and practices helps professionals provide support and understanding to the families involved. However, my study has highlighted practical as well as theoretical problems which face us when *there are no clearly laid down rituals and practices.*

In the *Article of Islam Acts*, article 601 states 'offering prayers for the dead body of a stillborn child is not ... recommended' (Khoei 1991: 129). Although it is obligatory to offer prayers for every Muslim including children aged 6 or more, my interviewee explained that prayers are not normally said for children under this age because:

> children are not considered to have any sins. In Islam, they believe you have a reward ... you lost the child ... that's not the end of it. This child could help you go to heaven ... You respect what God decides for you ... The saying is that the child you lost will stand in front of the door of heaven and [say] I won't go in unless I take my parents with me.

Within orthodox Judaism, the formal practices of mourning such as the *Shiva* are not observed for a baby who died in his or her first thirty days. The reason for the lack of obligatory mourning rites is a technical issue related to the viability of human life. In an interview with a Liberal rabbi, this was explained as follows: 'In its time, this was very enlightened. They were trying to stop ... limit the grief ... It was saying this wasn't quite a person yet ... wasn't a human being yet'. The rabbi recounted a recent case where twins were born and one died after twelve days: 'What I did was to have ... a truncated funeral service ... to respect Jewish tradition which doesn't have a funeral for a neonate ... and respect modern knowledge which is to say we need to facilitate the mourning process'.

The interviewee suggested that there was scope for innovations: 'women should be encouraged to write their own prayers and rituals'. These issues have been identified in a report (Goodkin and Citron 1994) which advocates: 'The publication of special prayers – for the loss of a baby through miscarriage and stillbirth ... [and] the loss of a young child ... under the age of one month' (1994: R3).

There were contradictions about the importance of baptism and the implications. A Roman Catholic priest told me that in his twenty-one years' experience he could remember one neonatal funeral. But he had never conducted a funeral for a stillborn or miscarried baby. He said that he would, if there was doubt about life, give a stillborn the benefit of the doubt and baptise. He pointed out that there is a special mass for an unbaptised child:

> a child who dies before they're able to sin ... their original sin is forgiven and we can be confident they go straight to heaven. .. [but] we know that only baptism forgives sins ... a child who is not baptised ... various theories are put forward about them in theology but *nothing very definite is said.* (my emphasis)

He continued that they are probably in limbo, adding:

> The lay idea of limbo is a sort of swirling place ... desolate ... but the theological idea is that it was a sort of natural happiness ... There wasn't that union with God that is heaven. It is sort of a happy limbo but without the beatific vision.

An opposing view was taken by a Church of England minister who regarded baptism of a stillborn or miscarried baby 'a pastoral gesture' saying: 'It doesn't make sense ... It's a nonsense. When the baby has died, as far as I'm concerned, the baby is in God's care'.

An Anglican hospital chaplain who heads a multi-faith team, carries out funerals for babies who die before or soon after birth. He also set up a counselling service, started five years ago, for parents and staff. This service evolved in direct response to the needs of staff:

> I don't see myself as chaplain simply to patients and relatives but also to staff. And in fact the majority of my time is spent with staff. ... At one stage, we were doing quite considerable numbers of late terminations for social reasons. This is extremely distressing for the staff and they needed some support and so the ward sister, who is now assistant counsellor, working in the field of miscarriage, asked me to facilitate a group. As a result of what came out, we then explored the possibility of creating a better system of disposal.

This quote brings out several issues. First, it demonstrates again how the distress and needs of the professionals paved the way for something to be done for the parents, and illustrates the necessity for caregivers' needs to be fully acknowledged. Second, it addresses the knotty issue of abortion – a topic raised spontaneously by most of the interviewees in my recent study and which cannot be ignored. When a woman becomes pregnant, she embarks upon a continuum which stretches from a fertilised ovum to a newborn human being. With advances in neonatal medicine, viability becomes ever earlier and, as Layne (1990) observed, ultrasound enables women to 'see life' before they 'feel life'.

The product of the pregnancy may be referred to as an embryo, 'abortus', foetus, baby, and these terms can be used interchangeably demonstrating some of the legal, medical and social definitional difficulties. In the United States, for instance, the legal definition of a foetus varies from state to state. This returns us once more to the problematic nature of definition which permeates these debates.

CONCLUSION

The issues discussed here aim to shed light on some of the reasons why death at the beginning of life has been such a neglected area riddled with ambiguities. Powerful groups have played their part in this neglect. As pointed out earlier on in this chapter, pregnancy and childbirth place a woman into a role where she is subordinated by medical men and patriarchal values. If the pregnancy goes wrong, there is a tendency for health professionals to minimise her lived experience and encourage her to 'try again'. Although, as has been indicated, there has been some progress, the nature of changes in the social management of these losses is still more in word than in deed with much depending on the individual style of a consultant. A midwife confided that while she was well aware of the new guidelines, 'quite honestly, there is still a theory–practice gap'. It takes time for the care to catch up with the rhetoric.

Similarly, within the religious context, professionals too, in spite of growing awareness, are slow to change their practice. Functionaries with experience ranging from two to twenty-five years, spoke at length about what they 'would do', but most had hardly ever conducted funerals (or other rituals) for early neonatal deaths, fewer for stillbirths and, with one exception, none for miscarriages. A Methodist minister admitted, 'We do our best, but it's still hit and miss.'

Here and there individuals – not necessarily within a religious tradition – are developing their own rituals. Self-help groups and organisations which protest the cultural denial of perinatal loss are trying to define miscarriage as a legitimate source of grief, although there is no co-ordinating umbrella organisation. Layne (1990) pointed out that groups are now widespread in Australia, Canada, Israel, Italy, West Germany, South Africa, the United Kingdom, United States and the Virgin Islands. She noted that participants tend to be mainly members of the white middle class and are thus not representative. It is important to gain an understanding of the religious beliefs and cultural traditions of all members of the community if we are to enjoy a genuinely pluralistic society. If attempts are to be made to empower the newly bereaved, enabling them to improvise, if necessary, this needs to be done within a context which makes sense to them.

In his description of death in a Hindu family, Laungani (1996) argues that unless we can appreciate the rituals, customs and traditions which give each culture its unique identity and meaning, there is a danger that the culture as well as the rituals may be lost. I suggest that culture thrives and can be enriched by adding fresh ideas which relate directly to human experiences. Individuals and groups within and outwith religious traditions are writing new prayers and creating their own rituals which can complement rather than compete with existing belief systems (Radford Ruether 1986, Willson 1989). Bereaved parents including the fathers, who tend to be overlooked, need opportunities to express their feelings and have their grief acknowledged. Too often fathers are expected to provide social support for their partners and more work needs to be done to access their needs.

Why have feminist movements remained so quiet? One reason could be that by focusing attention on the 'personhood' of the baby lost through miscarriage, stillbirth and early neonatal death, they might be seen as adding ammunition to the anti-abortion lobby. Does airing the neglect of miscarriage provide fuel for the pro-life, anti-abortionists? Does this debate present a danger of bringing women into conflict with other women? A woman who may have had an elective termination of pregnancy at one stage in her life may experience internal contradictions if she then subsequently loses a baby. While these tensions cannot be resolved here, they do need to be discussed more fully within the women's movement. Shying away from them leaves an opening for the opponents of women's rights to make decisions about pregnancy and childbirth and prescribe ways in which women's experiences are defined.

Instead of polarising a woman's experiences, it is more fruitful to try to build up connections. In making space to grieve over their miscarried babies, women do not have to forfeit – for themselves or anyone else – the rights at other times and places to make deliberate, difficult choices. In the search for meanings, it is up to the mother to define and shape her own reality and, at the same time, to be part of an all-embracing continuum.

ACKNOWLEDGEMENTS

Thanks are due to David Field, Veronica James and David Lovell for their constructive comments on earlier drafts of this chapter.

REFERENCES

Andersson Wretmark, A. (1993) *Perinatal Death as a Pastoral Problem*, Uppsala: Bibliotheca Theologiae Practicae, 50.

Ariès, P. (1974) *Western Attitudes Towards Death*, London: Johns Hopkins University Press.

Armstrong, D. (1986) 'The invention of infant mortality', *Sociology of Health and Illness* 8: 211–32.

Bailes-Brown, A. (1995) 'The dividing line', *New Generation* 14 (March): 20–1.

Borg, S. and Lasker, J. (1981) *When Pregnancy Fails. Families Coping with Miscarriage, Stillbirth and Infant Death*, Boston: Beacon Press.

Bourne, S. (1968) 'The psychological effects of stillbirths on women and their doctors', *Journal of the Royal College of General Practitioners* 16: 103–12.

—— and Lewis, E. (1991) 'Perinatal bereavement. A milestone and some new dangers', *British Medical Journal* 302: 1167–8.

—— Lewis, E. and Vallender, I. (1992) *Psychological Aspects of Stillbirth and Neonatal Death*, London: Tavistock Clinic.

Bruce, S. J. (1962) 'Reactions of nurses and mothers to stillbirths', *Nursing Outlook* 10 (2): 88–91.

CESDI (Confidential Enquiry into Stillbirths and Deaths in Infancy) (1993) Annual Report for 1 January–31 December 1993, Part 2, London: Department of Health.

Chalmers, I. and McIlwaine, G. (eds) (1980) *Perinatal Audit and Surveillance*, Proceedings of the Eighth Study Group of The Royal College of Obstetricians and Gynaecologists, London.

Cullberg, J. (1966) 'Reactioner info perinatal barnadod. 1 Psykiska foljder hos kvinnan', *Lakartidningen* 63: 3980–6.

—— (1972) 'Mental reactions of women to perinatal death' in *Psychosomatic Medicine in Obstetrics and Gynaecology, Proceedings of the Third International Congress*, Basel: Karger, pp. 326–9.

Davies, H. (1994) 'Early pregnancy loss – fetal disposal', Unpublished paper presented at National Childbirth Trust Conference, London: Queen Charlotte's Hospital.

Elias, N. (1985) *The Loneliness of Dying*, Oxford: Blackwell.

Estok, P. and Lehman, H. (1983) 'Perinatal death: grief support for families', *Birth* 10: 17–25.

Firth, S. (1993) 'Approaches to death in Hindu and Sikh communities in Britain', in D. Dickenson and M. Johnson (eds) *Death, Dying and Bereavement*, London: Sage, pp. 26–32.

Forrest, G. (1982) 'Coping after stillbirth', *Maternal and Child Health* 7: 394–8.

Giddens, A. (1991) *Modernity and Self-Identity*, Cambridge: Polity Press.

Giles, P. F. H. (1970) 'Reactions of women to perinatal death', *Australian and New Zealand Journal of Obstetrics and Gynaecology* 10: 207–10.

Gittings, C. (1988) *Death, Burial and the Individual in Early Modern England*, London: Routledge, pp. 60–85.

Goodkin, J. and Citron, J. (1994) *Women in the Jewish Community: Review and Recommendations*, London: Women in the Community.

Gorer, G. (1965) *Death, Grief and Mourning in Contemporary Britain*, London: Cresset.

HEC (Health Education Council) (1979) *The Loss of Your Baby*, Mind and National Stillbirth Study Group, London: HEC.

Hey, V., Itzin, C., Saunders, L. and Speakman, M. A. (eds) (1989) *Hidden Loss. Miscarriage and Ectopic Pregnancy*, London: The Women's Press.

Hugman, R. (1993) *Power in the Caring Professions*, London: Macmillan.

Jackman, C., McGee, H. M. and Turner, M. (1991) 'The experience and psychological impact of early miscarriage', *The Irish Journal of Psychology* 12: 108–20.

Jolly, H. (1975a) 'How hospitals can help parents to bear the loss of a baby', *The Times*, 5 November.

—— (1975b) 'The heartache in facing the facts of a stillborn baby', *The Times*, 3 December.

—— (1976) 'Family reactions to stillbirths', *Proceedings of the Royal Society of Medicine*, 69: 835–7.

Katz, J. (1993) 'Jewish perspectives an death, dying and bereavement', in D. Dickenson and M. Johnson (eds) *Death, Dying and Bereavement*, London: Sage, pp. 199–207.

Kennell, J. H. and Klaus, M. H. (1971) 'Care of the mother of the high-risk infant', *Clinical Obstetrics and Gynecology* 14: 926–54.

Khoei, I. (1991) *Articles of Islam Acts*, Pakistan: Islamic Seminary Publications.

Kohner, N. (1992) *A Dignified Ending. Recommendations for Good Practice in the Disposal of the Bodies and Remains of Babies Born Dead Before the Age of Legal Viability*, London: Stillbirth and Neonatal Deaths Society.

Lancet (1988) 'Disposal of the pre-viable fetus' (editorial), *Lancet* (ii): 611–12.
—— (1991) 'When is a fetus a dead baby?' (editorial), *Lancet* 337: 526.
Laungani, P. (1996) 'Death in a Hindu family: implications for health professionals', in C. M. Parkes, P. Laungani and W. Young (eds) *Death and Bereavement across Cultures*, London: Routledge.
Layne, L. (1990) 'Motherhood lost: cultural dimensions of miscarriage and stillbirth in America', *Women and Health* 16 (3/4): 69–98.
Lewis, E. (1972) 'Reactions to stillbirth', in *Psychosomatic Medicine in Obstetrics and Gynaecology, Proceedings of the Third International Congress*, Basel: Karger, pp. 323–5.
—— (1976) 'The management of stillbirth: coping with an unreality', *Lancet* (ii): 619–20.
—— and Page, A. (1978) 'Failure to mourn a stillbirth: an overlooked catastrophe', *British Journal of Medical Psychology* 51: 237–41.
Lewis, H. (1979) 'Nothing was said sympathy-wise', *Social Work Today* 10 (45): 12.
Lovell, A. (1983) 'Some questions of identity: late miscarriage, stillbirth and perinatal death', *Social Science and Medicine* 17: 755–61.
—— (1995a) *A Bereavement with a Difference*, Sociology and Social Policy Occasional Paper Number 4, London: South Bank University.
Lovell, A. (1995b) 'Towards a sociology of miscarriage and perinatal loss: the influence of the professionals', British Sociological Association Medical Sociology Group 27th Annual Conference, University of York, 22–24 September.
MacLean, U. (1971) *Magical Medicine*, Harmondsworth: Penguin.
McLenahan, I. G. (1962) 'Helping the mother who has no baby to take home', *American Journal of Nursing* 62 (4): 70–1.
Mead, M. (1956) *New Lives for Old*, London: Victor Gollancz.
Miscarriage Association (undated, received 1995) *Origins and Development of the Miscarriage Association*, Wakefield: Miscarriage Association.
Mooney, B. (1976) 'Brain clearing, awareness dawning, my hand felt my stomach. The nurse looked distressed: you had your baby . . . it was a little boy . . . he isn't alive', *Guardian*, 8 January.
Moulder, C. (1990) *Miscarriage: Women's Experiences and Needs*, London: Pandora.
Oakley, A., McPherson, A. and Roberts, H. (1990) *Miscarriage* (rev. edn) Harmondsworth: Penguin.
OPCS (1995) 'Perinatal and infant mortality: social and biological factors', *Mortality Statistics England and Wales 1992*, DH3 No. 26, London: HMSO.
Peppers, L. and Knapp, R. (1980) *Motherhood and Mourning*, New York: Praeger.
Pizer, H. and Palinski, C. (1980) *Coping with a Miscarriage*, London: Jill Norman.
Polkinghorne, J. (1989) *Review of the Guidance on the Research Use of Fetuses and Fetal Materials*, Cm 762, London: HMSO.
Radford Ruether, R. (ed.) (1986) *Liturgical Life and Women-Church*, London: Harper & Row.

Rajan, L. and Oakley, A. (1991) *Pregnancy Loss: Its Implications for the Family and Health Professionals*, Report for the Department of Health.
—— and —— (1993) 'No pills for heartache: support in pregnancy loss', *Journal of Reproductive and Infant Psychology* 11: 75–87.
SANDS (Stillbirth and Neonatal Deaths Society) (1995) *Pregnancy Loss and the Death of a Baby: Guidelines for Professionals* (rev. edn), London: SANDS.
Scheper-Hughes, N. (1992) *Death Without Weeping: The Violence of Everyday Life in Brazil*, Berkeley: University of California Press.
Thomas, J. (1990) *Supporting Parents When a Baby Dies Before or Soon After Birth*, Buckinghamshire: Mrs M. Brown.
Van Gennep, A. (1960) *The Rites of Passage*, London: Routledge & Kegan Paul.
Walter, T. (1994) *The Revival of Death*, London: Routledge.
——, Littlewood, J. and Pickering, M. (1995) 'Death in the news: the public invigilation of private emotion', *Sociology* 29: 579–96.
Willson, W. (1989) *Funerals Without God: A Practical Guide to Non-religious Funerals*, London: British Humanist Association.
Witz, A. (1992) *Professions and Patriarchy*, London: Routledge.

Chapter 3

'Shoring up the walls of heartache'
Parental responses to the death of a child

Gordon Riches and Pamela Dawson

INTRODUCTION

There is considerable debate about the relationship between a
child's death and marital breakdown (Rando 1991). Many studies
offer evidence of increased communication problems, emotional
isolation and mutual frustration between partners. Researchers
relate this increase in marital tension directly to differences in
grieving patterns between partners (Schwab 1992, Littlewood *et
al.* 1991). Studies also acknowledge cases in which partners report
that their relationship has been strengthened.

Grief response and gender are frequently linked and stereotypical accounts of strong men and emotional women may go
some way towards explaining variations in how parents cope with
the deaths of their children. While feelings of disorientation are
common in both partners, reports note that fathers appear to
grieve less deeply and for shorter periods of time than mothers.
Women appear to express profound distress more openly than
men, grieve for longer, experience more guilt, are preoccupied
more obviously with their loss and take longer to return to 'normal
functioning'. Men are more likely to grieve in practical ways.
These distinctive patterns are regularly reported regardless of
the age of the child and the cause of death, although researchers
occasionally report exceptions to them (Peddicord 1990, Vance
et al. 1995).

In our study it became clear that although many informants'
accounts reflected this pattern, some did not. While most fathers
appeared to be strong, to be supporting their wives and getting
on with their lives, some reported continuing depression and
expressed their emotions as openly as some mothers. While most

mothers reported recurring feelings of despair and were able to express emotions openly, a substantial number had returned to full-time work or were engaging in other activities relatively soon after their bereavement and appeared to be exhibiting coping styles more generally associated with men. Moreover, even those men and women who appeared to fit into typically gendered patterns of grieving included in their accounts exceptional behaviours and sentiments which did not fit neatly into these conventional distinctions.

In trying to explain these variations in our data, we noted that the type of social support available appeared to be linked to the ways in which parents oriented themselves to their loss and the extent to which they appeared disoriented by their child's death. We also found that parents' orientations altered during grieving, and not always in similar ways, irrespective of the time since the offspring's death. We suggest that movement from one grief orientation to another may be linked to the types of social network in which parents find support. Because the 'marriage' itself is a primary relationship, its nature also affects, and is affected by, the way in which each partner grieves.

Berger and Kellner (1964) argue that marriage is a process of negotiating mutual understandings about significant aspects of the world. It is likely that the death of a child may present a major challenge to parents' capacity to agree on the significance and meaning of their loss. Deal et al. (1992) argue that satisfaction in marriage can be directly linked to the degree of similarity of perspectives held by each partner. Given that over the last twenty years or so changes have occurred in the role of women and in the involvement of fathers in parenting, gender distinctions may be less useful in explaining marital tension following a child's death, than the degree to which partners share a similar understanding of the meaning of the child's death. Duncombe and Marsden (1995) argue that men undervalue intimacy and emotional expression while emphasising the importance of physical and economic activity. Grief work within the couple relationship can be described in terms of a division of discursive labour: women may draw upon emotional and expressive 'knowledge' to address the damage within their lived family experience, while men may draw upon organisational and cognitive 'knowledge' to address their adjustment within the public domain. Women's expression of grief is more likely to be informed by their experience of emotional discourses which characterise the private domain. Men's management of their joint emotional expression, of their support for their wives, and of their active supervision of arrangements concerning the death, is more likely to be informed by their access to discourses which characterise public living (Smith 1972).

Because the social and economic positions of men and women are changing, it may be necessary to rethink assumptions which link women with the private sphere and men with the public. While the resources available to bereaved parents may be predominantly gendered in origin, the increased economic activity of women and the long-term impact of feminist ideas on men may expose both parents to a range of discourses concerning the death of an offspring. Women in our own study who were in employment when their children died, and who adopted 'active' coping styles, confirmed the importance of work in 'coming to terms' with their grief and change of status, while some employed men failed to find such support, becoming preoccupied with their lost parental relationship. There is a need for a conceptual framework which, while accounting for gender variations in grief responses, also explains exceptions to this pattern and allows researchers to explore their consequences for the joint adjustment of couples to their child's death.

METHODOLOGY

Our conceptual model is derived from data collected on thirty-two bereaved parents. In eight cases, only one partner from the couple was interviewed, but in the remaining twelve cases, accounts from both partners were obtained, five together and seven separately. In total, twelve fathers and twenty mothers were interviewed. Parents' responses to the deaths of twenty children were explored. Eight died accidentally, six died as the result of illness, two were murder victims, and four were unborn or still-born infants. The time between the children's deaths and our interviews varied from eleven months to twenty-three years. We relied on a snowball sampling procedure and therefore make no claim to representative findings.

We used an ethnographic approach to investigate how parents perceived the role of their marital and other social relationships in coming to terms with the loss of their child. Qualitative data was collected through taped narrative interviews lasting between one and three hours. All quotations in this chapter are taken from those interviews. Interviews were conducted by three researchers – two female and one male. Each interviewer followed a loose agenda which sought to gain details of the child's death, experiences of feelings, emotions and events during and since the death, perception of support given, involvement with professionals and self-help groups, perceptions of partner's grief and perceptions of the effect of the child's death on marriage and family relationships. We also participated in a number of bereavement groups and support agencies. The agenda for the series was drawn up following an initial literature review and analysis of three pilot interviews. The diversity of these case studies allowed us to build a hypothesis which uses marital and other relationships to account, at least in part, for differences in parents' orientation to grief.

Taking a 'constructionist' approach, we are enabled by this data to identify those cultural discourses which parents use to make sense of their child's death and of their spouse's response to it. It also enables us to explore parents' perceptions of the relative value of different social networks in helping to reconstruct a damaged self-identity. We have viewed grief following the death of a child as a site of marital discourse. Each spouse contributes to the meaning and significance of the death within this discourse. Each partner's account offers insight into their perception of how the marriage and other close relationships have featured in their adjustment.

BEYOND GENDER: CULTURAL RESOURCES AND BEREAVEMENT ORIENTATIONS

The meaning and significance of death is culturally defined. Grief is a cultural product as well as a psychological response (Prior 1989). In modern societies distressing descriptions of child death and of extreme emotional responses can be found in public discourses (Walter *et al.* 1995). Parents will be familiar with these even before the death of their own child: 'With seeing it in casualty [Allison is a nurse] you would sometimes think subconsciously: "Thank God it's not my child ... How awful that would be if it were my child."' Although social relationships may facilitate the process of grieving, culture provides the content of grieving. In societies defined as late or postmodern, sensational images of child death proliferate, but after the media have gone the long-term task of making sense of personal tragedy is left to those directly affected.

While little research has been done into the ways in which grief is culturally produced, considerable work exists on the construction of illness and risk. Radley (1989), drawing on Durkheim's distinction between mechanistic and organic social relationships (1964), links heart disease patients' attitudes towards illness with their socio-economic status. Working-class patients were more likely to be fatalistic about their illness, denying its effect on their lives, while middle-class patients were more likely to perceive their illness as something to be managed. Couples use marital discourse to explore ways in which their lives can accommodate its effects. Radley argues that emotional responses are managed by the creation of an illness identity, constructed largely through conversation between the marital partners which draws upon wider discourses of class, gender and medicine.

Douglas and Calvez (1990) develop Durkheim's analysis into a 'grid/group' typology of risk and cultural sentiments. 'Grid' describes the strength of collectively held sentiments – structures of social positions, behaviours, beliefs and values within which role-based identity may be objectively located. 'Group' describes the strength of social processes and the individual's experience of affection – the subjective experience of identity as the product of relating with others. Their typology, although used to explain differences in perception of risk from HIV, is equally valuable in explaining variations in parental orientation towards grief. Their model demonstrates why gender has been so successfully used in the past to distinguish grief patterns. Sentiments about motherhood, expectations of parental roles and clear boundaries between male and female are basic features of the structure of traditional societies. It also demonstrates why gender may be less useful as an explanation in modern 'organic' societies where gender, sexuality and sexual orientation are increasingly open to negotiation and where boundaries between men's and women's work are blurred.

Following Radley and Douglas and Calvez, four identity-orientations can be identified to describe 'typical' ways in which the affection and sentiment encountered in social networks might combine to produce distinctive ways of making sense of a child's death. Bereaved parents may experience affectionate relationships in which significant others are supportive, accepting and affirming. Alternatively, they may either receive little affection, or their experience of significant others is critical, unsupportive or rejecting. At the same time, within these relationships, parents may encounter either strong prescriptive 'instructions' on how to react to the death or they may have to search hard even for weak, ambiguous or contradictory sentiments explaining the meaning of their loss. Four 'typical' orientations to parental grief based on the possible combinations of sentiment and affection appear: *isolation* – strong sentiments but weak affection; *nomic repair* – strong sentiments and strong affection; *sub-cultural alternation* – weak sentiments and strong affection; and *personal reconstruction* – weak sentiments and weak affection. The principal characteristics of these four orientations are summarised in Figure 3.1.

ISOLATION

Sentiments which define circumstances as hopeless discourage individuals from seeking close social support thus producing further seclusion and continued disintegration of self-identity. Most grieving parents initially experience cognitive and emotional disorientation, but many move through it as their feelings are drawn out through the conversation and grief of others. For those parents whose identities derive almost exclusively from their successful parenting, grief cuts them off from the affection of others. Correspondingly, it may be difficult for friends and family to give affection if they also base their self-identities on successful parenthood (or grandparenthood). Opportunities to develop other compensatory roles or fresh perspectives are minimised because there is no credible audience with whom to negotiate alternatives.

NOMIC REPAIR

In modern societies, identities within the dominant culture are likely to be composed of conventional role-clusters reinforced through family, work and consumer activities, held in place through liberal capitalist ideology. In our sample, parents recognised the value of outside activities such as work in providing 'psychological splints'. Familiar routines away from the home

Strong prescriptive sentiments

Fragmentation	**Nomic repair**
– self overwhelmed by grief	– quarantine of bereaved self
– normal role identities extinguished	– normal role identities re-emphasised
– preoccupation with loss	– diversion from loss
– grief as a destination	– grief as a threat
– marriage 'given' but irrelevant	– marriage 'given' and relevant

Weak or no   *Strong*

affection   *affection*

Personal reconstruction	**Sub-cultural alternation**
– self re-evaluated through grief	– self identifies with other bereaved parents
– normal roles and familiar relationships re-appraised	– bereaved self in opposition to mainstream society
– integration of loss	– development of sub-culture around loss
– grief as a journey	– grief as a relational bond
– marriage as part of a personal renegotiation	– marriage as part of a collective renegotiation

Weak or ambiguous sentiments

Figure 3.1 Orientations to the loss of a child

appear to offer diversion, if only temporarily, from emotional pain, and to affirm non-parental aspects of identity. In any event, whether familiar roles and routines are geared towards the management of mourning or towards minimising its impact, clear sentiments provide ready-made meanings through which identity can be repaired and re-integrated into former definitions. This orientation is characterised by acceptance of those sentiments which acknowledge that life must go on.

SUB-CULTURAL ALTERNATION

Radley and Douglas and Calvez identify the existence of counter-cultures whose members reject the dominant sentiments of mainstream society. Bereavement 'self-help' groups are dissatisfied with explanations arising from 'normal' discourses and with the everyday relations in which they are rehearsed. Bereaved parents generate alternative sentiments on the basis of shared loss and dislocation from mainstream living. The concerns and priorities of everyday life seem trivial and insensitive, thus foregrounding a bereaved parent's damaged identity rather than serving to repair it as in the previous orientation. Ball *et al.* (1996) identify a similar 'culture of childhood cancer' which develops within the trajectory of cancer treatment and which marks its members off from 'normal' living.

Amongst our sample, the death of an offspring marked a fateful turning point in which previous assumptions and former relationships became problematic. Dissatisfaction with 'mainstream' sentiments encountered amongst family, acquaintances, and in the media was frequently reported. In some cases they were actively challenged by crusades against, for example, the dangers of road conditions. On the other hand, many parents noted the support gained from other parents whose children had died. This orientation is characterised by acceptance of those sentiments which recognise that death somehow has irrevocably changed everything and is shared by a 'select' few in similar circumstances and avoidance of others whose lack of empathy denies the depth of their loss.

PERSONAL RECONSTRUCTION

In this orientation individuals act independently of social networks and prescribed sentiments, contributing creatively to change through innovation and independent action. Radley notes that some individuals discover a new meaning to life as a consequence of facing their mortality. Here the bereaved parent may arrive at a different destination in terms of sentiments and self-identity to those held within either the mainstream culture or bereavement sub-cultures. Our findings include parents whose search for meaning has taken them through other orientations but who, in the end, comprehensively changed their lifestyle and networks of relationships. Experience within this orientation may be compared and contrasted with nomic repair. Reintegration into mainstream culture involves a public rite of passage in which society 'permits' temporary deviant behaviour while the bereaved parent grieves and gradually returns to normal. The individual is able to carry through previous aspects of identity with the support of social networks, emerging, if not completely whole, then at least recognisably the same person. This orientation, on the other hand, is characterised by radical reconstruction, often appearing to result from a lonely refusal to give in to the despair of grief. In their search for meaning these parents scrutinise a range of sentiments as well as the limitations of previously close relationships. Exclusion from the routines of mainstream society may result in the shared ordeal of a bereavement sub-culture, but it may also result in an independent reconstruction of self with its comprehensive reappraisal of personal relationships. Marriage and other family networks will be included in this.

SUPPORT NETWORKS AND ORIENTATIONS TO GRIEVING: PARENTS' ACCOUNTS

Our case-study material indicates how central social support is in parents' narratives of their children's deaths and subsequent experience of grief. Social support frequently failed to recognise how profoundly awful their personal grief felt. The most valuable support was evidence of this recognition. Other people's expression of their own grief was far more comforting than sympathy. Medical explanations from professionals, reassurance from other parents who had undergone similar losses, direct sharing of the pain of loss with partner or other parents involved in the same accident, and, later, recognition of some positive good resulting from the death, all pointed to the value of sense-making discourse within intimate relationships. Disorientation and loss of self were commonly experienced after the death. Although gendered grief responses were frequently noted, exceptions included two fathers who continued to manifest marked emotional distress two years after the death, and eight mothers who adopted the more 'active' coping strategies conventionally associated with men. Work, education and voluntary activities appeared to provide positive support in returning to some semblance of 'normality'. Perceptions of spousal support also varied, with some couples feeling more frustration with partners' apparent lack or excess of emotional expression than others. Perceptions also varied in the degree to which the loss had been seen as significant in altering the couple's relationship. In three cases, the death of the child was followed almost immediately by permanent marital breakdown. These mothers accounted for their divorces largely in terms of their partners' inappropriate response to the dying and death of their child.

ISOLATION: RESIGNATION AND LOST PARENTAL IDENTITY

When a child dies the shock of the event may cut parents off from all social relations except those that have been lost (Cornwell *et al.* 1977: 656). While isolation might be seen as a passing response to the death, it appeared from our findings that it was not only those who lost children recently who showed a continuing preoccupation with the lost relationship and lack of interest in other potentially supportive ones. Cornwell's account implies that isolation is a function of the individual's psychological response to loss, yet unexpected or problematic deaths may also produce a social response in others. Emotional support may not only be hard to seek, it might also be harder to give, in as much as the event itself challenges assumptions about the given social order:

> I used to think it didn't happen but it does. People crossing the street or keeping their heads down. . . . It is probably the most horrendous thing that can happen in our society. Our culture doesn't gear itself up to this sort of thing very much.

It is not surprising that many bereaved parents find themselves in this position. Modern child-centred and health-valuing societies, with advanced medical systems and high expectations of longevity, tend to have few discourses which account for parental bereavement. Those discourses that do exist, emphasise (inaccurately) its rarity and abnormality. This orientation is anomic in the sense that the child's death now prevents the carrying through of strongly internalised roles of parenting, and the continuance of everyday routines attached to these roles. Personal control has been lost in the face of highly structured social and internal expectations. Self-identity, comprising to a greater or lesser extent parental role-identity, is called into question. Confusion, a sense of unreality and a loss of purpose were regularly reported:

and for four and a half months we were in this zombie stage – limbo state and it was terribly fuzzy. . . . I didn't really know what was going on very much, and I wasn't on any sort of drug – Valium – or anything like that.

Many of the informants in our study whose orientation towards grief was characterised both by preoccupation with the loss and a lack of reinvolvement with any social network had lost children in problematic ways and in many of these cases the sense of isolation appeared to have lasted. This may be explained in part by the absence of sentiments relating to problematic death response, and in part by an implicit conspiracy of mutual avoidance between the bereaved parent and potential support networks.

Stillbirth and miscarriage are circumstances where medical discourse, lack of opportunity for the father to share experience of the child's life and social expectations of successful motherhood place strong definitions of the situation on the bereaved mother while potentially offering few networks of support which appreciate the isolating factors in her loss:

The health visitor's response was 'You can always have another.' . . . I went off blaming George, and blamed myself I think, because he wouldn't fight back. If he had fought back we could have thrashed it out but it is like having an argument with a brick wall. . . . You end up just saying I can't be bothered. . . . So then you turn it all in on yourself, all the guilt.

Karen's account of her subsequent experiences included her apparent return to normal living, resumption of work, becoming sexually active as a wife soon after the death of her baby, and successful birth of another. It also recounts how she became 'post-natally depressed', was increasingly dependent upon alcohol and was apprehended for 'inadvertently' shoplifting. She recalled telling her husband about this event but was unable to explain to him how she felt about the lost baby and her confusion about her new one. Karen's doctor prescribed tranquillisers and referred her to a psychiatric clinic. Karen felt unable to tell her husband about any of these events because:

I thought he would leave me. I thought my mother-in-law would try and get my other kids then. Everything was getting a bit daft by that time. . . . I had left the baby at my mum's and not told her where I was going either. I said I had to go to the hospital for a stomach examination. . . .

Mary reported a similar sense of isolation following her first miscarriage, and further failure to be understood by her husband after a second miscarriage of twin daughters. She commented that it was only upon her ante-natal visit with the twins that a nurse acknowledged that this was her second pregnancy. She reported that her husband seemed embarrassed at formally burying their twins and taking flowers to the grave when no one in the neighbourhood had ever seen any children for them to lose.

In both cases of miscarriage, expectations to return to 'normal' and the failure of family, work colleagues or medical services to acknowledge that they had had a baby compounded the mothers' sense of anomie and confirmed the inauthenticity of their own experiences. Social support was available only if these women returned to their previous networks of family and work, in which the sentiments they encountered denied the importance of their loss. In both these cases, as in many others, marital and other close relations, rather than providing support, attempted to exercise control through support being conditional upon the acceptance of normative sentiments.

Deaths of children through murder or accident offer further examples from our data in which the circumstances of the loss contribute towards the continuing isolation of bereaved parents. Frustration then resignation may arise from contradictions between personal feelings and social constraints. Because of the involvement of the police, courts, coroner and pathologists, parents not only lose control of the body and the circumstances surrounding its disposal but there may be unresolved questions about the death. The harder the death is to 'make sense of' and the more unique the circumstances of the death, the more prolonged the parents' experience of this anomie is likely to be and fewer relationships appear capable or qualified to offer support. David and Janet, whose only adult son lived at home before dying in a motorcycle accident two years prior to the interview, exemplified how a couple could share this sense of isolated resignation. David had not returned to work at all and Janet only worked occasionally part-time, reporting that it did not help take her mind off her loss:

It feels hopeless. Everything you work for . . . your children. . . . We have no one to leave anything to. It's like your future is just chopped off. A lot of people say he [Robert] did a lot in a short time, but that's no consolation.

Of the four orientations outlined, it is this one which most strongly features the patriarchal sentiments which link women's fulfilment to motherhood. Where personal status is invested almost exclusively in successful motherhood, the social position of the bereaved parent can only be perceived by self and others as negative. Gender, especially in the case of stillbirth or miscarriage, can be seen to contribute substantially to mothers' inability to find others with whom they can share their grief. Health services, for example, are not geared to the needs of mothers whose unborn babies have died:

> when you go to hospital, the place where you have your baby removed is the same place you go when you are expecting your baby – it is the same complex. So I was going up in the lift with a women who was going to have a baby . . . and that was a bit horrific. . . . As soon as she got out . . . that was when I started to bawl . . . I was given no time as if they wanted it over and done with as quickly as possible and they treat it as if it is a minor thing.

Where fathers were in full-time work and mothers were at home with young children, the social circumstances seemed to contribute to typically patriarchal orientations within the couple relationship. However, the nature of the death as well as the absence of close social support might also have created an isolated orientation amongst some bereaved parents which had little to do with their gender.

NOMIC REPAIR: THE 'SPLINTING' OF PARENTAL IDENTITY

Nomic repair retains continuity with life before the bereavement. It also involves utilisation of prescribed and publicly available behaviours and sentiments to deal with the role identities most affected by the child's death. Thus discourses which reinforced continuing work and family roles provided some bereaved parents with touchstones of normality and enabled familiar relationships to be maintained. The problem may be greater for mothers if they have no work to return to and if, as many writers suggest, women's emotional responsibilities for parenting are more central to their sense of self than they are for men. If their child was an only child, or particularly favoured by one parent rather than another, or if the father had a lonely occupation in which little distraction occurred, then prescribed sentiments were insufficiently reinforced by social relationships to 'splint' the damaged parental identity. In such cases, gender continued to be a significant influence upon the cultural resources available, and for women who invested heavily in their parental role at the expense of others, nomic repair was not an available option.

This orientation possesses two distinct components: opportunities to gain reassurance from mainstream cultural discourses that the loss is meaningful and manageable; and opportunities to engage in activities connected to valued role-identities outside of the lost relationship. For example, Peddicord notes in his sample of perinatal grief, that a number of men were made conscious of cultural expectations of their role: 'Everyone was telling me to be strong for her and asking about how she was doing, but I was hurting too!' (Peddicord 1990: 266). There is also evidence of diversions within the family role as well as outside it. For example, couples who have a second baby soon after losing the first find its care helpful in diverting attention from the earlier death (Powell 1995).

Our data offer examples of ways in which parents have been supported by mainstream sentiments and relationships. A number of wives noted the value of having 'solid' husbands and the continuity which their dependability provided: 'I don't know what I would have done without him. He was always there. I never really knew what he was thinking . . . but I could always depend on him.' Noreen found support for her own grief through women friends and through groups of other bereaved mothers. Her husband, from the evidence of the interview, fitted classically into this orientation by continuing to 'protect' his wife and surviving children through his work and through his emotional control. Orientations to grief in this example, though different, are complementary and manageable within the family paradigm.

In contrast, Hillary, whose son died from a brain tumour at the age of 8 having already survived leukaemia when he was 4, recognised her conscious avoidance of her parent-identity, despite having two younger children:

but if I was at home with Sally – like a normal mother and child – I can't give her what I should be giving her . . . I can't. . . . I haven't the patience somehow. I put it down to the fact that I'm afraid of getting too close . . . because if I was as close to anybody as I was to Dean and I lost them again it would kill me. I just could not cope. I do think subconsciously you shun people you can get close to. . . . It affects the whole family.

Hillary's strategy for dealing with the dislocated parental identity was to undertake an activity (studying for A level psychology) which offered a new routine away from the house where she had nursed Dean, and away from the familial roles which reinforced her loss. In her case nomic repair involved minimising those role-identities relating directly to the loss and maximising those which offered new activity and diversion.

Frequently our data illustrated the value of work and work relationships in the nomic repair of self. Jennie noted how her boss took account of her loss and offered a flexible approach to her role, giving 'permission' for any deviant behaviour she might display in the work-place:

They were very good at work. They let me talk about it. The partner took me on one side and said if there was anything he could do, I only had to ask. If I felt bad, I could just take the rest of the day off.

Ron also acknowledged the way work provided diversion, affirmation and the space to practise being normal again:

You don't say 'That's it, I'm as fit as a fiddle again – as right as rain' – no way. I just think . . . you go back to work. . . . We have a good set of lads down there. Our factory is no different to any other. It is all football, sex – you know – general factory talk. You go to work in the morning and you get on with your job. I was a little bit fortunate in so much as I was foreman where I work and it was never very long before someone was coming to me with some sort of a problem as regards the job. So that sort of kept my mind occupied even more.

These examples are typical of the ways in which work enables grief to be set aside, if only temporarily, by bereaved parents while they engage in other relationships. Pressure of work, the support and esteem of colleagues, and acknowledgement of temporary abnormality all provide structural continuity which helps shore up parental identity. While in traditionally gendered divisions of labour, nomic repair through work might be a more likely option for men than for women, our data indicate that this orientation was readily available to some women involved in professional occupations or who had access to further and higher education. We found evidence of women discovering both in and out of work, routines and relationships which allowed diversion from their loss and which compensated, albeit in a small way, for the missing purpose to their lives. At the same time, there was evidence of men, even in full-time work, failing to find such diversion.

SUB-CULTURES: RE-EVALUATING BEREAVED PARENT IDENTITY

The value of established self-help groups such as The Compassionate Friends was noted by many of our informants, but, additionally, there was a clear recognition of a culture of bereavement which arose from shared experiences. The isolation created by a child's death can, for some parents, be mitigated through the discovery of other parents in similar circumstances, or of relationships which acknowledge in some profound or insightful manner the depth of their grief. The aftermath of a child's death may lead to a restructuring of outlook and a scrutiny of close personal relationships:

> people don't think you need anybody to lean on. They say, 'Oh she can cope . . .' so there wasn't anyone to lean on really. You find out who your friends are and they're not there, and the friends that I found out were friends, the friends actually that I made – that we, John and I made – were from the hospital – people in similar situations and they were really the friends that I was able to talk to and be with . . . To have empathy, you have to have gone through it.

Pat, whose son was murdered, overcame feelings of frustration with her close relatives and friends when she founded a self-help group for relatives of other murder victims. Possessing elements of a counter-culture, bereavement networks are bound together by their common experience of loss, of frequently feeling excluded from mainstream society and of being stigmatised because of the embarrassment of others: 'A lot of people keep their distance. . . . They are frightened of catching it.'

Personal loss and devastating grief are fundamental elements of a community of feeling from which care professionals are often excluded. Though conversant with the culture of bereavement, counsellors and health-workers may fail to acknowledge the uniqueness of perspective which can only be obtained through living the loss:

> I have got my opinions about psychiatrists – I don't know what your opinions are – but I have said to the wife, 'You might as well go and see the queen.' And we did go – she wanted me to go with her – and we went three or four times and, quite frankly, we might as well have gone to the chip shop. It was useless. No disrespect but he was saying . . . silly things . . . like don't go to the grave.

Common experiences and mutual recognition of each other's distress cemented the sense of shared ordeal amongst many bereaved parents. Support was experienced between parents who lost children at similar times, and amongst those who were 'further down the line' in terms of working through their grief. In one case, four sets of parents shared the hospital vigil after two daughters died in a road accident and the other two sons were in surgery. This generated a network which still survived six years later. Knowing others were experiencing the same loss and sharing the unfolding events of the tragedy provided a rite of passage which reinforced these eight parents' common identity and their difference from other relationships.

A common feature of the bereaved parent networks and support groups was both the preponderance and the leadership of women. The value of women's support was noted frequently. Una stressed that it was meeting other mothers of adult children killed in an air disaster which gave her most support. Noreen gained additional emotional relief from sharing her bereavement with her daughter's best friend who regularly came to stay. Una and Noreen became very close friends, even though they lived almost 300 miles apart, providing the focal point for a larger group of crash victims' relatives who continued to meet annually, regularly arranging flights back to the memorial erected at the crash site. Margaret similarly gained great support from her son's girlfriend, who also still visited her two years after his road accident. Jennie noted the level of intimacy achievable in such a group and its possible contribution to supporting marriage relations:

We were just twelve ladies in this discussion group and I think it was . . . me that brought the sexual side up. But once it had been brought up they all started to talk and everybody seemed to have the same sort of situation. That yes, they did love their husbands but they couldn't respond to him or found it very difficult to, and if they did it was just . . . very degrading and upsetting. . . . And I felt, it's not just me that's going mad. It's not just me that's off sex. . . .

Bereaved parent sub-cultures appear to share the 'communitas' which arises from a spontaneous expression of collectively felt emotion (Walter 1991). In addition, some of these sub-cultures reject professional accounts of death and bereavement – particularly those associated with the work of John Bowlby. Long-term refusal to 'detach from the loved one' is perceived by bereavement counsellors as 'complicated mourning' liable to turn into pathological grief (Worden 1982). One of the key sentiments of bereaved parent sub-cultures we observed was a defiant refusal to 'let go' of the dead child. Sustained contact with other bereaved parents allowed regular sharing of their children's lives: they reminisced, they showed photographs, they imagined what they might have done had they lived, they went back through the events of the death and, most importantly, they explored the radical changes to their lives which the child's death had caused. Many of the parents we spoke to were familiar with Bowlby and the grief trajectory framework. It was their unanimous rejection of this perspective which firmly set many bereavement groups against 'professional' approaches to grief:

It isn't in the past. Sarah is involved with us now as she always has been. I don't see any problem with it. I know people think you ought to get over things but I don't see anything to get over. It's part of me, part of what I am. This thing about getting over it I really resent. We went up to a TCF conference . . . and they had a speaker there who was a professional, got no children of her own but she knew everything, and she told you how long it would be before you got over it and she told you the stages of what would happen and that. I really wanted to get up and wring her neck to be honest. . . . I found it really, really objectionable.

Walter's 'new model of grief' incorporates many of these counter-cultural sentiments into an alternative theory which offers support to the notion that grief involves achieving a new relationship with the dead, rather than giving it up altogether (Walter 1996).

Of the three grief orientations outlined, sub-cultural support is the one which most strongly features the activities of women in re-evaluating the status of bereaved parenthood while at the same time totally rejecting mainstream sentiments about the finality of child-death. Our data offer evidence of the discovery by recently bereaved parents of a worthwhile identity which incorporated their loss. In particular, the exchange of memories of lost children helped confirm that they had actually lived. Parents took the opportunity to express their pride in their children's lives, to share their hopes for what they might have become, as well as to express their despair at their deaths. Jennie recognised the contribution which such a support group made to her esteem as a parent:

> I would come home from the meeting on a high. That was what I needed. Jim [Jennie's husband] said he would rather talk to people who knew Sarah and I said 'OK, I talk to anybody' ... and talking to people who didn't know Sarah – they instinctively knew. ... We had this bond, and I found that they were the easiest people to talk to. And I liked to hear about their [children]. ... I found this a great comfort. Not just talking for talking's sake but hearing about theirs ... such special things and I got a lot of comfort from that.

Within this orientation threatened self-identity is shored up through embracing parental grief as the common sentiment within a sub-culture of 'bereaved parents'. The birth and life of the child, no matter how short, has point and purpose because it is remembered, shared and further explored for deeper, more universal meanings. Bereaved parent sub-cultures confirm the enormity of their members' loss. They legitimate parents' need to share their children in the same way that parents of living children might.

SOCIAL AUTONOMY: PERSONALLY RECONSTRUCTING IDENTITY

A parent's sense of self and personal worth may well be devastated by the death of a child. Multiple losses are associated with grief. For example one husband left his wife for the baby-sitter six weeks after the death of their child. His wife subsequently became mentally ill, lost her job and was threatened with the loss of her remaining child. Following their child's death, many parents may either choose, or be forced, to replace many of the routines which previously connected them to their parenthood. Bereavement networks may not be helpful, failing to address the uniqueness of their lost relationship:

> I didn't feel I wanted to meet a group of strangers and go through saying. . . . You just want to talk about your own child and what they went through – all the treatment they had and what happened to them. . . . I didn't feel that I wanted to talk to strangers.

Experience of the child's death, the deeply personal nature of grieving, and a loss of anchorage in familiar routines may motivate some parents consciously (and often vigorously) to confront the implications of their losses rather than sinking into resigned isolation. In this intensely personal orientation, grief includes a scrutiny of the components which make up the self, including previous roles, relationships and assumptions. In the first three orientations, personal identity is anchored in lost parental role, work role and bereaved parent role respectively. In this final orientation the anchorage has gone entirely and all aspects of identity become problematic and open to review. Douglas and Calvez (1990) describe this orientation as 'individualistic', characterising its sentiments as entrepreneurial. While there may be little guidance as to how to deal with grief, there are correspondingly fewer constraints over appropriate responses. Independence from personal relationships combines with low commitment to conventional sentiment to trigger a significant review of relationships and assumptions about life and a comprehensive reconstruction of self.

Grief in this orientation provides a transitional social status in which fresh insights derive from personal rather than collective confrontation with meanings of their child's death. Among these insights is the 'privileged' viewpoint which can be found through searching for the person they have lost (Walter 1996). Some of our parents came to 'know' their children more deeply because they had died. Jennie learned what Sarah had meant to her through discovering what Sarah meant to other people:

> One of the privileges I find was learning about your child . . . things you would normally never know . . . what they were

really like. She was Margery Proops of the sixth form. It's a privilege to hear what people really thought of your child. What they have done, who they were with. Because you would never normally have known. . . . You see them much more as a person rather than your child.

This sharpened hindsight led to a re-evaluation of her relationship with her husband, her son and her work colleagues:

I think marriage in itself is a difficult road to travel, but when you have such a catastrophe you are just shattered and blown everywhere. . . . You're quite a different person afterwards. I am quite different now to how I was five years ago. . . . My boss said, 'You are much better with people now – you're much more sympathetic.'

During the four years after her son died each of Marion's principal roles disappeared: her parenthood, her marital status, her job in the family business and her home. Because John lived for over four years after the diagnosis of his tumour, Marion was heavily involved in his nursing care and developed close relationships with medical staff and other patients, as well as becoming closer to John himself. Even before John's death, Marion became part of a distinctive 'cancer' sub-culture and was committed to a demanding routine which provided a temporary suspension of her roles as spouse and business partner. Following John's death, Marion experienced a traumatic divorce, the death of John's dog in a car accident, finding work as a housekeeper, and a burglary in which many of her son's possessions were stolen. In surviving these upheavals, and in discovering herself still coping, Marion recognised that she was a changed and capable person. She had reconstructed an identity in which her son's life and death were incorporated into a new full-time occupation, into owning and running her own home, and into a range of social activities.

Many bereaved parents not only survive their child's death but in time turn it into a positive experience (Rando 1991). Allison, Pauline and Jennie, for example, all became local organisers of a national self-help network. Jennie sat on the executive committee. All three lectured at training sessions for counsellors and health workers, were involved in organising conferences, and were active in establishing local support groups. For these parents, bereavement sub-cultures clearly provided a valuable stepping-stone both for giving meaning to their children's deaths, and for offering opportunities through which to discover and develop personal skills. All three noted that their bereavement affected their marriages and their work roles, forcing them to re-evaluate their priorities. In two of these cases, this change grew from a need to face a deteriorating relationship.

Two other women had little to do with bereavement sub-cultures but were similarly emotionally independent from the constraints of either affectionate social relations or pre-existing sentiments during their attempts to come to terms with their loss. This is not to suggest parents like this don't grieve deeply, but rather that the very loneliness of their grief releases them from the social obligations to which others look for support. The size of our sample does not allow any conclusions to be made about the fact that this orientation appeared to fit only women's accounts. Theoretically, however, the continuing strength of the 'successful motherhood' discourse in modern culture, and earlier arguments concerning women's facility for emotional expression go some way towards explaining why mothers more than fathers might need to confront ambivalent feelings and, in doing so, are better equipped to resist explanations which dispute the enormity of the loss which they have experienced.

CONCLUSION

We have sought to demonstrate the value of conceptualising grief as a culturally constructed experience which involves parents making sense of their loss within the context of personal relationships and dominant discourses on family, gender and bereavement. We have illustrated that differences in parents' expression of grief may be explained in ways which go beyond gendered accounts of the domestic division of labour and of men's and women's distinctive approaches to emotional release. Following the initial shock of their child's death, parents may adopt an orientation to grief which allows them to reconcile damaged self-identity with available resources of social support and cultural sentiment. These orientations are not necessarily exclusive nor sharply distinguishable categories. Rather they summarise the range of positions which might be adopted when individuals are confronted by critical events and powerful emotions in themselves and in others and it is unlikely that any one parent would provide a pure example. The framework should therefore be read as a conceptual map upon which individual grief and identity change may be plotted and compared.

Gender analyses, though valuable in explaining differential adjustment of mothers and fathers to grief in patriarchal cultures, may be limited in their explanation of wider differences in late modern societies. Our data and published literature indicate notable exceptions to patterns of men dealing actively with grief and of women coping in more emotional ways. We have sought to address these wider variations by illustrating how both men and women draw upon a range of sentiments. Some of these sentiments may still rest on patriarchal assumptions about 'natural' differences between the sexes, but many of them are derived from the post-feminist, post-industrial discourses of late modernity. At the same time, we have noted that in the absence of unambiguous death and grief sentiments, both mothers and fathers are likely to be more open to alternative definitions of their loss and may be increasingly reliant upon negotiating these meanings within personal social relationships, including the relationship with the self. Marriage may therefore be seen as one important relationship amongst a number of relationships, which mediate interpretations of death and grief and which seek to impose appropriate responses. The orientations towards their child's death adopted by each partner, the cultural limitations placed upon their choices of these orientations, and the consequences of movement between orientations may all have a part to play in the impact which grief has upon self-identity and marital paradigm.

REFERENCES

Ball, S. J., Bignold, S. and Cribb, A. (1996) 'Death and the disease: inside the culture of childhood cancer', in G. Howarth and P. C. Jupp *Contemporary Issues in the Sociology of Death, Dying and Disposal*, Basingstoke: Macmillan, pp. 151–64.

Berger, P. and Kellner, H. (1964) 'Marriage and the social construction of reality', *Diogenes* 46: 1–23.

Cornwell, J., Nurcombe, B. and Stevens, L. (1977) 'Family response to loss of a child by sudden infant death syndrome', *Medical Journal of Australia,* 30 April: 656–8.

Deal, J., Wampler, K. and Halverson, C. (1992) 'The importance of similarity in the marital relationship', *Family Process* 31: 369–82.

Douglas, M., and Calvez M. (1990) 'The self as risk taker: a cultural theory of contagion in relation to AIDS', *Sociological Review* 38: 445–64.

Duncombe, J., and Marsden, D. (1995) 'Workaholics and whingeing women: theorising intimacy and emotion work – the last frontier of gender inequality?', *Sociological Review* 43: 150–70.

Durkheim, E. (1964) *The Division of Labour in Society*, New York and London: Free Press.

Littlewood, J., Cramer, D., Hoekstra, J. and Humphrey, G. (1991) 'Gender differences in parental coping following their child's death', *British Journal of Guidance and Counselling* 19: 139–48.

Peddicord, D. J. (1990) 'Issues in the disclosure of perinatal death', in G. Stricker and M. Fisher (eds) *Self-Disclosure in The Therapeutic Relationship*, New York: Plenum Press, pp. 261–73.

Powell, M. (1995) 'Sudden infant death syndrome: the subsequent child', *British Journal of Social Work*, 25: 227–40.

Prior, L. (1989) *The Social Organisation of Death*, London: Macmillan.

Radley, A. (1989) 'Style, discourse and constraint in adjustment to chronic illness', *Sociology of Health and Illness* 11: 230–52.

Rando, T. (1991) 'Parental adjustment to the death of a child', in D. Papadatou and C. Papadatos (eds) *Children and Death*, New York: Hemisphere, pp. 233–53.

Schwab, R. (1992) 'Effects of a child's death on the marital relationship: a preliminary study', *Death Studies* 16: 141–54.

Smith, D. (1972) 'Women's perspective as a radical critique of sociology', *Sociological Inquiry* 44: 7–13.

Vance, J. C., Boyle, F. M., Najman, J. M. and Thearle, M. J. (1995) 'Gender differences in parental psychological distress following perinatal death or sudden infant death syndrome', *British Journal of Psychiatry* 167: 806–11.

Walter, T. (1991) 'The mourning after Hillsborough', *Sociological Review* 39: 599–625.

—— (1996) 'A new model of grief: bereavement and biography', *Mortality* 1: 7–19.

——, Littlewood, J. and Pickering, M. (1995) 'Death in the news: the public invigilation of private emotion', *Sociology* 29: 579–96.

Worden, J. W. (1982) *Grief Counselling and Grief Therapy*, London: Tavistock Publications.

Chapter 4

Masculinity and loss

Neil Thompson

INTRODUCTION

The nature of grief as the emotional response to the experience of loss has been the subject of considerable debate and discussion (Raphael 1983; Stroebe *et al.* 1993). However, the gendered nature of such a response has received relatively little attention. This chapter therefore begins to address some of the important issues relating to grief as a social construct shaped to a large extent by dominant gender expectations, rather than a 'natural' response to loss. Grief is presented as an emotion that needs to be understood in the context of *mourning*, defined as a socially constructed and codified set of expectations as to how a loss should normatively be dealt with.

Just as grief itself is recognised as a socially constructed entity, so too must the received wisdom of what constitutes 'good grieving'. As Doka (1989) has argued, the established view of effective grieving is one characterised by the open expression of emotion, a view that tends to pathologise more instrumental, stereotypically masculine patterns of response. The question of what is necessary for the successful resolution of grief is a complex one, not least in terms of how issues of gender have an impact on the process. This chapter does not attempt to resolve this question but settles for the more modest aim of exploring some of the important ways in which issues of gender, masculinity in particular, intertwine with issues of loss, grief and mourning.

EMOTIONAL RESPONSES

The 'gendered' nature of social action and interaction has long been recognised (Tong 1989), as indeed has the gendered nature of language use (Pugh 1996). However, what has received far less attention are the ways in which emotions are influenced by gender norms and expectations:

> A recognized cost of masculinity is the phenomenon commonly known as 'emotional inexpressiveness', as captured in the phrase 'big boys don't cry'. However, it is important to note that this is misleading. It is not simply that men are discouraged through the socialization process from expressing emotion – it is only certain emotions which are seen as 'unmanly'. ... For example, the expression of anger or aggression is seen as suitably masculine, as is the expression of joy in certain circumstances, such as success at a sporting event. It is, therefore, not simply that women may express emotion while men may not. The range of emotions is structured according to gender – emotions reflect and reinforce differential gender expectations in society.
>
> (Thompson, forthcoming)

One of the implications of this is that responses to loss are likely to be different between men and women because of the influence of gender-structured patterns of emotional response.

Rando recognises the significance of gender in relation to issues of death, loss and grief when she acknowledges the need for bereavement counsellors to take account of sex-role stereotyping:

> when a male is grieving he may experience conflict, as the expression of feelings necessary for the resolution of the grief is often contrary to previous sex-role conditioning. When doing therapy with males, therapists frequently have to work through the societal and cultural dictates of stereotypical sex-role conditioning before the loss can be addressed. If these are not worked through, they will interfere with the adequate processing of grief and prevent mourning.
>
> (1984: 48)

Gender is therefore not only a feature of the external sphere of social relations – the 'objective' dimension of human existence – but also a significant aspect of the internal, subjective dimension of

human experience (Thompson, forthcoming). The social constructionist conception of social life as a dialectic between objective and
subjective factors therefore needs to take account of gender in
relation to both poles of that dialectic in so far as gender can be
seen to shape not only social institutions and patterns of conduct,
but also subjective experiences at a cognitive and affective level.

Another important concept is that of 'disenfranchised' grief, as
introduced by Doka (1989). This refers to types of grief that are
not socially sanctioned and therefore cannot be openly acknowledged or publicly mourned, for example the death of a gay partner
or an extra-marital lover. The lack of social support brought about
by such 'disenfranchisement' can be seen as a complicating factor
in the grieving process. In 1994, Doka took his analysis a step
further by considering some aspects of men's grief in terms of
'double disenfranchisement'. In the case of particular disenfranchised losses, where these are experienced by a man, the effect
of the disenfranchisement can be intensified by the social expectations that a man should not grieve openly.

Doka therefore argues that we need to understand men's experiences of grief in these terms, to understand masculine responses
to loss as different, rather than deficient. This is a point to which
I shall return below in discussing the dual process model of grief.

LIFE SKILLS

Writing from a gerontological perspective, Lund (1994) describes a
study of the responses of widows and widowers to the loss of their
partners. Focusing specifically on the male cohort within the sample,
he was able to identify the factors most likely to influence, positively
or negatively, the grieving process. Not surprisingly, loneliness
featured as a significant problem for those who had been bereaved.
However, in terms of the predictors of effective long-term bereavement adjustments, the three key factors identified were:

- having the opportunity to express thoughts and feelings openly;
- high self-esteem;
- competency in the tasks of daily living.

It is the third factor that I wish to consider further. The sexual
division of labour can be seen to apply both vertically (pathways
to management and other positions of power are gender-related
– see SSI 1991) and horizontally (in terms of types of work: men

in engineering, women in nursing and so on – see Witz 1993). This division of labour again reflects gender expectations (men as leaders, men as 'doers', women as carers) within the social structure, expectations that play an important role in the socialisation process. This division of labour in terms of paid work is also identifiable in terms of domestic labour, unpaid work tasks within the household. That is, certain tasks tend to be identified as 'women's work' (cooking, for example), while others are more closely identified as male roles (household repairs, for example).

Lund's work helps us to envisage a situation in which a couple have developed a gender-based division of labour that has become established as a family norm. However, when one partner dies, the other can be left in a situation where he or she is ill equipped to undertake tasks previously carried out by the deceased partner. Consequently, men may be left with domestic tasks in which they have little experience or competence. In view of the masculine preference for active coping, as identified earlier, this situation could prove to be very traumatic. This is because opportunities for active coping may be obstructed by a lack of competence in certain aspects of daily living. In this way, secondary losses arising from the primary loss of the person may undermine attempts to cope in an active way with a problem-solving focus. Socialisation into gender-related patterns of emotional response can therefore be seen to be compounded by a gendered division of labour, something which has significant consequences in terms of preparedness for the possibility of widowerhood.

RESPONDING TO CRISIS

Not surprisingly, the literature relating to loss has much in common with crisis theory – the overlap between the two areas of theory is of quite significant proportions. First, though, it is important to be clear about what we mean by a 'crisis':

> A crisis is a turning point, a situation which pushes our usual coping mechanisms beyond their limits of effectiveness and thus necessitates a different response, a different strategy for coping.
> (Thompson 1991: 4)

In this respect, the experience of bereavement can clearly be identified as a crisis. The fact that it constitutes a crisis does not mean that the individual is not able to cope – it is not a defining feature of pathology. It does mean, however, that the situation cannot go on as before – a new approach has to be adopted, major adjustments need to be made.

The outcome of a crisis or loss situation will depend to a large extent on the attempts made by the individual (and significant others within his or her social circle) to cope with the demands of the new situation, the steps taken towards re-establishing the balance of one's life. Although crisis responses tend to have much in common, there are also significant differences. These can be individual differences, personalised responses to a particular crisis situation. However, they can also be socially created differences in terms of variation according to class, culture and, of course, gender. Verbrugge (1985) argues that there are apparent patterns in coping responses according to gender. As Littlewood comments: 'Specifically, she concluded that women prefer to use social support and emotionally orientated styles (passive) whilst men prefer active, problem-solving and tension reducing ways of coping (active)' (1992: 70).

A characteristic masculine response to a crisis is therefore likely to be an active one, involving attempts to respond positively and constructively to the situation. In many crisis scenarios this can be a very appropriate and helpful response, as there can be a number of matters that need urgent attention. For example, in responding to a public disaster, health and social welfare staff will have very many tasks to perform in a short period of time (Raphael 1990), and so a direct action-orientated approach can certainly pay dividends in this context. However, when the crisis is one of a personal bereavement, an action orientation may be far less appropriate – the emotional 'grief work' that has to be done is not readily compatible with an outwardly focused action orientation.

An important concept here is that of 'ontological security', the ability (and need) to maintain a sense of coherence to our existence, to maintain a consistent thread of meaning. Such security can be challenged and undermined at the time of a loss, as Giddens argues:

> The maintenance of a framework of 'ontological security' is, like all other aspects of social life, an ongoing accomplishment of lay actors. Within the production of modes of interaction in which the mutual knowledge required to sustain that interaction is 'unproblematic', and hence can be largely 'taken for

granted', ontological security is routinely grounded. 'Critical situations' exist where such routine grounding is radically dislocated, and where consequently the accustomed constituting skills of actors no longer mesh in with the motivational components of their action.

(1993: 124)

Such 'critical situations', or crises, have the effect of turning our world upside down, leaving us with a major challenge in terms of re-establishing a sense of ontological security, a sense of personal wholeness. This again adds weight to the need for an approach governed more by psychological and emotional restructuring than actual activities – a focus on the cognitive and affective dimensions, rather than on the behavioural or conative.

At the time of a bereavement, there will be certain practical tasks that need to be achieved, including informing certain individuals and agencies of the death, making funeral arrangements, and so on. However, there are also certain emotional tasks that need to be accomplished (Worden 1982) in order to integrate the loss into our experience and enable us to move on. One of the problems of a gender-structured approach to grieving is that men are more likely to opt for the practical tasks, perhaps at the expense of the emotional ones.

Littlewood discusses the work of Barbarin and Chesler (1986) in relation to parental responses to the death of a child. They identify additional problems arising from gender-structured emotional responses:

they found that active coping styles (a masculine preference) were associated with potentially problematic parent/staff interactions. It may be possible that the greater tendency amongst men to use active styles of coping may inadvertently lead them to receive less appropriate support from hospital personnel. However, an alternative explanation may be that the hospital staff perceive the child's mother to be in greater need of support and consequently direct available resources towards her rather than her partner.

(1992: 70)

In sum, then, a masculine preference for active coping in situations of bereavement can be seen to be potentially problematic in terms of:

- a reluctance to undertake the emotional tasks of grieving;
- the greater likelihood of tension in relationships with professionals and other carers;
- the possibility of support not being offered when needed due to the perception of men not needing to grieve in the same way as women (or not needing to grieve at all).

THE DUAL PROCESS MODEL

One recent, and potentially very significant, advance in our theoretical understanding of grief work is the dual process model developed by Stroebe and Schut (1995). This model distinguishes between two orientations towards the experience of bereavement, a loss orientation and a restoration orientation. The former relates to a mode of being characterised by the intrusiveness of feelings of grief and the disruptiveness of breaking bonds and ties. In this respect, a loss orientation can be seen to be focused on the past, or specifically the lack of continuity between the past and the present brought about by the impact of the loss. The latter, by contrast, involves attending to life changes, making adjustments and going beyond the grief. It is geared towards the future, undertaking restructuring activities that clear the way for making progress, restoring a sense of purpose and direction, in short, rebuilding from the foundations of what is left after the loss.

As our earlier discussions indicate, these two approaches can be closely associated with gender expectations: a loss orientation, with its explicit acknowledgement of the grief inherent in loss, being seen characteristically as a feminine approach, while a restoration orientation, with its focus on activities, can be seen as a masculine one. This reflects strongly the dominance of patriarchal ideology, with its conceptions of men as active, instrumental figures and women as passive, nurturing figures.

However, Stroebe's and Schut's thesis is that these two orientations are best seen as an ongoing dialectic, rather than a simple binary choice. That is, although each approach can be identified with a specific set of gender norms, the two orientations are not gender-specific – it is a question of degree and emphasis, rather than a simple either/or. The two orientations also need to be seen in the broader context of the bereavement trajectory, that is, in relation to timescales. As time passes, people are likely to move from an emphasis on loss in the early stages to one on restoration in the later stages, a reflection of the 'healing' or growing entailed by grief work (Raphael 1983). In this way, restoration will gradually come to dominate in uncomplicated grief processes. Indeed, it could even be argued that patterns of complicated grieving involve a failure, for whatever reasons, of the restoration orientation to assert itself.

This theory also succeeds, to a certain extent at least, in accounting for the notion that 'mourning never ends' (Worden 1982: 18) or, as it is commonly put: 'You never get over it.' This can be understood as a description of situations where restoration is to the fore, but where the loss orientation has not been eliminated altogether, where it may remain largely submerged, only to reappear again at certain times – anniversaries and other such significant events being primary examples.

The theory is also helpful in accounting for cultural and societal differences in responses to loss. For example, some societies or cultural groups may be more likely to focus on one orientation far more than on the other. This presents good possibilities for the further development of an anthropology of grief and mourning leading to a much needed better understanding of cultural differentiation in patterns of response to loss.

A key aspect of the theory is the concept of 'oscillation'. That is, the grieving process is best seen in terms of a continuous oscillation between these two orientations, a continuous to-ing and fro-ing, with one or other orientation in the ascendancy. In the period following a significant loss, it is not surprising that feelings should be depicted as being in a state of flux, characterised more by turmoil and instability than uniformity and stability.

It is in this context that Doka's (1994) comments on men's responses to loss can be more fully understood. An action-oriented focus on restoration, as apparently preferred by men, does not necessarily have to be seen as problematic in its own terms. However, I would argue that what can be very problematic is a response to loss in which such an orientation is so dominant that it leaves little or no room for loss orientation, little or no scope for dealing with the emotional challenges a significant loss presents.

It could be argued that an action orientation is a means of coping with the emotional issues, a strategy of dealing with them indirectly, rather than a strategy of avoiding them altogether. The questions of what constitutes a successful strategy for effective grieving and to what extent oscillation between the two orientations is a basic ingredient of such effectiveness remain open. Clearly, this is an area that provides excellent scope for detailed empirical enquiry, for example to investigate the relative strengths, and costs, of differential approaches to the grieving process.

The dual process model of grief presents not only opportunities for empirical research but also further theory development. Stroebe and Schut have put forward a theoretical model that offers exciting possibilities for developing our understanding of important issues of death, dying and bereavement. Their framework offers a foundation from which to develop a more sophisticated theory of grief and mourning. For example, the tendency for men to have an elective affinity with the restoration orientation is not only part of an explanatory framework but also something that needs explaining in its own right.

IMPLICATIONS FOR SOCIAL THEORY AND PROFESSIONAL PRACTICE

A key element in social theory is the relationship between the personal and the social, and between agency and structure (Craib 1992). In view of this, both gender and loss can be seen as important issues for social theory and, by extension, for professional practice in the human services. This section therefore explores areas for development in both theory and practice.

The importance of gender has received a great deal of attention (Herrmann and Stewart 1994), despite being remarkably absent in some analyses. However, the consideration of gender as a significant factor has often been restricted to women's issues, without questions of masculinity being addressed (see Morris 1993 for a discussion of this in relation to disability). Consequently, the role of masculinity as a force for maintaining patriarchal hegemony has tended to be neglected, although this is now beginning to change (Hearn 1987, Segal 1990, Miedzian 1992, Phillips 1993).

Loss, however, has received even less attention. It is somewhat surprising that, although thanatological issues have been addressed to a certain extent at least in sociology, they have featured far less in social theory. How societies and cultural groupings deal with issues of death, dying and bereavement is of more than peripheral interest in terms of understanding the complex interrelationships between the individual and society.

Loss and gender are also both important issues with regard to the development of an approach to human services work that is premised on challenging and undermining the oppressive nature of sexism as it applies to health care, social welfare and other social practices. Traditional approaches to social policy have tended to be gender-blind, to see things from within an unproblematised masculine perspective (Williams 1989). It is therefore important that issues of masculinity, both in general and specifically in relation to loss, are taken into consideration if policy and practice are not to reinforce existing inequalities.

Loss issues have the effect of throwing the question of masculinity into sharp relief, as the following passage implies:

Armistead (1975, cited in Segal, 1990) suggests that the 'consciousness-raising' needed to change conventional masculinity may be hindered by men's tendency to 'resist sensitive exploration of each other's experience and feelings' (p. 6). In this sense, masculinity can be conceptualized as a self-perpetuating process in so far as one of the characteristics of masculinity is a resistance to self-analysis and the heightened level of self-awareness necessary to deconstruct patriarchal social relations. This is one of the barriers that the anti-sexist movement must strive to dismantle if genuine progress is to continue and accelerate.

(Thompson 1995: 461–2)

Frosh puts forward an argument that has much in common with this emphasis on the problematic relationship between masculinity and emotion. He expresses this in the following terms:

The *vulnerability* of men is an issue which feminists, including feminist psychotherapists and family therapists, have understandably not placed high on their agenda for analysis or concern. Nevertheless, it deserves such a place because it is from this vulnerability – the sense that masculinity is built on emptiness, including disavowal of the capacity to link with others in a mode of reciprocal neediness and intimacy – that much of men's violence has its origins. Under contemporary conditions, the traditional masculine defence of flight into rationality and repudiation of the feminine can no longer bolster the fragility of masculine identity.

(1995: 230)

This, in turn, has much in common with the existentialist notion of 'contingency', the lack of fixity and certainty that characterise human existence. Traditional masculine actions and attitudes can be seen as an attempt to deal with this contingency. This brings us into the field of ontology, the study of being (Thompson 1992). It is beyond the scope of this paper to pursue these matters in any detail but we should at least note that the question of masculinity is a very profound one with significant consequences in terms of the individual's relationship with the social world and, consequently, the relationship between agency and structure.

CONCLUSION

The relationship between masculinity and loss is an intricate and multifaceted one that requires a great deal of further attention from theorists, researchers and practitioners. It is not simply the case that men are unable or unwilling to express grief openly, nor is it simply a matter of uncritically proclaiming the need for more or better emotional expressiveness. A critical perspective on the gendered nature of grief and mourning stands in need of considerable further development, a perspective that can be closely associated with existing work that explores the social and personal costs of rigid patriarchal conceptions of masculinity. With regard to loss, these costs include: a 'disenfranchisement' of the expression of grief in the public sphere (Doka 1994); an ill-preparedness for practical coping following the loss of a partner (Lund 1994); challenges to ontological security (Thompson 1991), together with a range of other potentially problematic situations (see Lund, forthcoming).

Much has been written about loss, grief and mourning, although perhaps not as much as this important topic deserves. The specific question of loss and masculinity, however, has tended to be neglected, as indeed until fairly recently has the question of masculinity within the framework of gender studies. The work of writers such as Doka and Lund gives us important insights into aspects of masculine approaches to loss that can be used to develop our theoretical understanding further and provide the basis for empirical investigations. Similarly, the innovative work of Stroebe and Schut offers a firm foundation for taking forward our understanding of masculinity in the context of thanatology. However, we should not allow ourselves to become complacent. One thing that is very clear is that our understanding of masculinity and loss is still very much in its infancy – we still have a great deal to learn about this important topic.

In parallel fashion, the movement from theory to praxis is also very much in its infancy. The steps that need to be taken to develop non-oppressive, anti-sexist approaches to human services practice in the field of death, dying and bereavement are only vaguely sketched out, leaving considerable scope for further progress in establishing strategies for challenging and undermining the patriarchal structures, practices and discourses that place barriers in the way of effective grief work. In this context, the particular role of men needs to be acknowledged and re-appraised. Traditionally, as we noted above, gender has been equated with women's issues, and responsibility for tackling sexism has been seen to lie with women. The complications in the grieving process that arise as a result of socialisation into masculine patterns of mourning can be conceptualised as a potential spur to men taking a more active role in countering sexist oppression. Loss presents major challenges to us as human beings – rigid sex-role stereotyping only adds to the pressures and distress.

REFERENCES

Armistead, N. (1975) 'Men's liberation and men against sexism', *Men Against Sexism or the Pig's Last Grunt*, Spring.

Barbarin, D. A. and Chesler, M. (1986) 'The medical context of parental coping with childhood cancer', *American Journal of Community Psychology*, 14: 221–35.

Burck, C. and Speed, B. (eds) (1995) *Gender, Power and Relationships*, London: Routledge.

Craib, I. (1992) *Modern Social Theory: From Parsons to Habermas* (2nd edn), Hemel Hempstead: Harvester Wheatsheaf.

Doka, K. (ed.) (1989) *Disenfranchised Grief: Recognizing Hidden Sorrow*, Lexington, MA: Lexington Books.

—— (1994) 'Double disenfranchisement: the male disenfranchised griever', paper presented at the Helping the Bereaved Male Conference, London, Ontario (May).

Frosh, S. (1995) 'Unpacking masculinity: from rationality to fragmentation', in Burck and Speed (eds) (1995).

Giddens, A. (1993) *New Rules of Sociological Method* (2nd edn), Cambridge: Polity.

Hearn, J. (1987) *The Gender of Oppression: Men, Masculinity and the Critique of Marxism*, Brighton: Wheatsheaf.

Herrmann, A. C. and Stewart, A. J. (eds) (1994) *Theorizing Feminism: Parallel Trends in the Humanities and Social Sciences*, Oxford: Westview Press.

Littlewood, J. (1992) *Aspects of Grief: Bereavement in Adult Life*, London: Tavistock/Routledge.

Lund, D. (1994) 'After 40 years of marriage, I'm now alone: the bereavement experience of older men', paper presented at the Helping the Bereaved Male Conference, London, Ontario (May).

—— (ed.) (forthcoming) *The Male Experience of Grief*, Amityville, NY: Baywood.

Miedzian, M. (1992) *Boys will be Boys: Breaking the Link between Masculinity and Violence*, London: Virago.

Morris, J. (1993) 'Gender and Disability', in Swain *et al.* (eds) (1993).

Phillips, A. (1993) *The Trouble with Boys*, London: Pandora.

Pugh, R. G. (1996) *Effective Language in Health and Social Work*, London: Chapman and Hall.

Rando, T. A. (1984) *Grief, Dying and Death: Clinical Interventions for Caregivers*, Champaign, IL: Research Press.

Raphael, B. (1983) *The Anatomy of Bereavement*, New York: Basic Books.

—— (1990) *When Disaster Strikes: A Handbook for the Caring Professions*, London: Unwin Hyman.

Richardson, D. and Robinson, V. (eds) (1993) *Introducing Women's Studies: Feminist Theory and Practice*, London: Macmillan.

Segal, L. (1990) *Slow Motion: Changing Masculinities, Changing Men*, London: Virago.

SSI (Social Services Inspectorate) (1991) *Women in Social Services: A Neglected Resource*, London, HMSO.

Stroebe, M. and Schut, H. (1995) 'The dual process model of grief', paper presented at the meeting of the International Work Group on Death, Dying and Bereavement, Oxford (June).

Stroebe, M. S., Stroebe, W. and Hanson, R. O. (eds) (1993) *Handbook of Bereavement: Theory, Research and Intervention*, Cambridge: Cambridge University Press.

Swain, J., Finkelstein, V., French, S. and Oliver, M. (eds) (1993) *Disabling Barriers – Enabling Environments*, London: Sage.

Thompson, N. (1991) *Crisis Intervention Revisited*, Birmingham: Pepar.

—— (1992) *Existentialism and Social Work*, Aldershot: Avebury.

—— (1995) 'Men and anti-sexism', *British Journal of Social Work* 25 (4): 459–75.

—— (forthcoming) 'The ontology of masculinity' in Lund (ed.) (forthcoming).

Tong, R. (1989) *Feminist Thought: A Comprehensive Introduction*, London: Routledge.

Verbrugge, L. M. (1985) 'Gender and health: an update on hypotheses and evidence', *Journal of Health and Social Behaviour* 26: 156–82.

Williams, F. (1989) *Social Policy: A Critical Introduction*, Cambridge: Polity.

Witz, A. (1993) 'Women at work', in Richardson and Robinson (eds) (1993).

Worden, J. W. (1982) *Grief Counselling and Grief Therapy*, London: Tavistock Publications.

Chapter 5

Women in grief
Cultural representation and social practice

Jenny Hockey

INTRODUCTION

As a Women's Studies tutor in the late 1980s, I looked for accounts of western women's experiences of bereavement in order to introduce students to aspects of gender and ageing. Little material about women's grief seemed to be available. Closer examination of the 'classic' literature of death and dying which emerged from the late 1950s onwards revealed that many of its general statements about the nature of loss have an unacknowledged gendered basis in research among widows. There would seem to be a parallel here with much pre-1970s sociological and anthropological research which drew on interviews with men to provide a more general account of aspects of social life (Oakley 1974, Ardener 1972). What is different, however, is the gender of the interviewees whose testimonies are taken to represent both male and female experience.

This chapter asks why material pertaining to women rather than men might have been used to provide a foundation for accounts of grief in *adult* life. To explore this question, the early bereavement literature is examined alongside other representations of grieving women – for example, the image of the Victorian widow in full mourning dress, the weeping mother of Christ, the full-face newspaper photos of girls and women bereaved in major tragedies, nineteenth-century grave sculptures of women grieving with abandonment, accounts of women wailing during death rituals in traditional societies.

I will contrast these images and narratives of women with actual social practices associated with bereavement and go on to argue that neither women nor men are likely to grieve in public in the manner depicted in cultural representations of this kind. Both sexes are susceptible to the British imperative to conduct their grieving in private. In public, what is required is a display of signs that an appropriate emotional response is taking place, but elsewhere – in the private setting of the home (Walter, forthcoming). However, when it comes to cultural representations – media images of disasters, full-face photographs on the jackets of self-help books on bereavement, and paintings and statuary of the Virgin Mary cradling the corpse of her dead son – emotional expressivity is highlighted rather than hinted at. Furthermore, it is an arena within which women become prominent. They confront the viewer or the reader with an exposure of emotion which is not only unconstrained but also gendered. Thus, cultural representations of overtly grieving women stand in marked contrast with the social practice of providing no more than what Walter calls a 'competent performance' of grief.

AN EMOTIONAL DIVISION OF LABOUR?

A privileging of women's grief might seem predictable in the light of the well documented division of emotional labour within contemporary western society (Eichenbaum and Orbach 1983). Thus, it is argued, the gendered division of labour extends into the sphere of the emotions with the result that true femininity requires intuitive sensitivity and emotional expressiveness, in contrast with true masculinity which is predicated upon rationality and emotional control. Both Doyal (1979) and Showalter (1987) have traced the linkages between emotionality and femininity, in part, to nineteenth-century medical discourses which foregrounded women's reproductive cycles as having an overriding influence upon their nervous systems. In that this discourse also underscored men's intellectual abilities, their independence and their capacity for instrumental action, it represented a framework of ideas which emphasised the oppositional natures of the two sexes. This oppositional view of the natures of women and men is reflected in late-nineteenth-century responses to a bereavement. Thus, for example, in 1889 the magazine *Woman's World* expressed the view that 'the custom of mourning presses far more heavily on women than on men. In fact, so trifling are the alterations made in a man's dress . . . that practically the whole burden of mourning wrappings would seem to have fallen on women.

... they [men] positively manage to mourn by proxy ...!' (Morley 1971: 63).

Evidence of an emotional division of labour which appears to reflect an essential female expressivity can be found in accounts of grief in other parts of the world. From another culture therefore, rather than another time, Cline offers the example of the behaviour of a Greek woman, bereaved of her son, which took place in the presence of her American daughter-in-law:

> She entered the room and shrieked, threw herself on his body and just wailed. She shook him and she kissed him and she beat the hell out of him. ... I realised that this was what Greeks do. Greek women can wail. They're allowed to wail.
>
> (Cline 1995: 16)

Historical and cross-cultural comparison would therefore seem to yield parallels with a contemporary western privileging of the grief of women. It is what we have come to expect and, moreover, it appears to represent something of a universal and essentially feminine response to death. However, as I will argue in this chapter, these apparent 'parallels' cannot be read straightforwardly. They form part of an assemblage of cultural images or narratives of grief which, while visible elements within mainstream western society, do not reflect what actually happens at the time of a death. They are representations which are mediated by historical time and cultural space. For example, the Victorian widow is currently prominent in literature which either implicitly or explicitly tells contemporary readers how mourning should properly be conducted. In her time, however, she was a far less visible entity, being for the most part confined within the private space of the home. Her current 'visibility' is as a retrospective representation of grief. The Greek mother whose behaviour epitomises female emotional expressivity is foreign and therefore Other. She figures within a British author's account of grief because of her difference. Her behaviour is not what we expect or comfortably accept in practice. This point is exemplified by a Free Church minister, interviewed during a study of Sheffield funeral practices. He described a Ghanaian funeral where 'there was a great expression of grief and emotion which, in a different congregation I would have called hysteria' (Hockey 1993: 143). Another minister within the same study said, 'continental weeping and wailing which is the thing to do over there is very very difficult to deal with . . . we have people try and act with quiet dignity' (ibid.: 144).

In practice, therefore, what we have come to think of as women's universal emotional expressivity is not expected in modern Britain to constitute a highly visible aspect of social behaviours at the time of disposal and bereavement. Instead, women, like men, are susceptible to the requirement that nothing more than a limited set of clues as to the presence of grief should be manifested in public. The evidence for an emotional division of labour as an explanation for the prominence of women in representations of grief is therefore less straightforward than it might, at first glance, appear. Such a division seems to feature within conceptions of femininity and masculinity but is far less evident in the way women and men actually behave in public at the time of a death. How can we therefore explain the high visibility of grieving women when it comes to cultural representation, rather than social practice?

WOMAN AS OTHER

If we shift from the domain of grieving to the closely related sphere of dying, we find arguments to suggest that the proliferation of representations of dead women in western art and literature from the eighteenth century onwards can be seen as a complex cultural preoccupation with death which serves to distance masculinist readers or viewers from their own deaths (Bronfen 1992). In giving visibility to the deaths of young women in particular, death is made accessible, but by proxy. It is the death of the Other and not the self which is contemplated. Describing the female body as 'the superlative site of alterity' (or otherness), Bronfen articulates a process whereby such images 'repress by localising death away from the self, at the body of a beautiful woman, at the same time that this representation lets the repressed return, albeit in a disguised manner' (1992: xi).

Central to this approach is the notion that these kinds of representation allow access to areas of life and death which are too dangerous to be approached directly, yet which nevertheless haunt the imagination. It is a gendered approach to the ways in which death, dying and disposal are viewed in that it highlights the masculinist bias within the processes of representation. It provides us with a way of thinking about the representation of the aftermath of death, its grievous losses, through images and accounts of women in mourning and in grief. Central to this chapter, therefore, is the argument that in a society where grief is often experienced in private and signalled in public, such representations play a core role in illuminating that which, for many members of society, is a threatening yet hidden aspect of life. Walter, Littlewood and Pickering, for example, have argued that the media use of photographs of grieving individuals to highlight corporate disasters has developed in response to a lack of information about how to conduct oneself in public when bereaved (1995). This results from the loss of established death ritual, the requirement that private grief should somehow be signalled through a competent public performance, and a belief that expressing grief is the 'natural' and 'healthy' response to a death.

THE GENDERING OF SOCIAL PRACTICE

Those individuals who are most publicly and visibly associated with the event of a death are often men. They take the lead as doctors revealing bad news, funeral directors, clergy, lay persons giving funeral addresses, and solicitors. While some women are now taking on these roles, they are the exception rather than the rule – as are full-face images of sobbing men within the sphere of representation. It is in the lower-status or more covert practices of nursing and bereavement counselling that the presence of women comes to be associated with the experiences of dying and grieving. In summary, while in images and narratives of death and dying, women have high visibility as the providers of psychological 'instruction' (Walter *et al.* 1995), in practice it is predominantly men, both professional and lay, who frame the experiences of dying and bereaved people, be they patients, parishioners, clients or relatives. The exposure of women within representations of emotional expressivity which are accessible to a patriarchal collectivity, can be said to provide a way of contemplating not only human mortality, as Bronfen has argued for the female corpse, but also human vulnerability. Representations of the publicly grieving woman provide relatively unproblematic access to volatile, highly dangerous and hence irrepressible dimensions of human relationships.

In order to exemplify these arguments I will now give more detailed consideration to some of the culturally specific representations within which the association between women, death and dying come to constitute a cultural 'given'. As noted, they can be seen as a set of inversions, but one which forms part of a single system whereby the associations between masculinity, social power and rationality provide the dominant framework through which the unpredictability of death is brought to order. As noted, those individuals who become publicly visible around the time of a death are likely to be men. It is they who give public form to death and its aftermath. One of the ministers interviewed about funeral practice in Sheffield described it as his job to 'say those things which relatives are in no position to say for themselves at that time' (Hockey 1992: 17–18). Furthermore, there is an implicit understanding as to the precise form which visible, public responses to a death should take. Thus, clergy stressed that they themselves had to retain emotional control while articulating mourners' grief. As one said: 'Whatever you feel inside, that has to be held in check.' When it came to an address from a lay member of the congregation, that same emotional control was seen to be essential:

> sometimes people would like to do it and then really emotion-
> ally can't cope when it comes to it and so you have an upset-
> ting thing in the service instead of ... you know, someone
> breaks down when they're trying to speak and that doesn't help
> the relations.

> (Hockey 1993: 133)

Lay addresses are rarely given by women. I would argue, there-fore, that these are gendered social practices which take place in public space and which draw upon the institutionalised authority of male professionals. When it comes to representations of responses to death, however, it is a feminised image to which we are exposed. While such images and accounts appear to offer the reader or the viewer a model of normal and indeed generalisable responses to the inevitability of death, I would argue that they are the product of a series of cultural strategies which are grounded in the alterity of their subjects. Thus, among the exam-ples to follow, none can, in fact, be said to represent either ordinary death or indeed normal social practice. As Walter, Littlewood and Pickering point out, when discussing the example of media representations of grief, 'news discourse is, by definition, antithetical to social ordinariness' (1995: 583). As I will show, this is so not only for those women who are depicted in the media, but also women imaged or accounted for through other forms of representation. Despite their aura of normality, they are mad women, romantically voluptuous women, women from a lost past, foreign women, holy women or women fallen victim to major tragedy. In that women's bodies have been described as 'the superlative site of alterity' (Bronfen 1992: xi), their grief-stricken faces, abandoned postures and wild gestures provide both a point of identification as well as a place set apart for the masculinist viewer. They connote a familiar yet safely distanced image of human vulnerability in the face of mortality. It is a distance which is constituted first through their Otherness as women, but also compounded by their positioning in other kinds of social and indeed spiritual space and time, and by the extreme nature of the deaths which have afflicted them.

THE MAD WOMAN IN GRIEF

Those women whose interview material became public in the form of early texts on death and dying probably conducted their grief in seclusion. This private grief found its way into the public domain via the one-to-one interview or the psychiatric consultation, then to be transformed into a representation of grieving through the published accounts of men. Finding original form in 1950s and 1960s medical sources, such as the *British Medical Journal* and the *British Journal of Psychiatry*, what later became known as 'the bereavement literature' began to emerge in the late 1960s and early 1970s in Britain and America. It is exemplified in the work of psychiatrist Colin Murray Parkes' *Bereavement: Studies of Grief in Adult Life* (1972). John Bowlby, in a foreword to this work, described Parkes' account as 'an authoritative description of what today we believe we know about grieving in both its healthy and less healthy forms'. A knowledge claim was therefore being made, one which was legitimated by its grounding within scientific, medical discourse. Bereavement was accounted for in universalistic terms with little distinction being made between the responses of members of different social categories. Closer examination shows that in studies such as this, which 'describe the nature of the principal components of the reaction to bereavement', the 'components' presented were grounded predominantly in studies of women's experiences of the death of a partner. For example, Parkes' 1970 study of 22 London widows provides a constant reference point in what is represented as an account of 'grief in adult life'. He also cites a key study by Marris in 1958, where 72 East London widows were interviewed, a similar study by Hobson in 1964 which gathered material about 40 widows in a Midland market town, and Maddison's and Walker's 1967 survey of 132 American widows. It would appear therefore that the generalised stages of grief – numbness, alarm, searching, anger and guilt – which were described and popularised through work such as that of Parkes, are in fact highly gendered. Using women's experience to represent something universal parallels what was initially identified by feminist academics such as Ann Oakley in the mid-1970s. Within disciplines such as sociology and social anthropology, *male* experience was often the unacknowledged focus of research, its findings nonetheless being presented as representative of human experience more generally (Oakley 1974).

In the early bereavement literature we have a representation of the experience of the widow which at the time was made to stand for the nature of bereavement within the adult population. The vulnerability to which all human beings are exposed, what Parkes calls 'the cost of commitment', was exposed for contemplation but located at the site of the female Other. What also needs to be recognised is that we are dealing with a representation of the bereaved Other which is not only feminised but also 'psychiatrised'. That is to say, Parkes' account of grief in adult life is not only tied to the experiences of women rather than men, but is also couched within the categories of psychiatric thought. Bowlby's foreword describes bereavement as 'a major hazard to mental health' and Parkes opens his discussion of its effects with Breuer's and Freud's 1893 account of the case of a mad woman, Anna O, whose 'hysterical symptoms' were believed to have been occasioned by the terminal illness and death of her father. Furthermore, Parkes not only draws on his 1970 study of London widows, but also on an earlier study carried out at the end of the 1950s among psychiatric patients at the Bethlehem Royal and Maudsley Hospitals in London. Women outnumbered men by seventeen to four in this study. Because of the lack of existing studies of widowers, a comparison between bereaved psychiatric patients and 'normal' bereaved people was restricted to women. When a set of technical criteria emanating from a medical discipline is brought to bear upon responses to death in this way, grief comes to be categorised as 'healthy' or 'pathological'. It is thus that loss is 'psychiatrised'.

Radical feminists such as Phyllis Chesler, who explored mental health issues using a social constructionist or labelling theory approach, argued that the generalised profile of many forms of madness was in fact predicated upon the assumed experiences of a quite specific social category – women (Chesler 1972). Thus, in Chesler's view, a diagnosis of mental illness, which would seem from the evidence of health-care consumption to be largely a female problem, is often read off from symptoms which are synonymous with stereotypical representations of femininity – being easily hurt, having low self-esteem, passivity, conformity, low achievement motivation. As a result, those women who embrace femininity too wholeheartedly, as well as those women who fail to conform to such a profile, risk, in similar measure, a diagnosis of madness. Chesler's assertion that madness among women is but a construct of male psychiatric categories has been challenged by later feminists who have highlighted the social pressures which can lead to very real mental suffering among women (Ussher 1991). However, this is not to argue that the psychiatric diagnosis and treatment of women's mental health problems is a neutral, ungendered process.

The formulation of early models of bereavement by psychiatrists such as Parkes rests upon a similar unreflective use of gendered material and indeed stereotypes. For example, it is central to Parkes' theory of bereavement that the death of someone close can mean a loss of the self, such that something of the bereaved individual is buried along with the deceased. Evidence for this perspective is found in statements such as 'I feel as if half of myself was missing', 'It's as if my inside has been torn out and left a horrible wound there.' This material stems from in-depth interviews with women bereaved of a male partner. A generalised viewpoint is grounded in the experiences of a quite specific social category. Parkes says of such women:

> In large measure the newly bereaved widow confronts the same problems as the adolescent school-leaver. A new set of expectations and roles faces her and she must learn a new repertoire of problem solutions before she can again feel safe and at ease. Like the adolescent she may feel that too much is expected of her and she may react with anxiety, insecurity and irritability.

She may attempt to hold on to the ideas that she is still the cherished wife, protected from the world by a loving husband.
(1972: 115–16)

What we have therefore is a theory of bereavement based on a stereotypical representation of women's roles, status and self-identities as being defined in relation to a male partner. Bereaved of her husband, she is reduced to the lowly status of an adolescent school-leaver, someone who for the first time has to face the world 'unprotected'. Her experience underpins a model of bereavement which reflects a narrow if not typecast representation of the sheltered housewife whose identity is totally defined by her relationship with her husband. What we seem to be dealing with is a representation of grief which is not only framed within the categories of psychiatric thought but, like other forms of mental 'disorder', draws upon the experiences of women who conform very closely to traditional patterns of heterosexual marriage where domestic commitments are privileged over an independent career. Closely aligned, the profiles of madness and grief are epitomised in some of the most taken-for-granted representations of women. As such they constitute an implicitly localised and therefore acceptable representation of that which cannot otherwise be repressed.

THE SAINTLY WOMAN IN GRIEF

While Protestant worship requires the direct contemplation of God as represented by the body of his crucified son, Jesus Christ, Catholic worship takes place via the intermediary figure of the Virgin Mary. Thus at times of major lifecourse transitions – birth, marriage and death – as well as during weekly worship, practising Catholics are exposed to images of a woman who suffered what is felt to be a singularly tragic bereavement, that of her son in his early adult years. In the *Pietà*, she displays the most intense emotion to be inspired by a (male) death, the tears of the *mater dolorosa*. In an echo of paintings of the Virgin and Child, the Virgin of the *Pietà* similarly occupies the focal point of many images, her son, now dead, but still positioned beneath her, supported upon her knees. In their structural resemblance, each representation evokes the other. Warner argues that it is via representations such as these that the intermediary figure of the Virgin

Mary 'focussed human feeling in a comprehensible and accessible way' (1976: 211). Indeed, she goes on, 'through her, the Crucifixion, the Deposition, and the Entombment came to life. Through her sorrow, the man or woman in prayer could feel the stab of loss and agony' (ibid.). In Titian's *Entombment of Christ*, its three male figures adopt an instrumental role, evidenced by their hands which grasp the body of Christ as, between them, they lower it into the grave. By contrast the hands of the Virgin Mary play an expressive part, being clasped together, helplessly, in grief. A female attendant signals the overwhelming nature of Mary's emotional distress by barring her way forward with an outstretched arm.

What we have here are religious images of grieving which are readily and regularly available for many members of western society. Indeed their resonance extends well beyond the sphere of practising Catholics. In their condensed symbolism they evoke not only grief but also femininity, motherhood, purity and devotion in a single idealised figure. As both saint and woman, the Virgin Mary constitutes a powerful mediating figure. Neither human in that she is saintly, nor supremely divine in that she is female, she represents a volatile conjunction of similarity and difference. In keeping with the alterity of the bereavement literature's representations of grief, religious images of women in mourning work to make accessible that which is repressed by localising it away from the self. Indeed, Warner argues, the Virgin Mary represents a form of grief which, in its associations with the resurrection of Jesus Christ, is understood as a blessing. 'The Mater Dolorosa consoles the bereaved because she shares their sorrow; but also, at a more profound level, she satisfies a hunger of the believer, for the tears which gush from her eyes belong to a universal language of cleansing and rebirth' (1976: 223).

THE TRAGIC WOMAN IN GRIEF

One of the most readily accessible sources of images of grief is the media. As Walter, Littlewood and Pickering (1995) argue cogently, these images can be read as a form of emotional invigilation. In 1993, after a school mini-bus crashed on the M40 motorway in England killing a teacher and eleven school children, the headlines which framed the photographs of weeping teenage girls carried the injunctions of a psychological counsellor: 'I told the children they've all got to cry.' Though in this instance boys as well as girls were enjoined to cry, Walter *et al.* note that the images themselves are gendered. Thus, while the teenage girls represent emotional abandonment, being shown 'out of control in their grief', the head-master adheres to the customary practice of private grieving when he shields his face from the public gaze with his hand. Similarly, the father of Jonathan Ball, the small boy murdered in Warrington by the IRA in 1993, is depicted first supporting his wife in her loss, and then, after succumbing to grief, struggling bravely 'in a time-honoured masculine, British way, to regain control as quickly as possible' (1995: 590).

What Walter, Littlewood and Pickering note is the high visi-bility of these kinds of images of death in a society where death is said to be sequestered or taboo. Arguably, they can be said to contribute to the sequestration of ordinary death in that the disas-ters which are routinely introduced into the everyday world of tea-time television are in reality extraordinary. They represent the unthinkable tragedies to which other people fall victim – hence the search for causes and explanations which localise the death at the site of the specific individual who failed to have the wiring checked, who took the short cut across the deserted car park, who let his or her child wander too freely in the shopping precinct. By contrast the event of an 'ordinary' death is publicised only in the restrained small print of the 'Death Announcements'. Hardly riveting reading, such columns convey the manner of the death and the experience of loss via highly coded, almost terse termi-nology, the 'long illness bravely borne' being the only public clue that death took place after the private agony of cancer. The argu-ment that, in a world of privatised and professionalised losses, there is a need to know about grieving, and indeed that there is an identification with the dead and the bereaved, is persuasive. What is also evident, however, is that such 'knowledge' is made accessible via distancing strategies which locate it at the site of tragic female figures. Indeed, the viewer's degree of identification is further mediated by news editors' careful censoring of 'shocking' or 'offensive' photographs.

THE NINETEENTH-CENTURY WOMAN IN GRIEF

Alongside a bereavement literature which was generated from within the publications of psychiatrists, stands material produced by historians such as Phillipe Ariès (1981) and others, such as Geoffrey Gorer (1965), who drew on a historical perspective. They looked critically at the deathways of the twentieth century and, among other sources, drew on nineteenth-century mourning practices as a model for more therapeutic ritual responses to bereavement (Hockey 1996). As a result, high profile has been given to the Victorian widow, epitomised in the figure of Queen Victoria herself. Made into an iconic representation of an entire system of social practices, every aspect of her appearance appears to represent an open acknowledgement of that which is now seen to be hidden or sequestered – the mortal nature of human life. Thus Trollope's Duchess of Omnium, in answer to the question 'Was the widow weeping?' reports, 'Not actual tears. But her gown, and her cap, and her strings were weeping' (cited in Morley 1971: 64). Indeed the crape streamers which dangled from the widow's mourning cap were named 'weepers' and Queen Victoria's mourning handkerchief was speckled with black and white embroidered 'tears'.

However, the prominence given to this death-encumbered figure is a latter-day phenomenon, a cultural representation of what, at the time, was a social practice which can be described as conspicuous invisibility. As Walter notes, the Victorian widow's mourning dress was as much shield as display (1995). Social restrictions ensured that whatever she actually felt, grief or relief, it was safely relegated to the private sphere, separated off from the public world by a heavy black veil and the solid four walls of a well-staffed, middle-class villa.

In the Victorian widow we have a representative of a category of women who were well provided for and clearly disqualified from any form of labour by their constraining crape and bombazine garments. The 'invisibility' of their bodies can be seen to represent a set of explicit class-based assertions of their position within an unstable social hierarchy. Their clothing had the paradoxical effect of making them appear to disappear from public life, a form of retreat which signalled the social value of their dead partner. Not only was the widow shown to grieve her spouse wholeheartedly, but in her physical seclusion from society she indicated the material endowment which made her extended mourning possible. Recategorised as a widow, a term derived from the French word *vide* meaning empty, she constitutes a kind of conspicuous black hole. Morley, for example, suggests that 'the desired optical effect of mourning was the abolition of reflection' (1971: 63). Mrs Pipchin, a character from Charles Dickens' *Dombey and Son* (1848), spent forty years of her widowhood in a dress of 'black bombazeen, of such a lustreless, deep, dead sombre shade, that gas itself couldn't light her up after dark, and her presence was a quencher to any number of candles'. The 'sombre and intimidating' effect of the full mourning dress worn by women during the first year of widowhood is emphasised by Morley. Indeed, at the funeral of the Duke of Wellington the newly installed gas light was all but absorbed by the sombre, unreflecting cloth worn by the congregation (Morley 1971).

In the form of a gendered cultural representation of emotional abandonment the Victorian widow now has a highly visible public profile. What I have argued is that as a set of nineteenth-century social practices Victorian widowhood was a very private affair, albeit one which resonated powerfully throughout an entire social system. Late-nineteenth-century resistance to the ostentation of women's mourning dress met with a media outcry which drew parallels with the abandonment of mourning dress by French aristocrats prior to the Revolution. The *English Woman's Domestic Magazine* of 1876 speculated 'with a shudder whether these, too, are signs of the times to be followed by as awful a retribution' (Morley 1971: 63). The bombazine and black crape cloth into which the Victorian widow appeared to disappear seems therefore to have been integral to the fabric of her whole society.

While the Victorian widow's body was enclosed within heavy veils and mourning wrappings, and secluded within the four walls of her marital home, the unclad body of another kind of woman, often depicted in a state of 'erotic surrender', might well be exposed publicly upon the grave of the widow's husband (Oates 1995). Grave statuary, as depicted in David Robinson's collection of photographic images *Saving Graces* (1995), is a representational form which, in common with other images of grieving women, would seem to be at odds with the social practices of its time. Such statues are not only highly visible and supremely expressive; they are also quite clearly not representations of the women who were mourning the men whose corpses were interred in the graves below the statues. Oates notes that among them, 'there are no grieving widows of any recognisable type, no middle-aged or older women; no mothers or children. There are no hefty, or emaciated, or plain-faced, let alone unattractive mourners. No sons, brothers, fathers –

no masculine figures at all' (1995: Foreword). Indeed the Saving Graces, in Oates' view, are not nineteenth-century women at all. They belong to a different, distant era, to 'an entirely other dimension of mythologised experience'. As expert embodiments of ritual mourning, they signal the required intensity of emotional distress which the death of a man might bring about, never embracing the graves of women. Adorning the tombs of the wealthy they represent the enormous losses sustained by women who were defined almost entirely by their relationship with a male partner. However, they hold the gaze effectively in that they do not depict what such women might actually be experiencing in private. Being other women, they are safely set apart – by their age, their beautiful, barely clothed bodies and by their expansive gestures of despair.

THE FOREIGN WOMAN IN GRIEF

The death ritual of pre-modern, non-western societies has recently come to be seen as a source of inspiration for more 'enlightened' approaches to contemporary western death (Walter 1994/5, Hockey 1996). As a result, it is not uncommon to find references to the 'healthier' or more 'natural' mourning practices of 'old customs and other cultures' (Riley, cited in Hockey 1996). However, many of the ethnographic accounts which are drawn upon in critiques of current practice are themselves constructed in the image of much that is familiar. For example, Wilson's account of death ritual among the Nyakyusa of Tanzania (1939) shows a gender-divided ritual within which women are required to wail, while men are expected to dance. Participation in funerals is one of the ways in which members of Nyakyusa society escape suspicion that they have contributed to the death through witchcraft, and indeed fear pervades this ritual, whether it be of the spirit of the deceased, of the afterworld, of contagious diseases or of witchcraft accusations. It is as an expression of this fear, and therefore in order to assuage the spirit, that women wail and indeed bind their bellies with bark cloth to stem the trembling they are expected to experience. Later, men dance, in celebration of male potency, both sexually and in war.

Durkheim (1965), similarly describes the centrality of women in the death ritual of the Warramunga, a native Australian group who practise violent self-mutilation and noisy wailing after a death. Women's voluble display of grief is heightened through a contrast with their subsequent stage of mourning which prohibits normal speech. Entire villages of women communicate by sign only, some inhabitants never finding speech again. Durkheim argues that emotional displays such as these engender appropriate feelings of grief, thereby producing the collective sentiment which, in his view, is central to the stability of society. Warramunga women do not grieve in place of men. Instead their wailing is represented as the necessary stimulus which precipitates the required collective mourning. Both these accounts highlight the emotional responses of mourners, their analyses providing a rationale either for the nature of the feelings themselves, as in the case of an underlying threat of witchcraft accusations, or for their expression – that is, they ensure social solidarity through collective sentiment. It is this aspect of mourning, the emotional responses of survivors, which has gained ascendancy within post-Reformation practices of disposal. No longer required actively to steer the soul towards God, western mourning has come to focus, increasingly, on the needs of the bereaved. As argued throughout this chapter, it is the irrepressible nature of the contemporary experience of loss which is reflected in the proliferation of feminised accounts and images of grief. In the examples referred to above, we again see grief represented through accounts which give prominence to women, narrative forms which are generated within a society where the grief of both women and men is likely to take place in private.

CONCLUSION

Clergy interviewed about social practices associated with the disposal of the dead described situations where women had grieved in ways which resembled the cultural representations described above:

> My colleague had a funeral recently of a baby ... mother was uncontrollable ... spent most of the funeral walking up and down. All he could was try and get things over as quickly as possible with as much dignity as possible in very difficult circumstances.
>
> (Hockey 1993: 134)

> one girl started crying and the girl next to her started crying and by the time I'd finished I was dealing with this hysterical crowd of girls ... and so I really had to sort of say 'That's it.

No more of this. This is silly.' And I really had to do that, which is not exactly how you like to do a funeral. . . . you just have to be the big, brave, nasty horrible vicar who . . . and stop it.

(ibid.: 143)

This material suggests that in practice women who grieve publicly in the ways represented in grave statutary or media imagery contravene the requirements of male-controlled funeral behaviour. Interviews revealed clergy uneasily on the alert for mourners who shake uncontrollably, who wail and cling to the coffin, who demand to have it opened and who threaten to spring down into the grave at a burial (Hockey 1992: 27). If they have to resort to an undignified speeding up of the liturgy or a school-masterly reprimand, these are strategies which they find inconsistent with models of professional competence. What is expected from mourners, both female and male, is a set of bodily indications that grieving has been taking place. Indeed, we could argue that these indications are governed by an implicit set of rules; damp, reddened eyes, a pale complexion, solemn expressions, sighing and a subdued voice are all recognised as authentic clues as to the hidden presence of grief. The body itself is expected to remain more or less unchanged, though a degree of weight loss and a tendency towards drab clothing are signs of an appropriate level of private distress. Should there be gross changes in body size, coupled with failure to maintain personal hygiene and tidy dress, these can be taken as indications of an unacceptable, indeed 'pathological' yielding to despair.

As this chapter has demonstrated, such indications of grief contrast markedly with images or accounts of grief as an explicit and intensified expression of emotion. Crucially, they are feminised representations of grieving which serve to distance that which is nonetheless inescapable. Demonstrating the experience of intense pain, they signal the expected response to the deaths of significant relatives and friends. Just as mortality is intrinsic to human embodiment, so bereavement and loss are represented as essential to human sociality. If the death of a close Other does not spontaneously precipitate such distress, we may well take steps to obscure the fact. Bronfen argues that in a western society where 'cultural discourses construct the self as masculine' with the result that 'they ascribe to femininity a position of Otherness', mortality can be safely, indeed pleasurably contemplated via the image of the female corpse (1992: 181).

Cultural representations of a feminised grief, when framed within texts, photographs and statues, are a not unfamiliar rendering of death-at-a-distance. Questions remain, however, as to the significance of such representations for a female rather than male viewer. The assertion that, as viewers and readers, women and men are similarly positioned in a patriarchal society, such that Woman is universally read as Other, is a limited account of women's experience. It implies the false consciousness of women. By contrast, Bronfen concludes her work on representations of the dead woman by exploring ways in which the dead woman-as-muse has, or might, become the dead woman-as-creatrix (1992). On the one hand it could be argued that the woman who is represented is not the woman who views. The former is mad, semi-nude, foreign or saintly and therefore perceived as Other, not just by men but also by women. Irigaray argues that 'women ... maintain a relationship to the real environment but they don't subjectivize it as their own. They remain the locus for the experience of concrete reality, but they leave the matter of its structuration to the other' (1993: 35–6). However, she asks that, as the 'locus for the experience of concrete reality', women generate a set of representations which are not gender-neutral, but sexed. In their difference from the kinds of masculinist images and accounts described here, such representations contain the seeds of an independent, autonomous female subjectivity. Ultimately, it is towards this possibility that my chapter points.

REFERENCES

Ardener, E. (1972) 'Belief and the problem of women', in J. La Fontaine (ed.) *The Interpretation of Ritual*, London: Tavistock.
Ariès, P. (1981) *The Hour of our Death*, London: Penguin Books.
Bronfen, E. (1992) *Death, Femininity and the Aesthetic*, Manchester: Manchester University Press.
Chesler, P. (1972) *Women and Madness*, New York: Doubleday.
Cline, S. (1995) *Lifting the Taboo. Women, Death and Dying*, London: Little, Brown & Co.
Dickens, C. (1948) *Dombey and Son*, London: Nelson
Doyal, L. with Pennell, I. (1979) *The Political Economy of Health*, London: Pluto.
Durkheim, E. (1965) *The Elementary Forms of the Religious Life*, New York: Free Press.
Eichenbaum, L. and Orbach, S. (1983) *What Do Women Want?* Glasgow: Fontana/Collins.

Gorer, G. (1965) *Death, Grief and Mourning in Contemporary Britain*, London: Cresset.

Hobson, C. J. (1964) 'Widows of Blackton', *New Society*, 24 September, p. 13.

Hockey, J. (1992) *Making the Most of a Funeral*, London: Cruse-Bereavement Care.

—— (1993) 'The acceptable face of human grieving? The clergy's role in managing emotional expression during funerals', in D. Clark (ed.) *The Sociology of Death*, Oxford: Blackwell, pp. 129–48.

—— (1996) 'The view from the west: reading the anthropology of non-western death ritual', in G. Howarth and P. C. Jupp (eds) *Contemporary Issues in the Sociology of Death, Dying and Disposal*, Basingstoke: Macmillan, pp. 3–16.

Irigaray, L. (1993) *Je, Tu, Nous. Toward a Culture of Difference*, London: Routledge.

Maddison, D. C. and Walker, W. L. (1967) 'Factors affecting the outcome of conjugal bereavement', *British Journal of Psychiatry*, 113: 1057.

Marris, P. (1958) *Widows and their Families*, London: Routledge.

Morley, J. (1971) *Death, Heaven and the Victorians*, London: Studio Vista.

Oakley, A. (1974) *The Sociology of Housework*, London: Martin Robertson.

Oates, J. C. (1995) 'Beautiful mourning', *Independent on Sunday*, 29 October.

Parkes, C. M. (1972) *Bereavement: Studies of Grief in Adult Life*, Harmondsworth: Penguin.

Riley, J. L. (1984) 'The psychology of bereavement: a personal view', *Update*: 179–83.

Robinson, D. (1995) *Saving Graces*, New York: Norton.

Showalter, E. (1987) *The Female Malady*, London: Virago.

Ussher, J. (1991) *Women's Madness. Misogyny or Mental Illness?* London: Harvester/Wheatsheaf.

Walter, T. (1994/5) 'Natural death and the noble savage', *Omega* 30 (4): 237–48.

——, Littlewood, J. and Pickering, M. (1995) 'Death in the news: the public invigilation of private emotion', *Sociology* 29: 579–96.

—— (forthcoming) 'Emotional reserve and the English way of grief,' in K. Charmaz, G. Howarth and A. Kellehear (eds) *The Unknown Country: Experiences of Death in Australia, Britain and America*, Basingstoke: Macmillan.

Warner, M. (1976) *Alone of All her Sex. The Myth and Cult of the Virgin Mary*, London: Picador.

Wilson, M. (1939) 'Nyakyusa conventions of burial', *Bantu Studies* 13: 1–31.

Chapter 6

Death and the transformation of gender in image and text

Elizabeth Hallam

INTRODUCTION

Experiences of death are shaped by gender relations and identities. Gender also informs the divisions of labour within the practices which surround death, ensuring that the contributions of women and men within the dying process are different. This chapter examines a further gendered dimension of dying and death: the ways in which death forms a site at which gender and power relations are negotiated and transformed. Death, as a disruptive and destabilising force, opens out personal and social relations to critical reflection and in doing so releases a potential for significant shifts in interpersonal hierarchies. This has particular relevance for gender relations, understood as sets of social and symbolic categories which structure and inform social relations and practice. Anthropological approaches to gender have emphasised the importance of the analysis of variation in gendered experience as well as attempted to avoid assumptions about woman as a unified and universally subordinate category. Sanday identifies 'a move away from some of the constraining labels and blanket judgements implicit in past formulations in favour of addressing the conflict, variability and contradictions that we have all encountered in ethnographic field research' (Sanday 1990: 1). Gender categories are complex and their meaning shifts over time in relation to particular social and cultural relations.

This chapter explores a range of representations which engaged gender and death in early modern England. It is particularly concerned with the gender politics which emerged within popular, religious and legal representations of dying and death. In printed visual images, texts and legal documentation from church court

cases, the relationships between women and men, their differences, qualities, duties and capacities with regard to dying and
death, were explored and elaborated. Death formed a significant
arena in which access to power and authority was contested.

The first section examines the politics of gender in representations of dying and death. Early modern conceptions of order and
gender hierarchies within the household gave rise to particular
ideas about the relations of power and authority. Women as disorderly, disruptive figures were linked to sin and death and this
reinforced images of male authority. The impact of these representations was, however, dependent upon their reception and
incorporation in social practice. The chapter's second section
moves on to examine death as a life crisis during which gender
and power relations were negotiated and transformed. A further
set of representations of death and gender relations produced
within the Canterbury church courts offers perspectives on the
everyday relationships and practices which surrounded death.
Here witnesses' accounts of disease and the dying process reveal
the ways in which women's relationships with death were figured
in more positive ways. The final section is concerned with particular accounts of women's practices and responses to disease and
death. Women attendants at the deathbed were valued and, to a
certain extent, empowered when they were required to manage
the dying process.

GENDER POLITICS AND REPRESENTATIONS OF DEATH

Gender and power relations were negotiated through a range of
cultural representations surrounding dying and death. Early
modern visual images and texts, including printed pamphlets,
engravings, paintings, material objects and funeral monuments,
formed a rich field in which the moral, social, spiritual and physical dimensions of death were explored (Llewellyn 1991).The
significance of gender within these representations and the ways
in which they reproduced certain ideas about the condition and
location of women and men within social and moral relations
remain important areas of investigation.

The different phases of the life course of women and men were
depicted in engravings of the *Ages of Woman* and the *Ages of
Man*. These detailed socially significant stages from birth to death

Figure 6.1   The Ten Ages of Woman (*c.* 1570) represents the life course of woman from childhood to death in ten-year phases. The last image in this series shows woman at 90 years and then at 100 years when she is about to enter the grave.

and referred to the distinct life stages, capacities and qualities of woman and man. They formed visually complex representations of gender, age and status differences. In a sixteenth-century version of *The Ten Ages of Woman* the female figure was seen as a child, a maiden, a housekeeper, a matron, a grandmother and then at various stages in advanced years until, at 100 years, she was greeted by death (Figure 6.1). At the final stage of life the dying woman stoops beside a young child, suggesting the interlocking cycles of death and birth (Kunzle 1973: 206–7).

The visual representation of the passage through life stages was informed by notions about the appropriate conduct and duties of women. Gender relations, especially those within the household, were often represented in terms of an orderly hierarchy within which relations of authority between husband and wife, parent and child, master and servant were clearly established. Through household manuals, advice books and sermons, the orderly household, in which duty and respect reinforced gendered inequalities of power, was represented as a social and moral necessity. Within this model of the family the authority of the husband and master was secured through the obedience of the wife, children and servants (Amussen 1988: 34–66).

This concept of order was highlighted by representations of disorderly women who threatened the stability and harmony of the household. In popular cultural representations the politics of gender centred around women's struggle for dominance over men. The inversion of relations of power and the threat of the unruly woman who refused to remain subordinate formed a central dynamic in printed pamphlets, visual images and festive performance (Davis 1987: 124–51). The interrelationships between these representations and routine stories, rhymes and insults ensured that images of disorderly women were invoked within the gendered politics of everyday discourse (Hallam 1994, Gowing 1994). In their efforts to dislodge men's authority women were represented as a dangerous force and were often linked to images of destruction, decay and corruption:

> If not the devil, woman's other double was death. In the realm of imagination woman was the cause of death, the daughter of Eve, who by her vulnerability to temptation had brought death to humankind. Her sexuality and her beauty, ephemeral and false, made her a source of death.
>
> (Borin 1993: 216–19)

This set of related notions about the condition of woman was explored within religious images. *The Tree of Knowledge and Death* (Figure 6.2) represents Eve as the root of man's moral downfall and links her sin with death. Eve's fertility, sexuality and weakness in the face of temptation is emphasised as she gestures towards the serpent's fruit. Strong visual contrasts between the fleshy living body and death's withered frame indicate the fatal consequences of Eve's actions.

Figure 6.2   Tree of Knowledge and Death (1587) represents Eve as a source of disorder and moral corruption. Sin and death are linked to the female body.

Gender conflict and difference were represented in early modern pamphlets through a complex symbolism of the suffering body. Representations of women as fruitful, productive, healing, cleansing and nourishing vessels contrast with images of the female body as a source of disease or as a consuming, dangerous trap, which may appear beautiful but the true condition of which is filthy and borne by the devil (Henderson and McManus 1985). Joseph Swetnam's *The Arraignment of Lewd, Idle, Froward and Unconstant Women* (1615) employs a complex imagery to convey his picture of women who are said to be lascivious and crafty, whorish, thievish and knavish. Gender differences are constructed through insect and animal metaphors which convey the moral superiority of men. Men are industrious whereas women are harmful – 'the simple Bee gathereth honey where the venomous spider doth her poison'. The images of the harmful and damaging habits of women are extended by associating them with noisy, stinging 'Hornets, venomous adders, serpents and snakes'.

Women are also represented in this text as a powerful persuasive force. They will be fulfilled, if not by veiled persuasion, then by direct abuse. Men cannot hope to control women: a 'froward woman in her frantic mood will pull, hawl, swerve, scratch and tear all that stands in her way'. The physical and financial damage that women inflict upon men is represented through images of the consuming female body: 'They lay out the folds of their hair to entangle men into their love, betwixt their breasts is the vale of destruction; and in their beds there is hell, sorrow and repentance. Eagles eat not men till they are dead, but women devour them alive' (Henderson and McManus 1985: 216).

These moral commentaries upon the relations between women and men employed images of death to convey the problematic nature of women. Death was also represented as a solution to gender conflict. Marital strife initiated by the disobedient wife was a common theme elaborated in cheap, illustrated prints. *A precious good, hallowed recipe for men who have shrewish wives* (c. 1620) tells the story of a husband who suffered as a result of the misconduct of a noisy, quarrelsome wife (Kunzle 1973: 230–3). He is advised by a neighbour to beat her soundly. The wife then takes to her deathbed and after her funeral the husband celebrates in triumph (Figure 6.3). The print parodies advice and household manuals, which offered instructions regarding marital harmony. It presents an exaggerated version of gender hierarchies in which man's control of the disorderly wife was unlimited.

Representations of dying and death were deeply informed by notions of gender and power relations. The ways in which death was imagined and experienced were shaped by socially dominant ideas about the nature, qualities, and conduct of women and men. The gendered content of representations of death and the ways in which textual and visual images of death were deployed within early modern gender politics tended to reinforce dominant notions about women's subordinate status. A model of women, men and their relations which emphasised male authority was embedded

Figure 6.3   A precious good, hallowed recipe for men who have shrewish wives (c. 1620) represents the fate of a disorderly wife. Following the advice of his neighbour, a husband beats his 'quarrelsome' wife. The wife dies, and after her funeral the husband celebrates.

within commonly used images associated with death. The repeated and conventionalised use of such representations constituted their cultural resonance and power.

Relationships between representations of death and their contextual effects and interpretations within social practice are complex and subject to change over time. In a discussion of gender, power and cultural representations Moore foregrounds the problem of

> how we theorise the relationship between dominant representations and cultural discourses about gender and what people actually think and do. How is it possible for people both to consent to and dissent from the dominant representation of gender when they are encoded in the material world all around them?

(Moore 1995: 75)

This raises questions about the gender relations involved in the production and the reception of cultural representations within changing social contexts. The 'true' nature of gender relations or what women and men 'actually do' is seldom accurately reflected at the level of representation. So, for example, women's work is often represented as trivial when compared with that of men. In addition women are likely to produce positive representations of themselves which value their labour. Despite this, particular representations, which favour men, are maintained as dominant. Moore offers an explanation for this – the female perspective is not an alternative model but one which seeks to locate women *within* cultural structures, rather than to subvert them. As such, women's perspectives are contained through renegotiation. Women's representations of themselves are attempts to value themselves and to participate within the dominant social frame. In this way women contribute to the maintenance of dominant male structures (Moore 1986).

The concept of a continual process of renegotiation, in which different and competing representations of women and men emerge, is especially useful in the analysis of historical gender relations. It allows room for examination of the ways in which women were able to question or challenge their positions within gender relations and it opens the way for an analysis of complex and changing gender and power relations over time. The emphasis on contradiction, conflict and renegotiation at the level of everyday social practice and representation opens the analysis of competing perspectives and offers an approach which foregrounds women's own strategic social practice.

CRISIS, DEATH AND TRANSFORMATION

A certain potential for the negotiation of gender relations was presented throughout the life crises surrounding death. Life crises have long been recognised within anthropological studies as critical points in the life course during which changes in social relations, statuses and identities are marked and ritualised (e.g. La Fontaine 1972). With reference to the early modern period Llewellyn observes that 'Death is both a moment in time and a ritualised process; it refers to a physical transformation and a social phenomenon' (Llewellyn 1991: 7). The transformation of the body, its changing appearance, gestures and actions, were closely observed throughout the dying process and especially during the later stages before death. These bodily 'signs' and 'tokens' were interpreted as indicators of the dying person's physical, moral and spiritual condition. They were also regarded as meaningful 'statements' about the dying person's relationships with family, kin and friends. Therefore the transformation of the dying body was linked to shifting personal and social relations.

Death initiated a range of personal and social adjustments which were managed and mediated by family and kin as well as by medical and legal specialists. Documents generated by the Canterbury church courts during will disputes provide detailed accounts of the gendered relations and practices surrounding death in early modern Kent. Witnesses were required to disclose detailed information about the deceased and their everyday interactions with family, kin, friends and neighbours during the often extended period before death. Their accounts reveal a gendered division of labour which tended to emerge at the deathbed. Women were valued as longer-term attendants, a labour which often secured their position as knowledgeable and trusted witnesses in legal procedures when wills were contested. Men, as notaries, gentlemen professionals and church officials, were more centrally involved in the ritualised production of the will. These practices were, however, shaped by the life stage, social status and wealth of the dying person. So, for example, women were more centrally involved in the making of women's wills or when the will was produced in spoken rather than written form (Hallam 1996).

While early modern visual images and printed texts reveal some of the ways in which women were represented as subordinate and dangerous through their association with disease, physical corruption and death, the texts produced in the church courts commonly represented women's work during the dying process as necessary and valuable. Indeed it was regarded as a wife's duty to attend her husband at the deathbed and the fulfilment of this duty enhanced a woman's status among her 'honest' or respectable neighbours. The crises associated with dying and death opened the possibility for critical reflection upon the gendered relations of power within the family. The preparations for death drew women, as wives, kin and neighbours, into a process which offered them a certain power. Although constrained by their exclusion from professional and official positions within the church, their practices at the deathbed were significant and extended women's capacity to shape and control the dying process. The destabilising force of death tended to open and expose relations in family and kin groups as they shifted to accommodate imminent personal loss. Women's positions as trusted attendants and witnesses within this process allowed them to consolidate their influence and to enhance their authority.

'IN PASSIONS': WOMEN, DISEASE AND FEARS OF DEATH

A further field of representations suggests that the spaces of death, especially those which were regarded as infectious and therefore dangerous for family, kin, officials and specialists usually accustomed to managing the dying process, offered certain women a central part in death practices. Through an analysis of the interpersonal relations that developed within these places it appears that these women, who were represented as socially marginal or subordinate within household hierarchies, found their way into the centre of households rendered highly unstable with the onset of fatal infectious disease. A set of witnesses' accounts from the Canterbury church courts allows for a detailed reconstruction of the social relations involved in the movement of women from the margins to the centre throughout the dying process.

Although accounts produced within a legal context were constructed and constrained by social and power relations within and beyond the courts, they formed a significant field of representations which arguably provides access to women's perceptions, actions and relationships. Within the frameworks set by the legal practices of questioning and record making, witnesses presented extensive narratives relevant to the dispute under investigation.

Testamentary disputes heard in the church courts generated descriptions of the dying process, especially the practices involved in will-making. The social and cultural content of those descriptions, including their language and imagery, requires close analysis in order to interpret the gender and power dimension of dying and death. This analysis was pursued through an anthropological study of these archival materials.

One particularly detailed case describes the actions of young women servants, their responses to outbreaks of smallpox and their talks about the resulting deaths, in Hythe, Kent. The women witnesses in the case of Simons v. Jenken (1635) presented evidence to the court and their accounts highlight the importance of relationships between women in their preparations for death. In February 1635 Susanna Grigg and Anna Nethersole travelled to Canterbury to provide testimonies in the case surrounding the disputed will of Mary Jenken. These three women had previously lived in the house of Alice and John Knight in Hythe where they were employed as servants. In court both Susanna Grigg and Anna Nethersole described an occasion when all three women were together in the kitchen discussing smallpox. It was a month before Jenken died in September 1634 and they were 'talking and communing of the rifeness of the disease' in Hythe and the 'mortall nature of catching it' and 'how many died of it'. Grigg stated that Jenken 'never had the small pox and that she feared she would dy of them if she should have them as some of their next neighbours which had them newly did' (CCAL, MSS., PRC 39/46, ff. 50–1).

Such were Mary Jenken's fears that she declared her will to her friends. Susanna Grigg recalled the details. Jenken had declared that

> her meaning was that if she died or that after her death her Aunt Coleman (meaning the wife of Henry Coleman of Stanford) should have all her clothes where upon this depo-nent and her fellow servant asked her if she would give none of them to her sisters who answered that what she had her Aunt Coleman should have and if she pleased to give her sisters anything she might use her discretion and gave this for her reason and motive that her aunt Coleman was one of her chiefest friends [. . . Mary] being then in health of body and about 16 years of age.
>
> (CCAL, MSS., PRC 39/46, f. 50)

Mary Jenken's responses to the death of neighbours and her fears of disease initiated the preparations for her own death. The spoken will, witnessed by her fellow servants, formed a ritualised language in which to express her concerns and affection for kin and friends. In this context women within the same household provided support and performed the duties necessary for the confirmation of the final will. By acting as witnesses Susanna Grigg and Anna Nethersole would ensure that Mary Jenken's wishes were carried forward. These women would have recognised the social and legal obligations involved in the witnessing of a spoken will. They were required to remember the contents of the will and to ensure that the property was properly disposed of after Jenken's death.

A network of relations between women kin and friends centring around Jenken was consolidated and ritualised through the distribution of Jenken's possessions. Jenken confirmed her affection for her fellow servants, her aunt and her aunt's servant by giving her clothing as gifts and tokens of friendship. In this case the spoken word and material objects formed representations of the values women assigned to their relationships and it was exclusively through women's involvement that these representations were sustained.

Further important aspects of women's work in relation to disease and death are suggested by descriptions of the impact of infectious disease upon the preparations for death. In 1635 Maria Woolgate described the experiences of her aunt who died of smallpox: 'in the time of her sickness [she] was sometimes in passions and teachy through the malignity of her disease' (CCAL, MSS., PRC 39/46, f. 61v). The nature and effects of smallpox tended to distance the dying from those who would usually have been expected to visit and attend the deathbed. John Sole of Ulcome stated in court in 1641 that the houses of residents with smallpox were 'shunned as infectious' and Thomas Hilles from the same parish described smallpox as 'a disease which proved so mortal to many and therefore the house wherein it was held soe infectious that few or none durst adventure to visit any friend or other for fear therof' (CCAL, MSS., PRC 39/48, ff. 239, 235, 236v.)

In situations where the fear of infection disrupted relationships between the dying and their kin, friends and neighbours, servants would be expected to fulfil further duties and assume additional responsibilities. Alice Turner, a servant in Great Chart, explained in a testamentary case that she had attended Francis Stephens while he suffered from smallpox in 1641 'by reason of which infection noe body then coming unto ye said deceased but this deponent' (CCAL, MSS., PRC 39/51, f. 171). Francis Stephens' wife was absent from the house where her husband lay sick and Alice Turner was to cope with her master's needs at the deathbed, witnessing and guarding his will. Such preparations for death were usually conducted and controlled by family, kin and neighbours with the assistance of legal specialists. At the deathbeds of those isolated by fears of infectious disease, women servants acting as carers and mediators would assume duties which afforded them an authority they were usually denied.

In isolated households without services and assistance open to them, changes would have occurred in relationships within the household. A redistribution of responsibilities and duties took place and servants were obliged to cope with increased demands. These requirements, as well as the strategies which were used by a household to minimise the threat of infection, depended upon the various stages in the life cycle which its member had reached. For example, William Hovenden lay sick in Cranbrooke with smallpox in 1643 considering his wife, 'who he took such care of and love soe well that he would not be quiet till he had gotten her to leave the house for fear of ye infeccon of the pox she being then as he said with child' (CCAL, MSS, PRC 39/48, f. 267v). In such cases servants would again move into positions of authority with regard to the management of the dying process.

In addition to descriptions of women servants in central positions within the space of death, witnesses noted the presence of women who were prepared to attend the deathbed in infected houses (CCAL, MSS, PRC 39/48, ff. 243–4, 267). Widow Sayer, together with Elizabeth Gillow from Walmer, who were 'Kin to the testator [Gillow] by marriage', were described as John Gillow's tenders when he was ill in Deal in 1642 (CCAL, MSS, PRC 39/48, ff. 244v, 267). In John Sole's house at Ulcombe, Sole's daughter (who had recovered from smallpox) cared for her intended husband, and one Goodwife Adams was also noted as an attender to the deathbed (CCAL, MSS, PRC. 39/48, ff. 234, 235). Women with reputations of being skilled and knowledgeable were prepared to nurse the dying in situations considered threatening to family and kin. When Timothy St Nicholas, from Ash, caught smallpox in 1638 he was visited by his wife and her mother but only one woman, Margaret Newham, a widow from Ash, was described as his nurse. Others were apparently 'fearful to go near unto him [...] because the testator was sicke of the infectiouse disease' (CCAL, MSS., PRC. 39/48, f. 232).

Women, either as servants or as skilled attendants, were able to play a central part in the deathbed practices of those considered dangerous and infectious. They were also valued and trusted by other women in the making of wills and the distribution of their estate. These representations of women as central to the management of the dying process tend to conflict with images of women as marginal and disruptive. The crises associated with death initiated social and cultural processes within which women were variously positioned. Socially dominant concepts of household hierarchy which marginalised women servants and widows were, in a sense, inverted when they moved into positions of authority in 'dangerous' or infectious houses. Representations of women's proximity to disease and death could operate in various ways. Women were, on the one hand, a source of disease and death and, at the same time, they were known to occupy central positions in the management of the dying process. These contradictory representations highlight the complex cultural associations between gender, power and death.

CONCLUSIONS

This chapter draws together two fields of representations concerned with dying and death in order to examine the ways in which gender and power relations were constructed and negotiated. Widely disseminated printed texts and visual images formed a significant cluster of cultural representations which reproduced and elaborated upon social, religious and moral themes concerning gender relations and death. The church court materials including witnesses' accounts of the everyday relations surrounding death formed a further field of representations which provides access to the ways in which women's interpretations, actions and relationships informed their practices within the dying process.

Printed visual images and texts which engaged with the theme of death reproduced socially dominant ideas about gender differences and the nature of relations between woman and man. The representation of women within the site of death was complex. Women were identified as the root of sin, ultimately to blame for corruption and therefore in need of direction and control. They were represented as disobedient and troublesome wives whose punishment for the disruption of harmonious marriages was death. Alongside these images stand representations of the everyday relationships and practices surrounding death. These tend to incorporate women's interpretations of their positions within the dying process and they highlight the valued aspects of women's practices in the space of death. Cultural representations of death encompassed conflicting images of women and power and as such they were embedded in the negotiation of gender relations. Contradictions within the representation of women and death signal the significance of this life crisis as a space in which gender and power relations might shift and transform.

REFERENCES

Primary works

Manuscript sources

Canterbury Cathedral Archives and Library (CCAL), Canterbury Archdeaconary Court Depositions, 1635, 1638, 1641. DCc.PRC 39/46, DCc.PRC 39/48, DCc.PRC 39/51.

Printed sources

Swetnam, J. (1615) *The Arraignment of Lewd, Idle, Froward and Unconstant Women*, London: Edward Ailde.

Secondary works

Amussen, S. D. (1988) *An Ordered Society, Gender and Class in Early Modern England*, Oxford: Blackwell.

Borin, F. (1993) 'Judging by images', in N. Z. Davis and A. Farge (eds) *A History of Women in the West. Renaissance and Enlightenment Paradoxes*, London: the Belknap Press of Harvard University Press, pp. 187–254.

Davis, N. Z. (1987) 'Women on top', in N. Z. Davis *Society and Culture in Early Modern France: Eight Essays*, Cambridge: Polity Press, pp. 124–51.

Gowing, L. (1994) 'Language power and the law: women's slander litigation in early modern London', in J. Kermode and G. Walker (eds) *Women, Crime and the Courts in Early Modern England*, London: UCL Press, pp. 26–47.

Hallam, E. (1994) 'Crisis and representation. Gender and social relations in Canterbury and its region, 1580–1640', unpublished PhD thesis, University of Kent at Canterbury, currently being prepared for publication.

—— (1996) 'Turning the hourglass: gender relations at the deathbed in early modern Canterbury', *Mortality* 1 (1) (March): 61–82.

Henderson, K. U. and McManus, B. F. (eds) (1985) *Half Humankind. Contexts and Texts of the Controversy about Women in England, 1540–1640*, Urbana, IL: University of Illinois Press.

Kunzle, D. (1973) *The Early Comic Strip. Narrative Strips and Picture Stories in the European Broadsheet from c. 1450–1825*, Berkeley: University of California Press.

La Fontaine, J. (1972) 'Ritualization of women's life-crises in Bugisu', in La Fontaine (ed.) *The Interpretation of Ritual: Essays in Honour of A. I. Richards*, London: Tavistock Publications, pp. 159–85.

Lehner, E. J. (1971) *Devils, Demons, Death and Damnation*, New York: Dover Publications.

Llewellyn, N. (1991) *The Art of Death. Visual Culture in the English Death Ritual, 1500-c.1800*, London: Reaktion Books.

Moore, H. (1986) *Space, Text and Gender: An Anthropological Study of the Marakwet of Kenya*, Cambridge: Cambridge University Press.

—— (1994) *A Passion for Difference. Essays in Anthropology and Gender*, Cambridge: Polity Press.

Sanday, P. R. and Goodenough, R. G. (eds) (1990) *Beyond the Second Sex. New Directions in the Anthropology of Gender*, Philadelphia: University of Pennsylvania Press.

Chapter 7

Beauty and the Beast
Sex and death in the tabloid press

*Mike Pickering, Jane Littlewood
and Tony Walter*

INTRODUCTION

In a previous paper, we challenged the conventional sociological
view that death in contemporary western society is 'publicly
absent but privately present' (Mellor 1993, Mellor and Schilling
1993). By looking in particular at press coverage of the extraordinary deaths of otherwise ordinary individuals, we were able to
show that in Britain there is widespread coverage of death and
death-related issues by the media. We also contested the influential view of Gorer (1995) that death-related issues in their public
representations are emotionally sanitised in the manner of
pornography by showing that, at least as far as the press is
concerned, their treatment is saturated with emotion, however
sensationally treated that may be. Far from being subject to some
sort of taboo, the grief-torn feelings of relatives and friends of the
deceased in cases of extraordinary public deaths are actually the
focus of intense press interest. We offered three possible ways of
accounting for this kind of attention, which of course extends
beyond reporters to those who buy and read the newspapers for
whom they write, though not in ways that can necessarily be
assumed from any analysis of news texts themselves (see Walter,
Littlewood and Pickering, 1995). The three accounts were as
follows:

- People who have been bereaved and their comforters do not
  know what to do or say following the decline of mourning
  rituals. Therefore, there is interest in newspaper stories about
  death-related issues.
- People who have been bereaved in (white mainstream) Britain
  affirm the cultural value of stoicism but also wish to indicate,

indirectly, how deeply they feel their loss. The difficulties associated with this account for interest in this area.

- It is increasingly considered harmful to repress tears and negative feelings, and therefore there is interest in such expressions.

In this chapter, we wish to build on the earlier paper through an examination of the ways in which sex and gender feature as central structural components of front-page stories concerning death in the tabloid press. Our examination shows that the tabloid representation of death and death-related issues in general is structured around an 'inversion' of the contemporary discursive ordering of death in western societies, and that sex and gender are fundamentally implicated in this process. Added to these, the crime of murder figured as the third major thematic strand woven into stories concerned with the category of death. It is through the interweaving of these gender-linked 'inversions' in connection with stories of murder that their major ideological focus of disruption to conventional order is characteristically developed. In other words, those stories which involve, or can be presented as involving, the triple 'threats' of death, sex and crime, are held to be particularly newsworthy and so are then ripe for journalistic plucking from the general tree of events.

Initially, we intended our examination of the press coverage of such stories as a pilot study, and for this reason we concentrated on front-page stories over a three-month period, focusing on the tabloid press simply because such newspapers achieve the highest circulation of newspapers in the UK. We chose to look at stories covered during 1992 on the grounds that the time elapsed between the presentations of the original material and our analysis of it would be long enough to minimise any possible additional distress to relatives or friends associated with the stories, or subsequent further coverage of them. The months of May, June and July were randomly chosen, and we sampled all British tabloid newspapers. During this period, we found that three stories in particular were the most widely covered. These concerned the deaths of Alison and Matthew Manwaring, Alison Shaugnessy and Rachel Nickell. All of these people were the victims of brutal forms of murder, and in the press coverage of these acts of homicide, issues relating to sex and gender came very much to the fore.

DEATH'S PUBLIC STING

Perhaps the most significant finding resulting from our content analysis of this three-month period, was the extent to which death itself bulked large in the general spread of topics covered by the press. Within this period, and in one guise or another, death featured on 41.5 per cent of all front pages. The coverage ranged from that of the now defunct *Today* newspaper (56 per cent) to that of the *Sun* (33 per cent).

The commercial motivation behind such widespread coverage would seem to have been based on the assumption by editors and reporters that death as a topic of public discourse is a matter of interest and concern to their publics. This raises a number of complex issues, but the assumption itself is obviously supported by sales figures and the maintenance of those figures over and beyond the period in question. More importantly the central point of our earlier paper is empirically borne out; death was conspicuous by its public presence rather than its absence. Death has a public sting.

The death-related issues covered by the tabloid press over the period in question were, in declining order of frequency, as follows:

- murder and grief
- unexpected fatalities
- unlawful killings
- dying children
- celebrity deaths
- public health issues and AIDS
- child suicide
- compensation for loss of life.

What is striking about almost all of these deaths is both their timing and their location. First, their timing is, in the vast majority of cases, characterised by their untimeliness (Parkes 1972). Almost exclusively, they feature the deaths of young people and children – those who have met their mortal end long before any sense of a natural lapse of time. There were in fact only three deaths of elderly people covered during our sample period. Of these one was of an 'ordinary' citizen, Matthew Manwaring, whose death we shall deal with in a subsequent section. The other two concerned media celebrity stars – Frankie Howerd and Marlene

Dietrich. What is perhaps most interesting about the coverage of their deaths is the contrast between youth and age. The photograph accompanying the story about the death of Frankie Howerd, the celebrated English comedian, represents him as elderly. The famous actress, Marlene Dietrich, was in fact much older than Howerd when she died, and while her age of 90 years at death is included in the text covering this event, the photographs accompanying this text portray her as a young woman. The headlines announcing her death clearly encouraged public remembrance of Marlene Dietrich as a young woman, rather than as she looked in her dotage. The *Daily Star* (7 May 1992) carried a photograph of her in her youth with the headline 'Sexbomb Dietrich dies at 90', while *Today* (7 May 1992) reproduced a different photograph, but also one taken in her youth, and accompanied by the headline 'The Death of an Angel'. Indeed, this particular front page of *Today* contained three death-related stories and associated images which involved Ms Dietrich's photograph being placed between the photographs of two men. To her left was a picture of a murdered woman's fiancé, Gordon Healis ('Tragic Alison and me'), and to her right a picture of a football player, Trevor Steven, who had been involved in a fatal football stadium accident ('Grief of Hero Trevor').

Second, the physical locations of the deaths covered under the categories we have cited are also intriguing in that they all occurred either at home or in a public place. These sites are at variance with the vast majority of mortalities, which take place following chronic illness among the elderly populations in a hospital or similar institution.

It may be the case that these deaths are newsworthy precisely because of their potential to threaten the conventional ordering of death-related issues. Death *should*, in the conventional order of things, be publicly absent and privately present. It is precisely *because* it is not that death is in the news. Specifically, the conventional order of death, that is, of an elderly person from a chronic illness in an institution, is 'inverted' in these stories which tend to cover the sudden deaths of young people or children occurring at home or in a public place. This tendency is exemplified by the coverage of the three stories given the most extensive coverage by all of the tabloid press during the period of study, that is, the deaths of Alison and Matthew Manwaring, Alison Shaugnessy, and Rachel Nickell. Details of these deaths are given below. It is suggested that these stories were given extensive coverage because murder, sex and death could be effectively utilised to promote both a sense of threat and an increase in sales.

TWO ALISONS AND A RACHEL: MUTILATED FEMALE BODIES AND THE NEWSPAPER COMMODITY

In proceeding to examine the three news stories dealing with death which attained the most widespread coverage during our sample period, it may be useful to begin by recapitulating the bare details associated with them. First, Alison and Matthew Manwaring were killed and dismembered in their home and were found, eleven days after their deaths, buried in their own back garden. They were reported as being grieved by brother and son, Mark, and by Alison's fiancé, Gordon Healis. News coverage of the story involved the discovery of the corpses and the immediate aftermath of their deaths, a pattern repeated in the case of Rachel Nickell, who was raped and stabbed as she walked with her young son and pet dog on Wimbledon Common. In this second case, the press focused on the grief of her partner, Andre, her parents and her son, Alexander, who was tragically the immediate witness to the crime. Third, Alison Shaugnessy was the victim of a multiple stabbing at her home, and was shown as being grieved by her husband John, her brother and her parents. The coverage of the story involved the trial and subsequent conviction of two sisters, Michelle and Lisa Taylor, for her murder.

Analysis of the news reporting of these murders reveals a distinct focus of interest on the female bodies of the victims. This is perhaps most clearly shown by the differential treatment given to Alison and Matthew Manwaring, both of whom died at the same location and at roughly the same time, and both of whom were dismembered. These common details notwithstanding, the youth and gender of Alison, as opposed to the elderly category into which her father Matthew was placed, made her the subject of considerably greater attention. For example, all newspapers carried a photographic image of Alison, while only two, the *Sun* and the *Daily Mail*, carried an image of Matthew. The *Sun* (4 May 1992) presented equal-sized photographs of Matthew and Alison. These head-and-shoulder images were placed side by side, but the caption to Matthew's read 'Mutilated ... Matthew Manwaring died with his daughter', whereas that underneath the image of his daughter explicitly stressed the macabre nature of her death: 'Horror . . . Alison Manwaring's body was hacked to pieces'. The gender-directed contrast manifest in this was supported by the more clinical vocabulary chosen when describing Matthew's dismemberment ('mutilated') and the melodramatic description of Alison's which was further highlighted by being prefaced by the single lexical item – 'Horror'. The contrast was further reinforced by the way Matthew was reported as having died 'with his daughter' rather than the other way around, and by the subsidiary headline – 'Alison and dad carved up with butcher's knife' – where it is the woman who is identified by her first name and given priority in the process of naming. Similarly, the *Daily Mail* on the same date carried a photograph of Alison which was double the size of that of Matthew. Even these exceptional cases therefore fall into the more general pattern of an almost exclusive focus on Alison's death and the details surrounding it, with Matthew relegated to the sidelines of the coverage. According to the front pages of the tabloids, all of the grief was for 'our Alison'.

While the other two murders occurring during our sample time-frame were made salient by virtue of routine commercial news values, what was considered most story-worthy was, as with Alison Manwaring, the victims' youth and gender in direct relation to their gruesome deaths. Alison Shaugnessy was represented in a smiling wedding-day photo, and images were reproduced of Rachel Nickell with her partner and young son or, again, in an enlarged shot of her face, fringed by blonde hair and wearing a winning smile. The point was decoratively established by the *Sun*'s prominent use of this photograph to underwrite its banner head-line 'Beauty Slain by the Beast'. The stark contrast between the stereotypical features of a sexually attractive young woman and the horrific nature of her 'rape' and murder – a double physical violation – were then further glossed by this mythological reference. The structural opposition of beauty and beastliness resonates with fear and fantasy in ways which extend beyond this reference, as Schlesinger and Tumber (1994) have suggested in their analysis of the very similar story of the murder of a young woman, Tessa Howden, following a sexually motivated attack while she lay sleeping in her bedroom. On the one hand, there is the public fear of violent crime encroaching into the sanctity of private space, which as a public fear may be said to be predominantly felt by women, while on the other there is the private appeal to voyeurism in tabloid 'human interest' stories, which as a private appeal may be said to be publicly targeted at men. What then specifically concerns Schlesinger and Tumber are 'forms of reporting that might pander to male fantasies of destruction visited upon the bodies of women' (1994: 247). This concern, along with analyses of the fantasies themselves, is nothing new (see, for example, Dworkin 1981, Kuhn 1985, Kappeler 1986, and Theweleit 1990), but regrettably, yet unsurprisingly, on the basis of our own analysis it would seem that the news coverage of Tessa Howden's death was by no means atypical. It is precisely these types of death which are most extensively reported in the tabloid press.

Despite the fact that only Rachel Nickell's murder was directly associated with a sexual attack, both Alison Manwaring's and Alison Shaugnessy's deaths were treated in a similar manner, and the clear intent behind such treatment is exposed by the need, when all else fails, to resort to speculation. So, for instance, the *Daily Star* (7 May 1992) claimed that, 'It is *believed* Alison, 25, *may* have been forced to watch her father's murder at their home ... before being stripped naked and taken on a terrifying journey to her own death' (our emphasis). The warrant for this speculative account was provided by the fact that, at the time of writing, the manner of Alison's death was not known, whereas it had been established that Matthew had been killed with a shotgun – the blast had 'shredded' his heart. Yet this would have been true of other significant aspects of the murder inquiry, and these were not taken up as the basis for painting the lurid details of hypothetical scenarios. The one exception to this immediately follows the supposition already put forward, where the bodies of both victims were described as having been 'chopped up', *probably* on waste ground in North Woolwich, south London (our emphasis) – even though they were then subsequently buried in the back garden of their house in Barking, Essex. This conjectural, derelict location simply adds to the horror factor, an effect emphasised by the use of a crosshead – the word 'chopped' in bold lower-case letters – as well as the word 'butchers' in the main headline. These unsubstantiated details blur the line between the objective reporting which journalists perennially lay claim to, and the fantasies of violence to women's bodies which worry Schlesinger and Tumber.

It is indeed unclear whose fantasies are in the frame here, as with the other main stories of death during the period of our study. Alison Shaughnessy, for instance, was portrayed as the victim of fifty-four stab wounds made by a 'five-inch knife', though her case differed somewhat in that press coverage concentrated more on her killers and their trial for her murder than upon the way Alison died. In Rachel Nickell's case, her death was represented by some of the tabloids, without any sense of moral disquiet, as seen through the 'eyes' of her infant son. For example the *Daily Mail* carried the headline 'Murdered as her Little Boy Watched' (16 July 1992), and reported that, 'A boy of two lived through an unthinkable nightmare yesterday when a sex attacker slit his mother's throat as they walked in the park. For 45 minutes, the toddler clung to the lifeless, half-naked body.' Alexander Nickell was so traumatised by his experience that he was unable to speak. Despite this 'unthinkable nightmare' he was reported to have been taken back to the scene of the crime six days later, accompanied by a blonde woman (simulating his mother) and his father, André. The likely impact of this apparently crude and morally suspect police strategy was ambivalently handled by the tabloids. The *Daily Mail* (22 July 1992) picked up on its previous theme with the headline 'Return to a Nightmare' but in this case did not speculate about the rationale for treating a young child in this manner. The *Daily Star*, however, following the headline, 'Where Mummy was Murdered' (22 July 1992), suggested that a reconstruction might 'jog the toddler's memory'. Alexander was two years old. In light of this, the *Star*'s account of his response was almost gratuitous: 'The tot just looked confused, as if he didn't really know what was going on' (22 July 1992). Significantly, though, the blonde friend of Rachel's who simulated her part was described as looking 'absolutely distraught' and quickly breaking down, whereas André 'put on a very brave face' for his son's sake. This contrasts dramatically with previous accounts of his having 'broken down' and 'sobbed' (see, for example, *Daily Express* and the *Sun*, 17 July 1992). After a relatively short spell of time, gender-appropriate role behaviour was thus shown as restored, following movement out of the gender-atypical phase of liminality deemed appropriate to being plunged into the first throes of grief. Within days the masculinity of the father had emerged cleansed and intact.

TWO ALISONS AND A RACHEL: WHAT MANNER OF WOMEN WERE THESE?

In her analysis of press coverage of women who have been raped, Helen Benedict has emphasised the 'inescapable virgin–whore dichotomy' underlying the media's portrayal of women 'The women at home are the virgin types.' 'The alluring sirens of the ads are the whores' (1992: 22). According to Benedict, for a female victim of sexual crime to be treated sympathetically, as virgin rather than vamp, she must:

- not know her assailant
- have been threatened with a weapon
- be of a different race to her assailant
- be of a higher class than her assailant
- be of a dominant ethnic group
- not be young
- not be too pretty
- not deviate in any way from the traditional female sex role.

While the three women in our stories were sympathetically treated by the tabloids, it would seem that women who have been raped and/or murdered are treated differently from women who survive a sexual assault. In this respect, the details outlined by Benedict are divergent from those cited in these stories; it was speculated that Alison Shaugnessy and Alison Manwaring knew their killers, making matters 'worse' for the women; weapons were mentioned as having being used before or after death in all three cases; all three women were described as young and pretty; and although the killers of Alison Manwaring and Rachel Nickell were unknown, Alison Shaughnessy was allegedly murdered by two sisters of similar class and ethnicity. These differences notwithstanding, all of the tabloids were at pains to portray the adherence of the victims to traditional female sex roles, most particularly in their relationships with men: Alison Manwaring as a fiancée, Alison Shaughnessy as a bride (despite having been married for eleven months prior to her murder), and Rachel Nickell as a partner and mother who had given up her career as a model to spend more time with her son. All three women were shown as exhibiting the traditional 'warmth expressiveness' cluster of female characteristics which includes nurturance, sensitivity, warmth and affectivity (Betz and Fitzgerald 1987: 30).

In Benedict's terms, they were represented as 'at home virgin types'. The point of this, in relation to the above divergences from her analytical schema, is that any sense of threat is narratively heightened in press coverage when 'being good and staying at home' fails to secure immunity from male aggression.

The moral of this narrative treatment is tellingly emphasised when compared with a different discourse identified by Sandra McNeill (1992) relating to the deaths of women who try to leave the domestic sphere. Stories which employ an interpretive system of 'woman-killer as tragic hero' are used in connection with men who kill women and subsequently go on to commit suicide; the couples involved are then sentimentally treated as being 'united in death'. The structure of such treatment is dependent on a critical omission: 'One significant detail that the newspapers ignored or buried was the fact that in every case the woman was leaving the man, or had left, or had asked for a divorce – that is, she was leaving to start a new life, which, at all costs, the man was clearly not going to allow' (McNeill 1992: 179). Arguably, the reportorial omission of this detail is sufficient either to shift the representation of the woman involved into the 'whore' category, however loosely this may be realised, or to lead to an uneasy association with it because of the way the killer is heroically elevated in death. The 'tragic hero' figure can then begin imperceptibly to merge with the 'folk hero' status and identity which may accrue to the name of famous killers of women, and this further association with 'whore killing' encourages the shift to the binary opposite of the 'stay-at-home virgin type'. In this respect, Deborah Cameron has shown how the 'centenary' of Jack the Ripper involved forgetting the fact that he brutally murdered, and ritualistically mutilated, a series of women: 'Jack the Ripper has been thoroughly sanitised, turned into a folk hero like Robin Hood. His story is packaged as a bit of harmless fun: only a spoilsport would be tactless enough to point out it is a story of misogyny and sadism' (1992: 188).

Similarly, Nicola Ward-Jouvé has expressed concern over the attitudes of many men during the search for the 'Yorkshire Ripper': 'How is it that so many men, not only the fans, but thousands of hoaxers who phoned the West Yorkshire police hotline to play practical jokes, those who wrote to the papers pleading 'leave the Ripper alone, he's doing a good job' – could believe that killing was a job – or a joke?' (1988: 33). Ward-Jouvé claimed that the psychosexual myths and fantasies which possessed Peter Sutcliffe are embedded in the very structure of social relations between men and women in our society. While we would not want to generalise in this way, it seems clear enough that at times they resonate unmistakably with tabloid constructions of female murder and mutilation. Putting it somewhat bluntly, if 'heroes kill whores' is one disturbing equation made by the tabloids, then 'savage butchers from hell kill virgins' is another. In the cases with which we are dealing, Alison Manwaring was described as having been 'butchered' by 'scum' (*Daily Mirror* and *Daily Mail*, 4 May 1992), Alison Shaugnessy as having been 'butchered' in a 'frenzy of hatred' (*Daily Mirror* and *Sun,* 7 July 1992) while Rachel Nickell was attacked by a 'savage' (*Daily Mirror*, 17 July 1992) and a 'sex fiend' *(Sun,* 17 July 1992). It would therefore seem that those victims whose deaths are constructed in association with the stereotypical attributes of 'innocent virgins' are linked with demonic forces which are then 'packaged' as the antitheses of 'harmless fun'.

Yet what remains disturbing is the presence of fairy-tale imagery in connection with the murders of such women. We have discussed elsewhere (Littlewood, Pickering and Walter, forthcoming) the various ways in which readers may be distanced from this potentially disturbing material, but it is important to emphasise that headlines such as 'Beauty Slain by Beast' (*Sun*, 17 July 1992), 'The Sleeping Beauty Murder' (Schlesinger and Tumber 1994) and the slightly more inventive 'Axeman Murders Little Boy Lost' (*Today*, 25 May 1992), contain rather than convey a sense that a real human being has been brutally killed. Tabloid levity is also manifest in the insensitivity of their front-page composition. For example, a picture of Rachel Nickell was featured on the front page of the *Daily Star* (18 July 1992). The accompanying text noted that she had been killed by a 'sex monster' and supported this with the headline 'Family Torn Apart by Fiend'. Yet this story was overwhelmed by the main front-page headline of the day which related to a story about royal stalkers. While the banner headline accompanying this story is a classic of its kind – 'Eight Nutters Stalk the Queen' – it is difficult to evaluate such material without being left with a sense that death is being 'packaged' in ways which trivialise the harmful consequences that are actually entailed.

It is also important to point to a feature of the tabloid treatment of death which both the dichotomous and primitivist images of women have in common. Nichola Ward-Jouvé has noted that the reporting of the Yorkshire Ripper case concerned 'men, consciously or unconsciously trying to establish, not just that women have no right to freely walk the streets', but also that 'they should be denied as feeling and speaking subjects'. She went on: 'I am neither being flippant nor insensitive when I say that there have been no women in this case' (1988: 37). Nor are we being flippant in emphasising the virtual absence of women as 'speaking subjects' on the front pages of the tabloid press in the cases with which we are dealing. Overwhelmingly, women were portrayed as silent, hysterical or dead. The only woman who was quoted was Alison Shaugnessy's mother, and it is significant that she was not placed in either of these dichotomous categories. Whether as 'virgin' or 'whore' the voices of women were being comprehensively muted in the popular discourse of death.

GORDON, MARK AND ANDRÉ: IDENTIFICATION OR SOCIAL DISTANCING?

The impact of the deaths of these three women upon Gordon Healis, Mark Manwaring and André Hanscombe was portrayed in a similar way across the tabloid press. Specifically, they were all portrayed as crying, or their tears were the subject of the text. For example, the most commonly used photograph in connection with the Manwaring's deaths was that of Gordon and Mark laying flowers on the site where their bodies were found. Both men were shown kneeling on the ground and both were apparently weeping, with Mark placing his arm around Gordon's shoulders. *Today*'s (5 May 1992) caption for this image was 'Alison's grieving brother tries to console a weeping Gordon', while the *Mirror*'s for the same image on the same day was 'Tears for our Alison'. André Hanscombe was described as making 'emotional appeals' (*Daily Mail*, 17 July 1992) and 'Sobbing' (*Daily Star*, 17 July 1992). This focus on men weeping in public extended beyond the deaths given greatest coverage during our sample period. The impact of the funeral of the young footballer, Daniel Yorath, on his friends, for example, was described in a similar manner – 'Tears for a Team Mate' (*Daily Star*, 11 June 1992).

Such a focus on the emotional expression of male distress could be interpreted as appealing to the voyeurism in crime reporting that so concerned Schlesinger and Tumber. An alternative interpretation would be that it represents a general encourage-ment for greater openness and compassion between men, and for reader-identification with the psychology of that distress. However, it is significant to note here that the only bereaved woman to appear on the front page of a tabloid during our three-month period (the widow of Glen Goodman, a special policeman shot by the IRA) was described in terms of her bravery and portrayed as stoically repressing emotion in order to cope with her loss (*Daily Star*, 11 June 1992). Whichever interpretation is preferred it is clear that pornography in Gorer's sense is not in evidence, for the immediate aftermath of death was represented, in the case of men, as being awash with emotion and not 'sani-tised' at all. Further, in interpreting such representations of bereavement and grief we want to suggest that they should not be understood simply as either voyeuristic or expressivist, but rather as evidence of prevarications in contemporary (white main-stream) culture concerning how to grieve, how to relate to other people's grief, and how to manage effectively public stagings of personal grief. The public display of acute emotion is subject to cultural codes and enacted according to historically specific rhetor-ical practices in the dramatisation of social order. These are often attached to gender-appropriate roles and identities, yet these attachments often disintegrate under the force of strong personal emotion, while public expression of such emotion seems increas-ingly not to be subject to any fixed or even explicit ground rules of social action. As we have suggested elsewhere:

> Either a ritual of prescribed behaviour has been replaced by the prescription to feel but nobody knows how to express those feelings; or a ritual of prescribed behaviour has been replaced by a ritual of prescribed feeling but the prescribed ritual is very difficult to carry out. In both ways, one would expect intense interest in learning from others how to present grief, especially when the role-models are ordinary people who have only been catapulted into the glare of media attention as a result of extra-ordinary death.
>
> (Walter, Littlewood and Pickering 1995: 592–3)

However, to this we must add that, as previously noted, the three extraordinary deaths dealt with here represented a challenge to the conventional order of death in western societies – that is why they were story-worthy as news. It would seem reasonable to suggest that the conventional ordering of gender-appropriate affect may also be presented as overturned by proximity to these 'bad deaths'. If this is, indeed, the case then indirect evidence for our second hypothesis – that is, that the cultural value of stoicism, at least amongst men, represents the conventional ordering of grief – is provided by the news coverage of these particular stories (see Walter, Littlewood and Pickering 1995). Specifically, both conventions are overturned by proximity to a 'bad death'.

Ritualistically, then, what may be significant is the association between symbolic pollution and socio-cultural forms of transgression (Douglas 1966). This puts tears, stoicism and identification in an entirely different light. For if we are being encouraged to bear witness to a rite of passage (Van Gennep 1960) which commences with the discovery of a threat to the conventional order of death (that is, separation), then, to use Victor Turner's terminology, the 'liminal personae' in view were displaying gender-atypical affect associated with the symbolic exclusion from broader society of those polluted by their proximity to threatening deaths.

Whilst the communality originally associated with liminality by Turner (1969) was displayed in the case of Gordon Healis and Mark Manwaring (they were widely portrayed as hugging each other and were frequently described as being united in their grief), the manner of its presentation (that is, transition) may encourage social distancing rather than any degree of identification with the affected individuals. Further evidence of the role played by gender-atypical affect behaviour in the construction of a primitive tabloid ritual may be found in the coverage of the trials and verdicts of the stories we have been discussing. Specifically, the restoration of the conventional order (that is, reincorporation) was associated with verdicts of 'guilty' following the relevant trials.

JOHN, LISA AND MICHELLE: TRIALS AND VERDICTS

As Soothill and Walby (1991) have indicated, the end of a trial for sex crimes is a conventional point for the media to conclude a narrative about particular crime. Schlesinger and Tumber also indicate:

> A trial is an important moment in the ritual process of restoring social order when a criminal act has been committed . . . The

next phase, where guilt is proven, is imprisonment, which in effect constitutes the vanishing of the offender from society.

(1994: 231)

The relevant coverage of the death of Alison Shaugnessy was related to the trial and conviction of two sisters, Lisa and Michelle Taylor, for her murder. In many ways, the treatment of Alison's death was presented as a sex crime but the 'crime' in question was that of adultery between her husband, John, and Michelle Taylor.

This 'betrayal' was graphically portrayed by widespread use of John and Alison's wedding video tape on which Michelle Taylor and John Shaugnessy were widely portrayed as kissing each other in the presence of a presumably innocent Alison (*Daily Star, Daily Mail* and *Daily Mirror*, 10 July 1992). This theme of the adulterous betrayal of a bride was pursued with vigour despite Alison's death occurring eleven months after her marriage. For example, the *Daily Star* (9 July 1992) led with the presumably rhetorical question 'Did you kill your bride?' in a story which reported that John Shaugnessy 'broke down' and 'sobbed' as he denied any involvement in his wife's murder.

Alternatively, Lisa and Michelle Taylor were described throughout the trial as cool and calculating. More than that, they were portrayed as schooled in fighting skills inappropriate for their sex. *Today* (25 July 1992) noted in the banner headline that they were: 'Trained to Kill'. This point was further emphasised by the headline: 'Martial arts violence of sisters who killed Alison'. Yet Alison Shaugnessy was reported as having been stabbed to death. Again, gender-atypical affect and behaviour was indicated during the process of this particular trial.

However, the verdict was associated with a reversal of this affect and behaviour. Specifically, the 'violent martial arts' experts Lisa and Michelle 'held hands and wept' (*Daily Mail*, 25 July 1992). Alternatively, their conviction had a radically different impact upon John Shaugnessy. The *Sun* (25 July 1992) reported John as saying, of Lisa and Michelle, that 'I hate them' and that 'I'd hang them myself' only days after having been reported as breaking down and sobbing over the death of his wife. It was fortunate perhaps that he was prevented from doing so because Lisa and Michelle Taylor's convictions were eventually judged to be 'unsafe and unsound' and overturned – partly due to the belief that the relevant press coverage may have prejudiced the jury.

This 'reversal' to gender-typical affect following a conviction was a common feature of the trials which were reported upon during the period of the study. For example, on the one hand, the father of Lynne Rogers was described, following the conviction of her killer, as 'exploding with hate' and saying 'I'll kill you! I'll have you one way or the other!' On the other hand, Lynne's sister and aunt 'burst into hysterics' (*Daily Star*, 23 July 1992). Thus, the conventional moral order was symbolically restored at the point where the threat to that order had been identified and consequently removed from society.

Presumably the tabloid press then go on to identify the next threat to the conventional order of things which they deal with in a similar manner. To put it bluntly, they go on to tell us another one which is necessarily just like the previous one, because, in many ways the stories which were the subject of the most extensive press coverage were not different stories – they represent a specific discourse on death which is nothing but the same old story, except to those people who are unfortunate enough to be the subjects of it.

CONCLUSION

In many respects this chapter, while going some way towards answering our initial questions, raises even more questions than it answers. Perhaps most significantly, while death is very clearly publicly present, this very presence is portrayed as a threat to the conventional ordering of death-related issues. Consequently, it might be suggested that our analysis confirms as well as denies the publicly-absent privately-present thesis. Yet there are simply so many death-related stories covered by the tabloid press that it is likely that several different discourses are being conducted on an almost daily basis.

We also recognise that the three-month period of study was, in all probability, too short for sampling the full range of death-related topics which are reported in the tabloid press. For example, issues associated with voluntary euthanasia gain widespread media attention which is frequently reflected in the tabloid press, but no relevant cases were being discussed during the period of study. Consequently, it seems reasonable to suggest that we have under- rather than over-estimated the relevant scope of death-focused or death-associated themes. Added to this, the current study was concerned with front-page (unequivocally public) coverage. The full range of coverage of such themes in tabloid newspapers may be broader still, though what also needs more careful consideration is the variation in the extent of coverage of death-related issues across the tabloid press.

However, as far as the three stories given the most front-page coverage during our period of study were concerned, the presentation of the threat of 'bad deaths' was profoundly gendered. First, 'stay-at-home virgin types' were brutally murdered. Second, these deaths resulted in public displays of gender-atypical affect. Third, the conventional and profoundly gendered order of the tabloid representations of 'bad' deaths was only restored following the trial and conviction of those held to be responsible.

So, contrary to Gorer, the emotional aftermaths of these deaths was the focus of intense press interest, though it is difficult to know from this whether any degree of identification between news consumers and people who have been bereaved occurs. However, the structure of these stories would indicate that distancing, rather than identification, may be encouraged. The structure of these stories as they appear and disappear from the front pages of the tabloid press would appear to be relatively simple:

- a death-related threat to the conventional order is discovered;
- this threat overturns the conventional gendered order;
- the conventional order is restored by the conviction of those held to be responsible.

However, other discourses on death may generate identification and some readers may identify and others not.

Despite the limited scope of the present study, it has shown that the reporting of death and death-related topics was, within our given time-frame, profoundly gendered. Exactly who dies and who kills, and who grieved and how, are gendered issues which require much fuller documentation and analysis. Nevertheless, it would seem clear from the three stories given the most prominent coverage that gender was central to the construction of these particular death-related stories. Furthermore, while feminist research has, quite rightly, done much to indicate the importance of the impact of the negative stereotypification of women, particularly within the criminal justice system, the positive stereotypification of women is in many ways equally injurious to them. The beastliness of the tabloid construction of beauty may well defy any fairy-tale happy ending.

REFERENCES

Benedict, H. (1992) *Virgin or Vamp: How the Press Covers Sex Crimes*, Oxford: Oxford University Press.

Betz, N. and Fitzgerald, L. (1987) *The Career Psychology of Women*, London: Academic Press.

Cameron, D. (1992) '"That's entertainment?": Jack the Ripper and the selling of sexual violence', in J. Radford and D. E . H. Russell (eds) *Femicide: The Politics of Woman Killing*, Buckingham: Open University Press, pp. 184–8.

Douglas, M. (1966) *Purity and Danger: An Analysis of the Concepts of Pollution and Taboo*, London: Routledge & Kegan Paul.

Dworkin, A. (1981) *Pornography: Men Possessing Women*, London: The Women's Press.

Gorer, G. (1955) 'The pornography of death', *Encounter*, October (reprinted in Gorer 1965).

—— (1965) *Death, Grief and Mourning in Contemporary Britain*, London: Cresset.

Kappeler, S. (1986) *The Pornography of Representation*, Cambridge: Polity Press.

Kuhn, A. (1985) *The Power of the Image: Essays in Representation and Sexuality*, London: Routledge & Kegan Paul.

Littlewood, J., Pickering, M. and Walter, T. (forthcoming) 'Good wives and wicked women: they all died happily ever after', in J. Littlewood (ed.) *Misconstruing the Feminine Social Change and Social Control*, London: Macmillan.

McNeill, S. (1992) 'Woman-killer as tragic hero' in J. Radford and D. E. H. Russell (eds) *Femicide: The Politics of Woman Killing*, Buckingham: Open University Press, pp. 178–83.

Mellor, P. A. (1993) 'Death in high modernity: the contemporary presence and absence of death', in D. Clark (ed.) *The Sociology of Death*, Oxford: Blackwell, pp. 11–30.

—— and Schilling, C. (1993) 'Modernity, self-identity and the sequestration of death', *Sociology* 27: 411–32.

Parkes, C. (1972) *Bereavement: Studies of Grief in Adult Life*, New York: International Universities Press.

Schlesinger, P. and Tumber, H. (1994) *Reporting Crime: The Media Politics of Criminal Justice*, Oxford: Clarendon Press.

Soothill, K. and Walby, S. (1991) *Sex Crime in the News*, London: Routledge.

Theweleit, K. (1990) *Male Fantasies: Women, Floods, Bodies, History*, Minneapolis: University of Minnesota Press.

Turner, V. (1969) *The Ritual Process*, Chicago: Aldine.

Van Gennep, A. (1960) *The Rites of Passage* (trans. M. B. Vizedom and G. L. Caffee), Chicago: Chicago University Press.

Walter, T., Littlewood, J. and Pickering, M. (1995) 'Death in the news: the public invigilation of private emotion', *Sociology* 29: 579–96.

Ward-Jouvé, N. (1988) *The Street Cleaner: The Yorkshire Ripper Case on Trial*, London: Marion Boyars.

Chapter 8

Absent minorities?
Ethnicity and the use of palliative care services

Chris Smaje and David Field

INTRODUCTION

There is a widespread feeling in the British palliative care community that people from minority ethnic populations are under-represented among the users of services for the dying. Unfortunately, few systematic data are available which allow us to determine whether this belief is well-founded. Nor is there much evidence to inform an understanding of the context within which people from minority ethnic groups may use palliative care services, and their views and experiences of service provision. Nevertheless, there are more general data available which can help clarify patterns of service utilisation among minority ethnic groups, and there are some suggestions in existing research about the way that people from these groups interact with palliative care services.

One of the few British studies concerned with the use of palliative care services by people from minority ethnic groups is Rees' (1986) report on the use made of St Mary's hospice in Birmingham by immigrants, including those from Europe.[1] Rees found use by immigrants to be much lower than that of British-born individuals, with crude utilisation rates among the latter group nearly four times higher than among the immigrants. Yet of those who were referred to the hospice, immigrants were *more* likely to receive hospice services. From these and other results, Rees inferred that hospices were not discriminating against immigrants, as the crude utilisation figures might at first seem to suggest.

Although in this instance Rees is probably correct, the matter is rather more complicated than his analysis credits. The aim of the present chapter, as well to describe the relevant evidence, is to provide a framework which allows a systematic appraisal of the whole range of factors affecting people's use of services. This framework is outlined in the following section and its implications for an understanding of ethnic patterns in the use of palliative care services are then illustrated throughout the remainder of the chapter.

A MODEL OF HEALTH SERVICE UTILISATION

Health economists conventionally view utilisation as jointly influenced by the *supply* of services – their location, ease of access, quantity and quality – and the *demand* for services, that is, the felt need for them in the (potential) user backed up by the material or social resources to make that felt need an effective demand. By contrast, public health professionals tend to regard need as an objective criterion, regardless of whether it is 'felt' by the potential user or not. In the public health model it thus becomes possible to identify 'needs' which are not demanded and which may or may not be supplied. 'Demand' here becomes a third factor mediating the interaction between need and supply according to a social logic regarding the potential user's own valuation of their 'need'.

This is illustrated in Figure 8.1, which is derived from Stevens and Gabbay (1991). The figure shows that it is possible to have services which are either needed (field 1), demanded (field 2) or supplied (field 3) independently of the other fields. The aim of the health planner is to concentrate services into the intersection of the three primary fields such that they are needed, demanded *and* supplied (field 7). However, in looking at the use of palliative care services by people from minority ethnic groups we will be particularly interested in whether people from these groups are over-represented in:

- field 1 (services which are needed, but neither demanded nor supplied);
- field 4 (services which are both needed and demanded but not supplied); and
- field 6 (services which are both needed and supplied, but not demanded).

These all raise difficult policy questions which we address further in later sections.

In the specific context of palliative care services for people from minority ethnic groups, field 1 – which we have labelled *need* –

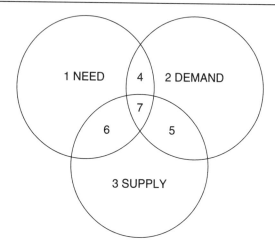

Figure 8.1   Factors affecting utilisation of palliative services

identifies the factors which predispose people to seek palliative care. At the level of the individual this is straightforward enough: the presence of a chronic, incurable and terminal condition. But at the level of the population – or more specifically, different population groups – the level of need will in turn be affected by demographic and epidemiological factors which vary from group to group. We must therefore examine how need for palliative care might differ between ethnic groups by considering variations in their demographic and epidemiological profiles.

Field 2, labelled *demand*, reflects the public health approach outlined above: while palliative care is generally only sought by those who need it (hence fields 2 and 5 can largely be ignored), this is not a sufficient condition for actual use, since there is a range of specifically social factors which intervene. For example, alternative sources of care and attitudes to the kind of care delivered by the various main providers, as well as individual preferences, may tend to vary systematically between people from different ethnic groups and affect patterns of utilisation at the group level. It is therefore important to consider how need for care may be mediated by varying demand for services. As we suggested in drawing attention to fields 1 and 6, people may 'need' palliative care, but might not want it, and it is important for care providers to consider the implications of this distinction.

The final set of factors relates to the *supply* of services. This encompasses everything to do with the distribution, organisation and delivery of care which might affect utilisation, particularly differential utilisation between ethnic groups. Such factors include both the quantity of services (e.g. their extent locally) and their quality (e.g. their cultural sensitivity). The critical question here is whether there are services which are needed and demanded by minority ethnic groups but which are not appropriately supplied.

What is perhaps elided in the figure is a sense of the *dynamic* interaction of the three major fields. So, for example, the lack of or dissatisfaction with the supply of services may condition future demand. In this sense, there is often a strong mutual determination between the three major fields, something to which more sophisticated variants of the present framework, such as the behavioural model of health-care utilisation, are increasingly attuned (Andersen 1995). This should caution the analyst against invoking an unchanging ethnic substrate as the critical dimension underlying ethnic patterns of utilisation. People are not fixed by their ethnicity alone into a timeless patterning of utilisation.

THE NEED FOR PALLIATIVE CARE

We now proceed to examine each of the major fields set out in the framework described above. The first task, therefore, is to determine underlying levels of need. Palliative care users are mainly comprised of people suffering from various kinds of cancer and to a lesser extent chronic obstructive lung diseases and, more recently, AIDS. Looking first at cancer, the incidence of this disease rises with increasing age, so, other things being equal, we would expect older people to be over-represented among users. Figure 8.2 indicates the age structure of some of the major ethnic groups in Britain, as enumerated in the 1991 census (OPCS 1993). It can be seen that, in comparison to whites, all other ethnic groups have a much younger age structure. For example, around three quarters of the Pakistani, Bangladeshi and African populations are aged under 35; this is true of less than half the white population. And, while 16 per cent of the white population is aged 65 or over, this is only true of 5 per cent of the 'black – Caribbean' population, and of even fewer of the other minority populations. This younger age distribution of minority ethnic populations is invoked by Rees (1986) to explain the low utilisation of hospice

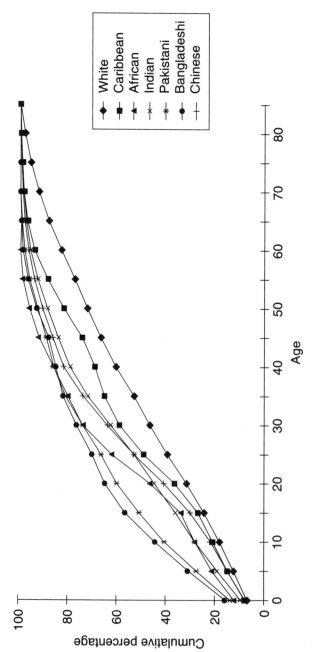

Figure 8.2 Age structure of ethnic groups

services in Birmingham, although he does not compute age-specific rates to confirm the point.

On the grounds of age alone, then, we would expect there to be a lower incidence of cancer among minority ethnic populations. However, ethnic differences in age-specific cancer rates must also be considered. Rees (1986) found that cancer appeared to be of earlier onset among the immigrant hospice users he studied, particularly Pakistani women. Nevertheless, epidemiological studies have shown that cancer incidence is generally lower among immigrant populations even after age has been taken into account. Table 8.1 illustrates this by showing age-specific cancer mortality rates for different migrant populations. Again, the data refer only to those born abroad and are therefore not an entirely adequate proxy for rates among the minority ethnic population as a whole. There is a limited amount of evidence to suggest that British-born minorities may be taking on the cancer patterns of the general British population (Barker and Baker 1990). But the great majority of people from minority ethnic groups currently suffering from cancer have been born abroad. In comparison to the general population of England and Wales, cancer mortality is lower for all of the migrant groups shown (although some other migrant groups, most notably the Irish, have higher mortality), generally falling between about half to three quarters of the 'all places of birth' rate for each age-group. Since these rates refer to specific age-groups, the results are not affected by the differences in age structure between ethnic groups mentioned above.

To give some idea of how these figures translate in terms of actual cancer deaths, if the rates in Table 8.1 are applied to population figures in the corresponding age ranges derived from the 1991 census we would expect there to be around 700 cancer deaths annually among South Asian people nationally, 500 among Caribbean people, and under 100 among African people: this compares to a total expected number of cancer deaths nationally of around 84,000. At the local level, the corresponding figures in Brent – an outer London borough with a particularly large minority ethnic population – are around 30 deaths in the South Asian and Caribbean populations, and 4 deaths in the African population, compared to a total expected number of deaths of 343. To express these figures in another way, for every person in England and Wales from the minority ethnic groups described above there are around 22 white people, yet for every cancer

Table 8.1 Cancer rates per million population by place of birth, England and Wales, 1979–83

| | Age group | | | | | | | | | | | |
| | 15–24 | | 25–34 | | 35–44 | | 45–54 | | 55–64 | | 65–74 | |
	Male	Female	Male	Female	Male	Female	Male	Female	Male	Female	Male	Female
Indian subcontinent	54	11	100	93	284	412	828	1207	3161	2774	8164	5987
Caribbean Commonwealth	85	54	127	156	322	456	1044	1146	3300	2895	9106	5285
African Commonwealth	51	48	141	159	314	451	944	1204	3645	3279	8038	6567
All places of birth	79	53	143	173	421	609	1693	1913	5609	4163	12949	6930

Source: V. Raleigh (personal communication)

death among people in these groups there are around 63 deaths among white people.

Several points should be made about these calculations. First, death rates have not been provided for people under 15 or over 74, mainly because the number of cancer deaths among people from minority ethnic populations in these age groups is very small. This means that the figures provided above underestimate the total number of cancer deaths. But since there are very many more elderly white people (with high cancer rates) than people from minority ethnic groups the figures also *overestimate* the proportionate share of cancer deaths among minority ethnic populations. Second, the application of now rather dated rates referring to *migrant* populations to *minority ethnic* populations is, as noted above, inappropriate in several respects, and may tend to underestimate deaths among minority ethnic groups. On the other hand, applying national cancer mortality rates to these groups – as Hill and Penso (1995) do in parallel calculations – almost certainly overestimates these deaths. Finally, the total expected number of deaths for Brent is likely to be an over-estimate, since the ethnic composition of the borough is very significantly different from that of the general population, upon which the calculation is based. For all of these reasons, the figures given above should be treated as no more than a rough guide to the expected number of cancer deaths. Nevertheless, they indicate that we are talking about fairly small numbers of such deaths among minority ethnic groups.

Although death rates from *all* cancers are lower among minority ethnic groups, there are some ethnic variations in mortality from specific cancers. With the exception of cervical cancer among Caribbean women, cancer mortality among most minority ethnic groups is lower for the four cancers (breast, cervix, skin and lung) for which national targets have been set (Cm 1986 [1992]). Conversely, there are some cancers which have a higher incidence in particular ethnic groups. For example, mortality from cancer of the lip, oral cavity and pharynx is higher in people born in the Indian subcontinent and the African Commonwealth; the same is true of liver cancer (Balarajan and Bulusu 1990). However, these cancers affect a very small number of people. Rees (1986) found few striking differences in cancer site between the immigrant and indigenous populations in his Birmingham study, although the number of cases was probably too small to draw firm conclusions.

It should not, however, be assumed that the patterning of cancer incidence is immutable. The fact of migration considerably complicates analysis and it cannot be assumed that disease patterns observed among now elderly 'pioneer' migrants will be replicated in more recent generations (Shanmugaratnam *et al.* 1989). Moreover, various factors may act to raise or lower rates considerably in particular populations. For example, McKeigue *et al.* (1988) report extremely high smoking rates among Bangladeshi men in East London; while this population is at present comparatively youthful, if high smoking rates persist this may be reflected in future raised cancer rates for this population.

The mortality rates described above do not tell us much about cancer-related morbidity, except in so far as they act as proxies for underlying patterns of morbidity. Clearly, however, it is the morbidity associated with cancer – the course of the 'cancer journey' – which is of most relevance to an understanding of the use of palliative care services. It may be that ethnic differences in the incidence of specific cancers are reflected in differences in the length and nature of the associated symptoms with a concomitant impact upon the need for palliative care, or indeed that ethnic differences exist in symptomatology which again may affect the need for care. Little evidence exists on these points and their likely impact on levels of need for palliative care is uncertain.

Turning more briefly to other diseases, research has painted a picture similar to that of cancer in the case of chronic obstructive lung diseases such as bronchitis and emphysema. Although these diseases are a much rarer cause of death in all populations than cancer, their incidence rises with age, and age-specific mortality rates are very considerably lower for most minority ethnic groups than for the general population. Thus, as with cancer, these groups currently exhibit lower levels of need for services associated with chronic obstructive lung diseases.

With regard to HIV/AIDS, this again currently affects a much smaller proportion of the population than does cancer. At the end of 1992 there were 5,591 reported AIDS cases among white people in Britain, 521 among black people and 119 among South Asian people (Balarajan and Raleigh 1993). These figures are rather unreliable and should probably be regarded as minimum estimates. Nevertheless, they give a rough indication of the scale of the issue. Unlike the other diseases mentioned, AIDS is more likely to affect younger people and, in this sense, may be of proportionately greater impact upon minority ethnic groups, other factors being equal. Figures for HIV distribution indicate that incidence is raised among black people and lowered in South Asian people relative to the UK population as a whole, and US experience underlines the potential for greater prevalence in economically disadvantaged, urban minority populations (Small *et al.* 1995).

A final point concerning levels of need for palliative care should be made. It has been suggested that some people from minority ethnic groups may return permanently to their countries of origin as they become older (Hill and Penso 1995). We have already seen that the proportion of elderly people among most minority ethnic groups is at present relatively low compared to the general population, and if this process of return migration is occurring on a significant scale it may be reinforcing this demographic pattern and helping to keep down the need for palliative care in these groups. However, it may be that return migration does not occur at random. It is possible that people who are terminally ill or in danger of becoming so are either over-represented among the returnees (perhaps reflecting the wish to re-visit or die in one's place of birth) or under-represented (perhaps as healthy people decide upon retirement in Britain to return to further projects in their countries of origin). Rees (1986) confirms the existence of return among terminally ill South Asians, but was unable to address its overall extent. Figures based on the International Passenger Survey (OPCS 1995) indicate that around 9,000 people left Britain to migrate to the Indian subcontinent or the Caribbean in 1993, a figure which does not appear to have changed markedly over the previous twenty years or so. Unfortunately, the age and ethnicity of these people cannot be determined. On the face of it these figures are not suggestive of a large-scale return migration effect. However, if the majority of the emigrants are indeed older people returning to their countries of origin, there may be a noticeable effect which *may* manifest itself through a change in age-specific death rates at older ages, although other factors also affect these rates. The most recent data available are still those linked to the 1981 census. This is now likely to be very inaccurate with regard to the question at hand. The impact of selective return migration upon the need for palliative care cannot therefore be assessed with confidence, but its potential significance must be noted.

It has been shown in this section that both the young age structure and the low incidence of cancer independently from age structure among these groups are such that we would expect a lower need for palliative care. When the relatively small absolute size of these groups is also taken into consideration, it *may* be the case that there is no under-utilisation of services and that low utilisation rates reflect genuinely lower levels of need. However, the data to hand do not allow us to do anything other than suggest this as a possibility; it remains entirely plausible that palliative care services are under-utilised by minority ethnic groups even when levels of need are taken into consideration.

Minority ethnic groups are highly concentrated residentially, with over 60 per cent of all people from 'non-white' ethnic groups living in a small number of major urban areas, particularly London, the West Midlands and the urban areas of West Yorkshire, where less than 20 per cent of the total white population lives (Owen 1994). As we saw, in areas of high minority ethnic residence such as Brent, a significant – though still fairly small – number of cancer deaths among people from minority ethnic groups will occur annually, and providers in these areas can be expected to have developed some experience and knowledge of the particular issues affecting the death and dying of people from local minority ethnic populations. In areas of lower density residence, there may be very little 'need' for palliative care services by minority ethnic groups, and health professionals may have little experience of providing the relevant care. It is therefore important that appropriate support and guidance is available to health professionals in this situation. In this sense, the epidemiological fact of a low level of 'need' for palliative care among minority ethnic groups underlines rather than undermines the importance of committed policy attention to the issue.

THE DEMAND FOR PALLIATIVE CARE

In this section we examine factors which may cause ethnic variation in the demand for palliative care services, looking in turn at resources for informal care, knowledge about the availability of services and attitudes to services.

A large proportion of the care which people receive for health needs of all kinds is self-administered or provided informally by the family or friends of the person in need. In the case of palliative care, the provision of such informal care assumes even greater importance since clinical intervention is of a relatively low intensity and the emotional needs of the patient and the people in their social network are of paramount concern. It is possible that recourse to formal services might vary between social groups – including ethnic groups – in accordance with the degree to which resources for informal care can be mobilised. Such resources may alter the level of demand for formally provided palliative care services, regardless of the level of need.

The view that people from certain minority ethnic groups – particularly South Asian ones – do not seek care because they 'look after their own' in supportive family networks has rightly been criticised as a stereotyped over-simplification (South Thames RHA 1994, Atkin and Rollings 1996). Analysts are increasingly emphasising the heterogeneity and dynamism of family forms (Ahmad 1996), and it is even sometimes argued that the traditional basis of informal care is breaking down within some South Asian families. These are valid points – although the notion of a *general* process of South Asian family breakdown is highly debatable – but we must be careful to avoid replacing sweeping generalisations that attest to the existence of well developed family care in certain minority populations with equally sweeping generalisations to the contrary. The existence of systematic ethnic differences in the patterning of informal care and the concomitant demand for services constitutes an empirical question as well as an arena for debate about the construction of stereotypes. It is, unfortunately, an empirical question which has barely begun to be addressed.

There is nonetheless some general evidence which is relevant to the question at hand. Several differences have been demonstrated between ethnic groups in patterns of family and household structure. Rates and age of marriage and divorce, the prevalence of lone parenthood, family size and the prevalence of multi-generational and multi-family households vary considerably between ethnic groups. Some of these differences can be explained in terms of the effects of age structure, but even when this is taken into account differences persist. Of particular note for present purposes are the greater proportion, in comparison to whites, of multi-generational and multi-family households among both Caribbean and South Asian populations, particularly among the latter (and particularly among Pakistanis and Bangladeshis). The greater mean family size among South Asian populations, and the high proportion of one-person or lone parent households among a number of other ethnic groups, including the Caribbean and African populations, are also relevant (Brown 1984, Berrington 1994). It is unwise to infer too much from these findings, but they at least suggest that there may typically be more caring resources available among South Asian families. This might also be true of some Caribbean families, but less true of others. It is of course possible that, on the contrary, the prevalence of multi-generational families in some minority ethnic groups is a *consequence* of poorer access to caring services, whereby infirm people are forced to reside with their relatives through lack of appropriate formal care. This possibility has not been researched but it is not borne out by US evidence (Worobey and Angel 1990) and it would not appear to be a likely explanation for all of the differences described above, although it may be a relevant consideration. At the same time, the family data described above show clearly that there are many elderly people from minority ethnic populations who live alone. Interpretive caution is therefore appropriate.

As well as the immediate family, many South Asian populations in particular are able to draw upon the resources of broader kin-based groupings – in different populations, the *biraderi*, *zat* or caste-associated groups. The role of these groups in Britain has not been well researched, but it appears that they can operate as resources of support. Anwar (1985) found that the majority of Pakistanis he surveyed in Rochdale turned primarily to their *biraderi* or a friend for 'financial and general help'. In a later article (1995) he reported that the *biraderi* provides services to people on specific occasions, including deaths. According to Anwar, 'Turning to *biraderi* when in trouble before using other agencies established for such purposes is the rule rather than the exception in Pakistani families' (1995: 240). Unfortunately, there is little evidence in Britain focused explicitly upon the role of kinsfolk, the *biraderi* and similar institutions in caring for the dying. Nevertheless, it appears that there may be additional resources for informal care among South Asian populations which may partially obviate recourse to formal services.

It is tempting to conclude that there are 'cultural differences' between ethnic groups which affect patterns of demand for pallia-tive care services. For example, Rees (1986) reports a greater use of domiciliary as opposed to residential palliative care services among migrants, especially Pakistanis, which he attributes to 'family structure and cultural traditions'. However, things may not be as simple as this since cultural and economic factors can interact in complex ways. For example, in the USA it has been found that elderly white people are more likely to use nursing homes for their long-term care, whereas black people are more likely to rely upon informal home care, even after controlling for differences in health status, demographic structure and income. Different patterns of service use among ethnic groups in the same income category might lead one to infer the presence of cultural differences, but Headen (1992) argues that the findings reflect a rather more complex relationship between cultural and material factors in which the social roles of family members as carers interact with their labour market position and human capital. Here we confront the difficult debate about the extent to which 'cultural' patterns are functionally related to socio-economic circumstances, a debate which – in the USA – has long been polarised around entrenched political positions on the question of race (Smaje 1996). Underlying cultural preferences for particular kinds of care may very well exist (Hill and Penso 1995, Holmes and Holmes 1995), but it is important to consider how such preferences may in fact be related to socio-economic circumstances.

It has been possible in this section to look at existing knowledge about family *structures* and to draw tentative inferences about resources for informal care, but little is currently known about the *meanings* placed upon family roles in palliative care contexts within different ethnic groups. It is here that new research could fill a major gap. From what is already known about social structuring we can, however, expect to find that such roles and meanings are inevitably contradictory. Far from finding distinctive orientations to dying and caring for the dying which are peculiar to a given culture or ethnic group as a naive culturalism would suggest, we are likely to find a multiplicity which is structured in particular ways across the lines of class, gender, age and so on. For example, the attitudes of an elderly man concerning informal care may differ in significant ways from those of a young female family member from whom he expects to receive it, and their interests as cared-for and carer may diverge sharply. This is not just a feature of social change in the context of migration to Britain – though it is possible that this constitutes an added complication – but is inherent in the caring relationship (Ungerson 1993). This raises some difficult policy issues: if palliative care services are 'needed' but not 'demanded' in accordance with the availability of unwilling family labour, what kind of intervention strategy can best vouchsafe the interests of all the parties concerned?

An entirely different set of demand-side factors involves aware-ness of or levels of knowledge about the range of palliative care services available. This question has been little researched. People in Leicester from a small minority ethnic sample already using palliative or oncology/radiotherapy services as patients or carers reported that they had received little advice about the relevant services, although the study was unable to address the extent to which this varied between ethnic groups (Haroon-Iqbal *et al.* 1995). A more general study of carers from minority ethnic groups in London also found that respondents often indicated their lack of knowledge about how to make best use of available formal services (McCalman 1990). In fact, several studies have shown that while there are high levels of GP registration among people from minority ethnic groups, use of other primary, community and social care services tends to be lower than among the majority population, particularly among elderly people; there appears to be little knowledge or use of district nursing services which certainly constitute one important source of palliative care (Donaldson 1986, Hek 1991, HEA 1994). By extension, one would also expect there to be low use of more specialist nursing services such as Macmillan and Marie Curie nurses.

The reasons for these findings are not entirely clear. Some researchers have found that elderly minority ethnic patients report that they would use services more frequently if they knew more about them, although others report a low level of expectation regarding the delivery of formal services (Atkin *et al.* 1989, McFarland *et al.* 1989). On balance, it would seem that a poor knowledge of services may act as a significant impediment to receipt of palliative care. In reviewing the evidence concerning access to palliative care services, Hill and Penso argue,

> Some black and Asian patients and their relatives/carers are very disadvantaged as they do not know what they are entitled to and hence what to ask for by way of services and benefits. They are mistrustful of the NHS and the Social Services, and

do not want to disclose their personal and financial affairs for fear this might attract racist reactions concerning their entitlement to the services.

(1995: 16)

These points underline the fact that, while poor knowledge of services may lower 'demand', it is supply-side factors which may largely be at issue.

The third set of demand factors involves attitudes to services. Again, there has been little research on this among minority ethnic groups. Haroon-Iqbal *et al.* (1995) found quite high levels of dissatisfaction with the way dietary and religious requirements were addressed in acute settings. They also found that a third of their sample reported experiencing racism during hospital treatment and a greater number reported that they had been 'treated differently' because of the way they 'looked, dressed or appeared'. More general research has found satisfaction with health services to be generally high among minority ethnic groups – as it is in the majority population – although several studies have found that the former are more likely to be dissatisfied with certain aspects of their care (Smaje 1995). The report on minority ethnic carers in London mentioned earlier (McCalman 1990) found that most respondents did not feel racism to be a factor when accessing services. Most, however, found it difficult to answer whether service delivery was in keeping with their cultural and religious background.

In view of the rather sketchy evidence, it is difficult to offer any firm conclusions about the effect on demand of attitudes about palliative care services among minority ethnic groups. It *may* be the case that there are more reservations about the nature of the services among minority ethnic groups, which might have the effect of depressing demand. Certainly, the levels of racism reported to Haroon-Iqbal *et al.* (1995) are grounds for considerable concern. Such findings certainly suggest that people from minority ethnic groups may be conscious of a poorer service which may have longer-term effects on their inclination to make use of formally provided services.

THE SUPPLY OF PALLIATIVE CARE

The discussion in the previous section raised several questions about the nature of supply which we now confront directly. The impact of the supply of services on ethnic patterns of palliative care utilisation may be manifested through either the *quantity* or *quality* of services provided. Taking quantity of services first, the question at issue is the extent to which the local supply of services matches need. We saw earlier that minority ethnic populations are heavily concentrated residentially into a relatively small number of major urban areas. If there is systematic variation in the quantity of palliative care services available which coincides with this geographic distribution, the result may be that minority ethnic groups have poorer access to services and exhibit lower levels of utilisation. It is difficult to assess this question with any degree of sophistication with the data to hand. An analysis of the palliative care facilities listed in the 1995 *Directory of Hospice and Palliative Care Services* (Hospice Information Service 1995) reveals no lack of palliative care units or beds in the main areas of minority ethnic residence. Indeed, if anything, the reverse is the case. However, there may be important considerations of catchment area and 'treatment density' which are impossible to gauge from a simple county-level listing. Nevertheless, the geographic distribution of services does not, on the face of it, appear to be an impediment to the receipt of palliative care among people from minority ethnic groups.

It may also be the case that geographic differences in the structure of service provision affect patterns of utilisation. For example, Boyle and Smaje (1993) found that there were around 30 per cent fewer places in long-term residential care per capita of the elderly population in London compared to the figure for England as a whole. Inner city areas outside the capital displayed an 8 per cent deficit. There was a concomitantly greater provision of community-based services in these areas. If pathways to care differ between ethnic groups – particularly if minority ethnic groups are less able to access care through community services, as the evidence discussed earlier might suggest – then the result again may be lower levels of palliative care utilisation among minority ethnic groups.

Indirect evidence for the importance of pathways to care can be found in studies of ethnic patterns in health service utilisation. Smaje and Le Grand (1995) analysed ethnic patterns in the use of GP and acute services, controlling for relevant confounding factors in a nationally representative sample. They found that whereas among most minority ethnic groups (the most striking exception being the Chinese) the use of GP services is generally either high or equivalent in comparison to the white population, use of acute (particularly outpatient) services is low. It may be the case – though this requires further analysis – that the role of the GP as 'gatekeeper' to other services is exercised with greater vigour in the case of people from minority ethnic groups and that this might affect palliative care services as well as acute services more generally. This is consistent with Rees' (1986) finding that a higher proportion of the migrants in his study who were referred for hospice care subsequently received it, since it could be that only those migrants with relatively greater need receive a referral in the first place. Clearly, there may be alternative explanations for Rees' findings. Nevertheless, the role of GPs in accessing the whole range of health services is critical for minority ethnic users and an appraisal of the GP's role should be a key dimension in any attempts to improve access to palliative care services.

Turning to the quality of services, it could be that poor provision for dietary, religious and other needs, ethnocentric attitudes to the experience of dying and individual or 'institutional' racism may all play a part in discouraging minority ethnic users from accessing palliative care services. Again, while one suspects that all of these points may have some bearing in reality, there has been little research specific to palliative care services which has addressed any of them. Hill and Penso suggested on the basis of primary and secondary research that hospices, while impressive in many respects, had 'not sufficiently addressed issues of cultural and religious differences and ethnicity' and that they were often 'uncertain of what they should be doing to make their services known and accessible to these communities' (1995: 14). One important step might be to encourage greater recruitment of palliative care staff from minority ethnic groups. No data are available on current levels of employment, but certainly hospices are often regarded as fairly 'white' institutions.

TACKLING INEQUALITIES IN PALLIATIVE CARE UTILISATION

While there is less 'need' for palliative care services among most minority ethnic groups than the majority population, the apparently lower levels of utilisation probably also stem from a range of other factors, including differences in patterns of informal care and ethnocentrism or perhaps racism in the provision of services. The appropriate policy responses to these factors vary.

The commonest response in the literature to the perceived ethnocentrism of existing palliative care provision has been to provide information about the beliefs, customs, religions and death and disposal practices of minority ethnic groups (e.g. Henley 1987, Neuberger 1987 and 1993, Green 1991, Firth 1993, Katz 1993). However, this so-called 'checklist' or 'factfile' approach has itself been the target of considerable criticism (see Gunaratnam, this volume). Its principal shortcoming is its tendency to reduce or reify ethnic difference to a set of particular practices – and in the palliative care literature, funerary rituals – so that the totality of, for example, being Hindu or Muslim can come to be represented by a few simple motifs.

We shall shortly add our voices to that critique. Before doing so, however, we wish to sound a note of caution. While the 'check-list' approach does tend to reify culture, it is nevertheless the case that some aspects of culture are indeed very reified. The most obvious examples are food prohibitions, such as the Muslim and Jewish strictures against the consumption of pork. More gener-ally, while it is true that 'culture' is too often seen as a fixed and definite quantity, alternatives which view it as entirely fluid and contextual are also problematic (Asad 1990). Culture and ethnicity might be described as processes, but parts of those processes involve the reification or objectification of difference. Certainly, for staff who are unfamiliar with the range of values and practices associated with the religions or cultures of the people with whom they are working, basic information of the sort provided by the 'checklist' literature can be very useful. As Neuberger (1987) argues, if a health worker displays some basic knowledge about the user's culture and its implications for their care this can indicate a thoughtfulness and respect which improves the quality of the encounter. Thus, if basic information about religions or cultures is used as a resource in the interaction between users and professionals rather than a prescription about what people belonging to the religion or culture are 'like', it may be of considerable benefit.

Nevertheless, the dangers of the 'checklist' approach need to be acknowledged. It is all too easy to obliterate the complexities of religious and cultural practice, ignore processes of change and of variation between individuals and sub-groups, and fuel the construction of ethnic stereotypes by characterising particular groups in terms of cultural exotica. The implicit model of culture is an external modulation of some essentially stable 'individual' whose behaviour, though perhaps culturally patterned in a distinctive way, is readily comprehensible as a response to the human universals of dying and death. Here 'cultural difference' merely encodes 'their way' of doing something in distinction to 'our way' of doing it – the 'something' in question being regarded as fixed. Such assumptions are questionable at best.

Yet, notwithstanding their intrinsic merit, analyses of this sort have not generated a very obvious policy agenda for health-care professionals concerned with providing services to people from minority ethnic groups. In fact, much of the energy in the 'ethnic health' field over recent years has been expended in increasingly stale critiques which favour socio-economic over cultural explanations for the ethnic patterning of health. Too often analysts have been either uncertain or inconsistent in identifying their position concerning the existence of distinctive health-care needs among people from minority ethnic groups. Gunaratnam (this volume) breaks out of this impasse creatively and points to ways in which health-care staff can appropriately engage with the needs of minority ethnic users. Here we offer some complementary suggestions which address the *structure* of service provision.

The policy agenda which emerges from the preceding analysis must be premised on the idea that dying people and their families in all ethnic groups can benefit from external support, albeit that the support may need to be offered in different ways. As Bhopal (1991) argues in the context of health education, health professionals often think that the needs of minority ethnic groups differ from the majority population but the means of fulfilling them do not, whereas the opposite is often the case. In palliative care, ways need to be found to tackle the apparently low utilisation of existing services among minority ethnic groups. This can be conceived at a number of levels. First, it is important that people from all ethnic groups know about the existence of services and how to access them. This in itself represents a considerable challenge, but can be achieved by a developing expertise in multicultural health education among health agencies nationally. Second, efforts must be made to tackle racism and ethnocentrism in the provision of palliative care. This is no small task in a society where social thinking and social position are racially structured in quite fundamental ways. Nevertheless, much of value can be achieved through staff training, high-level managerial action and appropriate audit procedures, as well as continued efforts to develop procedures and – in health-care facilities – environments which are able to address the cultural and religious values of all users (South Thames RHA 1994). Despite our criticisms of the 'checklist' approach, we believe that it has a role to play in this context. Finally, it is important that all users have access to the full range of relevant services – pain control, respite services for carers and bereavement support – in appropriate settings. However, the manner in which such services can usefully be offered may vary between ethnic groups.

The model for service delivery which is likely to meet with most success is a collaborative one in which palliative care professionals work with users, informal carers and local community groups to integrate services with community structures. But, as in the majority population, gender, age and other social relationships may be such that the perceived interests of some members of the population may be at the expense of the interests of others. This may raise difficulties for providers in defining interventions which can be seen as culturally sensitive. Nevertheless, some important innovations have already been made in areas such as respite care, and recent publications have enumerated a diverse range of issues which can usefully be addressed in order to provide palliative care services genuinely able to attend to the needs of all ethnic groups (South Thames RHA 1994, Hill and Penso 1995).

Existing knowledge about ethnic patterns in palliative care utilisation and about successful policy development is insufficient for us to be able to draw any very specific conclusions about how services ought to be configured in the future. We have therefore aimed to provide a systematic framework to shape and inform thinking about palliative care issues, and which points towards the kind of information now required to provide more detailed policy guidance. We have also identified some key issues which face palliative care providers in supporting dying people and their carers in such a way that their services are a genuinely multi-ethnic resource. Perhaps the most important issue is the need to think both structurally and culturally about the ways in which services may or may not be reaching different groups. This requires an appreciation not only of different cultural beliefs and ways of living but also of the ways in which the wider social structures of British society affect and shape the lifestyles and life chances of minority ethnic group members.

NOTE

1 For a variety of reasons, many studies concerned with the health of people from minority ethnic groups use data which refer only to immigrants (i.e. British residents born abroad), thus excluding from the picture people of minority ethnic status born in Britain. It is important to be aware of the potential bias that this introduces, although in the case of palliative care the demographic profile of most minority ethnic groups is such that most users are likely to have been born abroad.

REFERENCES

Ahmad, W. (1996) 'Family obligations and social change among Asian communities', in W. Ahmad and K. Atkin (eds) *'Race' and Community Care*, Buckingham: Open University Press, pp. 51–72.

Andersen, R. (1995) 'Revisiting the behavioural model and access to medical care: does it matter?', *Journal of Health and Social Behaviour*, 36: 1–10.

Anwar, M. (1985) *Pakistanis in Britain: A Sociological Study*, London: New Century.

—— (1995) 'Social networks of Pakistanis in the UK: a re-evaluation', in A. Rogers and S. Vertovec (eds) *The Urban Context: Ethnicity, Social Networks and Situational Analysis*, Oxford: Berg, pp. 237–57.

Asad, T. (1990) 'Multiculturalism and British identity in the wake of the Rushdie affair', *Politics and Society*, 18: 455–80.

Atkin, K. and Rollings, J. (1996) 'Looking after their own? Family caregiving among Asian and Afro-Caribbean communities', in W. Ahmad and K. Atkin (eds) *'Race' and Community Care*, Buckingham: Open University Press, pp. 73–86.

Atkin, K., Cameron, E., Badger, F. and Evers, H. (1989) 'Asian elders' knowledge and future use of community social and health services', *New Community*, 15: 439–45.

Balarajan, R. and Bulusu, L. (1990) 'Mortality among immigrants in England and Wales 1979–83', in M. Britton (ed.) *Mortality and Geography: A Review in the Mid-1980s*, London: OPCS (Series DS No. 9), pp. 103–21.

Balarajan, R. and Raleigh, V. (1993) *Ethnicity and Health: A Guide for the NHS*, London: Department of Health.

Barker, R. and Baker, M. (1990) 'Incidence of cancer in Bradford Asians', *Journal of Epidemiology and Community Health*, 44: 125–9.

Berrington, A. (1994) 'Marriage and family formation among the white and ethnic minority populations in Britain', *Ethnic and Racial Studies*, 17: 517–46.

Bhopal, R. (1991) 'Health education and ethnic minorities', *British Medical Journal*, 302: 1338.

Boyle, S. and Smaje, C. (1993) *Primary Health Care in London: Quantifying the Challenge*, London: King's Fund.

Brown, C. (1984) *Black and White Britain: The Third PSI Survey*, Aldershot: Gower.

Cm 1986 (1992) *The Health of the Nation: A Strategy for Health in England*, HMSO: London.

Donaldson, L. (1986) 'Health and social status of elderly Asians: a community survey', *British Medical Journal*, 293: 1079–82.

Firth, S. (1993) 'Approaches to death in Hindu and Sikh communities in Britain', in D. Dickenson and M. Johnson (eds) *Death, Dying and Bereavement*, London: Sage, pp. 26–32.

Green, J. (1991) *Death with Dignity: Meeting the Spiritual Needs of Patients in a Multi-cultural Society*, vol. 1, London: Macmillan Magazines.

Haroon-Iqbal, H., Field, D., Parker, H. and Iqbal, Z. (1995) 'The absent minority: access and use of palliative care services by black and ethnic minority groups in Leicester', in A. Richardson and J. Wilson-Barnett (eds) *Research in Cancer Nursing*, London: Scutari, pp. 83–96.

HEA (Health Education Authority) (1994) *Health and Lifestyles: Black and Minority Ethnic Groups in Britain*, London: Health Education Authority.

Headen, A. (1992) 'Time costs and informal social support as determinants of differences between black and white families in the provision of long-term care', *Inquiry* 29: 440–50.

Hek, G. (1991) 'Contact with Asian elders', *Journal of District Nursing*, December: 13–15.

Henley, A. (1987) *Caring in a Multiracial Society*, London: Bloomsbury Health Authority.

Hill, D. and Penso, D. (1995) *Opening Doors: Improving Access to Hospice and Specialist Care Services by Members of Black and Ethnic Minority Communities*, London: National Council for Hospice and Specialist Palliative Care Services, Occasional Paper 7.

Holmes, E. and Holmes, L. (1995) *Other Cultures, Elder Years*, London: Sage.

Hospice Information Service (1995) *Directory of Hospice and Palliative Care Services*, London: St Christopher's Hospice Information Services.

Katz, J. (1993) 'Jewish perspectives on death, dying and bereavement', in D. Dickenson and M. Johnson (eds) *Death, Dying and Bereavement*, London: Sage, pp. 199–207.

McCalman, J. (1990) *The Forgotten People: Carers in Three Minority Ethnic Communities in Southwark*, London: King's Fund Centre/Help the Aged.

McFarland, E., Dalton, M. and Walsh, D. (1989) 'Ethnic minority needs and service delivery: the barriers to access in a Glasgow inner-city area', *New Community*, 15: 405–15.

McKeigue, P., Marmot, M., Syndercombe Court, Y., Cottier, D., Tahma, S. and Riemersa, R. (1988) 'Diabetes, hyperinsulinaemia and coronary risk factors in Bangladeshis in East London', *British Heart Journal* 60: 390–6.

Neuberger, J. (1987) *Caring for Dying People of Different Faiths*, London: Austen Cornish and Lisa Sainsbury Foundations.

—— (1993) 'Cultural issues in palliative care', in D. Doyle, G. Hanks, and N. MacDonald (eds) *The Oxford Textbook of Palliative Medicine*, Oxford: Oxford University Press, pp. 507–13.

OPCS (1993) 'Ethnic group and country of birth: Great Britain', *1991 Census*, London: HMSO.

—— (1995) 'Table 18 – International migration: country of last or next residence', *Population Trends*, 79: 59.

Owen, D. (1994) 'Spatial variations in ethnic minority groups populations in Great Britain', *Population Trends* 78: 23–33.

Rees, W. (1986) 'Immigrants and the hospice', *Health Trends* 18: 89–91.

Rosenblatt, P. (1993) 'Cross-cultural variation in the experience, expression and understanding of grief', in D. Irish, K. F. Lundquist and V. J. Nelsen (eds) *Ethnic Variations in Dying, Death and Grief: Diversity in Universality*, Washington: Taylor & Francis, pp. 13–19.

Shanmugaratnam, K., Hin-Peng, L. and Day, N. (1989) 'Cancer in migrant populations: a study in Singapore', in J. Cruickshank and D. Beevers (eds) *Ethnic Factors in Health and Disease*, Sevenoaks: Wright, pp. 145–54.

Smaje, C. (1995) *Health, 'Race' and Ethnicity: Making Sense of the Evidence*, London: King's Fund.

—— (1996) 'The ethnic patterning of health: new directions for theory and research', *Sociology of Health and Illness* 18: 139–71.

—— and Le Grand, J. (1995) 'Equity, ethnicity and health care', paper presented to the Social Policy Association Meeting, Sheffield, 18–20 July.

Small, N., Ahmad, W. and Murray, R. (1995) 'Marginalised or demonised: racism, ethnicity and the HIV epidemic', paper presented to the Social Aspects of AIDS conference, London.

South Thames RHA (1994) *Palliative Care 1994: Service Provision for Black and Ethnic Groups – Specific Issues for Consideration*, London: South Thames RHA.

Stevens, A. and Gabbay, J. (1991) 'Needs assessment needs assessment', *Health Trends* 23: 20–3.

Ungerson, C. (1993) 'Caring and citizenship: a complex relationship', in J. Bornat, C. Pereira, D. Pilgrim and F. Williams, (eds) *Community Care: A Reader*, Basingstoke: Macmillan, pp. 143–51.

Worobey, J. and Angel, R. (1990) 'Poverty and health: older minority women and the rise of the female-headed household', *Journal of Health and Social Behaviour* 31: 370–83.

Chapter 9

Culture is not enough
A critique of multi-culturalism in palliative care

Yasmin Gunaratnam

INTRODUCTION

The need to provide accessible and appropriate care to Britain's growing numbers of Black and ethnic minority terminally ill people, has recently been recognised as a significant service development issue for many providers of palliative care. A report from the National Council for Hospice and Specialist Palliative Care Services (Hill and Penso 1995), identified a particular need for the provision of 'culturally sensitive' services in relation to the 'spiritual, language and dietary' needs of Black and ethnic minority service users. While such developments are both positive and welcomed, this chapter critically examines the predominant construction of Black and ethnic minority people's needs in terms of cultural and religious needs. In particular, the chapter focuses upon the resurgence in popularity of cultural 'factfile' or 'checklist' approaches, as support resources to meet the training needs of health professionals. These approaches can be typified by their cataloguing of largely descriptive information on the cultural and religious practices of different Black and ethnic minority populations. In practical terms, factfiles appear to make positive contributions to the training needs of health-care professionals and to the quality of palliative care provision itself. However, a sociological consideration of the conceptual framework of resources suggests more ambivalent repercussions, in which their use can also legitimate complex repertoires of discrimination.

In critically examining factfile resources, this chapter draws upon data collected by the author from eight focus group discussions with thirty-two members of staff at a London hospice. The

Considerations for the living

Sick patients in hospital would wish to be treated in the same way as everyone else and are unlikely to make special requests. Families may feel that the doctors are remote and unapproachable and feel unable to communicate with them and ask questions. Afro-Caribbean nursing staff may be able to help to bridge that gap.

Prayer is important for those who are regular churchgoers and the opportunity of privacy for prayer, and even for the singing of hymns, would be appreciated. Families would like to be able to be more demonstrative than the average white family and often feel emotionally restricted and inhibited in hospitals in the UK. Ward staff should anticipate the need for a side room for a dying patient.

Diet

There are no general dietary restrictions, but hospital food may seem very dull to long-stay patients. An occasional Caribbean dish would be greatly appreciated.

Care of the dying

Visitors are very important to the sick, not just family members but also church and community leaders. The extended family may wish to make frequent and prolonged visits, and close relatives will want to be present at the death. West Indian patients are likely to require facilities for more than the average number of visitors. It is important that the clergy visit and that prayers are said together. Sacraments are seen as less necessary than prayer but some will wish to take Holy Communion.

Post-mortems and body donation

Older members of the community may believe that the body must be intact for the after-life and will be deeply offended by its disfigurement. They are unlikely to give consent for post-mortem except for coroner's cases.

Blood transfusion

There is no religious objection to the giving or receiving of blood (except for Jehovah's Witnesses or Rastafarians).

Organ transplants

There is no religious objection to the reception of a transplanted organ, but those with belief in the sanctity of the body are unlikely to agree to organ donation. Younger family members may have different views.

Procedure at death

Routine last offices are appropriate. There are no religious objections to others handling the body as long as respect is shown. It may be preferred if a nurse from a similar ethnic background is able to fulfil this duty.

If death occurs at home, the laying out may be done by family and friends.

Funerals

In the UK, burial is the preferred method of disposal. The funeral is an important and elaborate occasion for the extended family and for all those who loved the deceased during life.

The entire community will wish to attend. Time will be allowed for the dispersed relatives to gather together. The body may be brought to the home before the funeral service, and may be viewed there and also during the singing of a hymn in church. This is a sign of respect, according to the wishes of the family especially in Pentecostal communities. (The body should ideally be embalmed, especially if the funeral will be delayed.)

Because of the importance attached to funerals, time off work to attend them is necessary for many people, not just the very close family. The funeral service may be long, varied to suit the individual and characterised by hymns, tributes, a choir, a steel band or other music, gospel-singing and flowers.

At the graveside the family will fill the grave in themselves, while the singing continues. The congregation will probably return to the church hall for a gathering, after which the family house remains 'open' for people to call on the relatives, and for prayer, for about a week.

Figure 9.1   An example of a factfile: the Afro-Caribbean Community

Source: Reproduced by kind permission of Nursing Times where this article first appeared, 19 February 1992.

data are part of a larger, qualitative study exploring experiences of terminal illness and care amongst Black and ethnic minority health service users.

I will begin by briefly outlining the origins and development of factfile resources. The limitations of factfiles will then be examined in relation to three main issues: the reification of cultural and religious practices; reductionism; and the failure to address professional and structural power relations. Data from the hospice focus groups will be used throughout the chapter to 'ground' the conceptual analysis of factfiles and to highlight the practical issues and dilemmas confronting multi-cultural practice.

THE FACTFILE APPROACH

'Culturalist' approaches (Pearson 1986) – which account for differences in the health-care needs of Black and ethnic minority people in terms of cultural variations – represent a longstanding, conventional wisdom within the health service. First emerging during the 1960s, culturalist paradigms pivot around the need for professionals to 'read' and respond to cultural signifiers, such as customs and rituals. Although this focus has remained unchanged, culturalist approaches have evolved from constructing cultural practices as 'barriers' which need to be 'overcome' by professionals (Dodge 1969), to present-day approaches which also emphasise accommodation (Green 1991, 1993).

Given the construction of the need for professionals to be literate in relation to cultural practices, it is not surprising that professional support and training resources have been developed within a descriptive and categorial framework. For example, an influential exponent of early factfiles was Alix Henley, who in a series of books and training packs sponsored by the Department of Health and the King's Fund, provided descriptions of the cultural and religious practices of different Asian populations (1979, 1982, 1983a, 1983b). In providing information about beliefs and customs that were seen as holding implications for health-care needs, Henley's work provided professionals with practical and accessible information on such issues as naming systems, dietary requirements, codes of personal hygiene, and rituals surrounding birth and death.

Henley's detailed work undoubtedly filled an information gap within a budding multi-culturalism in the health service. It also quite rightly identified the need for greater multi-cultural awareness and flexibility on the part of professionals. However, what is of particular interest is that the prevalence of the basic need for the benign description and cataloguing of cultural practices appears to have remained unchanged since the early 1980s. Indeed, the 1990s have seen a number of variations of the factfile approach re-emerging (Bal and Bal 1995, Karmi 1995), with particular contributions focusing upon death and dying (Green 1993). In addition to factfile resources, a significant part of the broader literature on ethnicity and death has also been constructed around culturalist themes, for example Irish *et al.* (1993) and Firth (1993).

However, while there is clearly a professional market for factfiles, it is equally apparent that despite many well-developed materials, information on culture has not been enough to facilitate meaningful changes in the nature of service provision (Johnson 1993). Health services generally, and palliative care services in particular, are still struggling to meet the needs of Black and ethnic minority service users:

> Hospices ... have not specifically addressed issues of cultural and religious differences and ethnicity. In many instances they were uncertain of what they should be doing to make their services known and accessible to these communities.
>
> (Hill and Penso 1995: 14)

I would also argue that factfile resources, as part of a broader professional discourse, can present barriers to the achievement of a genuine, anti-racist multi-culturalism within palliative care services.

REIFICATION

Factfiles vary considerably in their quality and content, from well researched and sensitive materials (Henley 1987, Neuberger 1987) to more compartmentalised and simplistic approaches (Bal and Bal 1995, Green 1991, 1993). Resources also differ in the criteria used to index populations, with some resources using taxonomies based upon ethnicity (Karmi 1992), others using religious affiliation (Neuberger 1987) and some covering a somewhat arbitrary mixture of both (Green 1993). Yet despite such variations, the basic structure of resources is the same, revolving around the categorising of populations according to cultural and religious beliefs and practices. Underlying such cataloguing is the assumption that unfamiliarity with cultural practices can present particular problems for professionals working with Black and ethnic minority people:

> These articles came to be written because the nursing staff in my health district asked for them. ... It was the Day of Atonement, the holiest day in the Jewish calender, when a Jewish patient died unexpectedly ... The family were not present. Nursing staff were ... unsure of what should be done.
>
> (Green 1989: 1)

> Of basic and particular consideration, however, and questions frequently asked by nurses, are whether there are last rites, whether there are rules about who can touch the body, questions about confession, about prayers, about leaving the dead person alone ...
>
> (Neuberger 1987: 4)

Factfiles thus appear to meet real and identified professional needs for guidance and information in relation to task-oriented practice issues. However, in attempting to describe and classify beliefs and practices, resources ultimately conceptualise and treat culture, and indeed identity, as some form of constant. As such the resources suggest that it is possible for professionals to relate ethnic and religious identities in a somewhat linear way to healthcare needs and behaviours. Although many resources recognise their limitations in being able to classify what are essentially dynamic social processes, the paradox remains that the very popularity of resources has lain precisely in their ability to provide one-dimensional snapshots of cultural and religious practices which are frozen in both time and context. Hence, all resources inevitably struggle with the fundamental tensions between sweeping generalisation and crude stereotyping and the need to recognise variation and idiosyncrasy.

At a conceptual level, it can also be seen that factfiles operate within a framework in which the cultures of Black and ethnic minority peoples are constructed as fixed and free-standing. That is, as having an existence *sui generis*, rather than being seen as highly contingent, negotiated and unstable social projects. In reifying the historical and social production of cultural processes, factfiles fail to recognise that culture can develop in complex and paradoxical ways (Gilroy 1987, Solomos and Back 1995) in which constructions of death-related practices, beliefs and attitudes are continually emerging and even co-exist with past constructions. For example, Williams' (1989) study of attitudes towards death amongst older Aberdonian people, found a predominant pattern of 'disregard' towards death, co-existing with both contemporary attitudes favouring control over the time of one's death ('controlled dying') and much older patterns of 'ritual dying', oriented towards a preparation for death. In linking these attitudinal patterns to historical changes in the religious, familial and medical spheres, Williams suggests that 'Contemporary attitudes to dying appear as historical strata laid down by a culture in motion' (1989: 121).

The fundamental issue here is not simply that factfiles reify and mystify the social production of culture at an abstract and theoretical level. It is also that as part of a professional discourse, such conceptualisations can have practical implications for professional practice. A postmodern analysis can be particularly useful in this instance, in unravelling the complexities, ambivalences and ambiguities inherent in such functionings:

> a 'postmodern' framing regards the production and representation of particular identities as relational: that is, as constructed through alterity, compassion, opposition and possible marginalization of other identities ... this creation takes the form of representations which construct a kind of mirroring, in which collective and individual identities are formed as much by 'reflections' of, and on, what the perceiving subject is not, as by what it is, as 'seen' in the mirror of self-regarding and other regarding texts and practices.
>
> (Rattansi 1994: 28–9)

Taking the stated aims of resources as a starting point, it can be seen that the categorising of cultural and religious practices into discrete packages can serve to allay professional concerns about the inaccessibility and the potential unmanageability of information about cultural practices. In terms of palliative care, such anxieties can be further exacerbated by professional awareness of the radicalising nature of death (in the threats posed to the ontological securities of individuals), and also in the very real constraints of time in the development of professional–user relationships. In fact, a recurrent theme in focus group discussions with hospice staff related to the impact of intersections of death and ethnicity on professional confidence, risk-taking and practice:

> 'There is a fear of dealing with people from different cultures – that you don't want to "get it wrong". It's harder to take the risks that you might do with people from your own culture ... It is also about dealing with people who are dying – death conjures up an atmosphere of danger.'

> 'I think it is the pressure, the speed, you know [laughs], it's now or never, basically ... I feel that sort of pressure to try and "get it right" and try and sort out problems ... because it's going to be too late very soon.'

Within such a context, the reification of cultural processes by factfiles can be seen to hold complex ambivalences for professional practice where multi-culturalism is also frequently accompanied by imposing and dualistic professional scripts of either 'getting it right' or 'getting it wrong'.

At one level, there is no doubt that patterns and continuities exist in cultural and religious practices. Professional awareness of the range of such patterns can be a vital starting point in addressing the needs of Black and ethnic minority users and carers (Harper 1995). For example, awareness about religious festivals, dietary prescriptions and death-related rituals can give real and symbolic affirmations to users, which can also enable the wider expressing and addressing of needs. As one nurse emphasised, such processes can also give reassuring feedback to professionals that they are 'getting it right':

> 'I think though, that you've got to have a basic knowledge of what their religion is about to be able to give people choices. For instance we had a Vietnamese lady ... who didn't speak any English, but her family spoke a little bit and I said to them, "Would you like to say prayers in the room?" ... "Can we ring bells?" "Yes, yes that's fine." ... I said to them, "Would you like to burn some incense?" "What is incense?" and I said, "It's a perfumed stick, that you sometimes have." "Oh yes. We did not know the word. But it is very important to us." So if I hadn't actually said that ... they wouldn't have been able to actually say to me "Can we burn incense?"'

However, although information on cultural processes can enhance professional practice, it can also have more negative repercussions. In particular, the attempts by factfiles to impose a closure upon the unruly nature of cultural processes can lead to the manufacturing of mythical stabilities which can feed into and off discourses of either getting it 'right' or 'wrong'. Moreover, if cultural practices are seen as rigid and uncontested, then the addressing of need can quickly turn into a 'task' rather than a 'process' issue, serving to short-circuit professional explorations and risk-taking. For example, factfiles translate cultural and religious practices into a series of visible and objectified 'needs' which can be met through practical measures such as the provision of Kosher food for Jewish users or through the availability of the Koran for Muslims. Multi-cultural practice can then be condensed into highly practical, task-based competencies which by-pass the need for professionals to engage with subjective experience and personal choice. Yet, by portraying cultural and religious needs as rigid and non-negotiable, factfiles can also threateningly concretise the possibilities of professionals 'getting it wrong'. So rather than allaying fears, reified information can paradoxically serve to heighten professional anxieties while also channelling practice into 'safe' and unimaginative areas.

Somewhat counter-intuitively, it may be precisely the lack of knowledge about cultural and religious practices, or the active suspension of existing knowledge that can liberate professional practice from constraining forces:

'I have done my most miraculous stuff with cultures I know nothing about. If you don't know anything about a culture, you are not tempted to come up with you own solutions for them.'

(Hospice nurse quoted in Noggle 1995: 88)

'And sometimes we're brave enough to say "I'm sorry, we don't know enough about what you would like to do . . . you know, normally what would you like to be able to do ?". . . And not using the information you've got before just in order to presume and act on those presumptions. But it takes some bravery, because you're, you're stepping outside your comfort zones as it were. You're stepping outside your experience.'

(Focus-group participant)

Such experiences serve to challenge the basic premise of fact-files, which present cultural and religious knowledge as the key solution to professional inadequacies in meeting the needs of Black and ethnic minority users. There is no denying the fact that professional multi-cultural awareness can have real benefits for service users, but it is also the case that the form and nature of such knowledge is equally important. Reified information on cultural practices has the practical benefit of simplifying and coding behaviours into manageable and 'digestible chunks' of information for professionals. Yet it can also lead to limiting and stereotypical presumptions about need. In this way factfile resources can become caught up in complex, multi-faceted reper-toires of discrimination in which multi-cultural awareness can also turn in on itself to constrain the nature and range of professional practices with Black and ethnic minority people. Processes of discrimination can thus be reconstituted, legitimated and even valorised by the multi-cultural discourses of factfiles.

REDUCTIONISM

In failing to address the dynamic social and historical production of cultural processes, factfiles also eclipse subjective experience through their emphasis upon the defining nature of cultural forces for Black and ethnic minority people. The relationships between individual identity, meaning frameworks and cultural contexts are thus constructed deterministically, without 'space' being accorded to the gaps which exist between self-identifications and culturally related behaviours (Hutnik 1991). Thus, although factfiles appear to offer reassuring guidance to professionals about cultural prescriptions, they offer little guidance about the nature of lived experiences, in which subjectivities are negotiated through 'fluc-tuating levels of absorption and detachment' from the social (Ellis and Flaherty 1992). So, while there is an abundance of descrip-tive information on cultural and religious prescriptions in relation to death, we still know next to nothing about Black and ethnic minority peoples' subjective and emotional experiences of death and dying.

In examining the effects of cultural reductionism for profes-sional practice, I will explore the particular theme of professional cognitive dissonance. In relation to work with Black and ethnic minority people, I use the term to refer to the uneasiness, dilemmas, incongruities and reconciliations that are thrown up for professional practice. A key source of this dissonance is seen as lying in attempts by professionals to negotiate their way around constructed dichotomies, between the subjectivities of Black and ethnic minority people and cultural contexts, and also between agency and cultural prescription. Such dissonance is seen as being particularly acute within palliative care, where professional scripts promote subjective explorations by users and emotional accompaniment by both professional and lay carers (Seale 1995).

It is also suggested that factfiles are implicated in the generation and reinforcement of professional dissonance through their privileging and separating out of cultural processes from individual and subjective elements. The danger here is that preoccupations with cultural identity can serve to stall and limit professional intervention and support. For example, a recurring issue for hospice staff was the willingness to ascribe culturally 'ambiguous' or improvised behaviours by Black and ethnic minority people to the realms of cultural prescription. Thus, non-compliance with drug regimens, closed awareness contexts and the photographing of dead relatives were all primarily defined as 'cultural' practices. The reframing and de-essentialising of such practices were only enabled – if at all – through 'referential groundings' in which ethnicity was controlled for through retrospective, contemporaneous and hypothetical comparisons with same-case white families/individuals. Embodied within such instances are the practical consequences of the reification of culture and cultural reductionism. In practice these two themes frequently dovetail to evoke nebulous notions of cultural 'authenticity' which create burdensome and often futile dilemmas for staff. The fundamental conundrum for practitioners is two-fold: how can they make informed judgements about the validity of their perceptions of what constitutes 'cultural' practice? And second, how can they disentangle individual practice and behaviour from cultural prescription?

It is precisely these very real 'process' issues which factfiles ignore, even though such deliberations can have repercussions for practice. The following case described by a focus-group participant, illustrates how the predominance given to cultural and religious prescriptions can obscure subjective experience, sidetrack therapeutic interventions and also lead to professional feelings of de-skilling. The case involved a young Sri Lankan woman, who when close to death did not want to eat. Tensions arose when her mother continued to try and feed her:

> 'there was a kind of thing around the ward, that maybe, um, that what they supposedly needed was an expert in Buddhism. ... But also what transpired ... was that it was not just cultural issues. It was the fact that this young woman nearly died as a baby from ... lack of food and actually she'd [mother] had to force feed. ... So it was also about her own history and her own experience. But ... even later on ... the wards were still saying things like "Get in a cultural ... expert in the field". And there's a way in which I found that very disabling and sort of like "Oh my God, I'm doing the wrong thing. I shouldn't be in here at all. I know nothing." ... What I did was I talked to her Mum in front of this young woman and ... I said to her "Your daughter is saying she doesn't want to be fed anymore." ... And then we talked ... and that produced a lot of distress ... and then of course by having started that conversation off, you're having the conversation about "No she's not going to get better. So feeding her isn't going to make any difference at all." ... I mean, it just, it just led on and on and on and then we got to, "Well I had to, you know, when she was a baby, if I hadn't fed her, she would have died."'

What such cases indicate are the complex ramifications that culturalist perceptions have for professional confidence and for the nature of support offered to Black and ethnic minority users and carers. It is my contention that factfile resources are implicated in mobilising cultural and religious prescriptions as elaborate smoke-screens, which dehumanise Black and ethnic minority people. In terms of professional practice, it is not just that by defining experiences primarily through exotic cultural differences, resources position Black and ethnic minority people as 'Other' (Bhabha 1983). It is also that such differentiation actively works against cognitive processes of empathetic alignment, which are often a key starting point for professional support. Established professional practices such as the exploration of subjectivity through the addressing of emotion (Hunt 1991) can thus become easily hijacked through the diversion of attention to cultural and religious needs. Responsibility for the emotional accompaniment of Black and ethnic minority people can then also be more easily and legitimately 'given up' to cultural/religious specialists, in an underground emotional economy in which professional confidence is simultaneously protected and undermined.

In considering the effects of cultural reductionism, it should be recognised that such dehumanising themes are also interlaced with romanticised conceptualisations of the role of cultural and religious prescription within Black and ethnic minority populations. What appears to characterise this romanticisation is both its practical 'usefulness' in disenfranchising Black and ethnic minority people from emotional support, and also its ideological role in providing a tantalising comfort about the continuing dominance of meta-narratives (particularly those relating to religion) in postmodern societies. The interrelatedness of these functions was evident in the hospice focus group data. For example, two re-emerging themes (which also parallel academic debates on death), related to assertions that public mourning rituals served to ensure the greater incorporation of dying and bereaved people within their communities (Ariès 1981, Elias 1985); and that cultural and religious practices played a central role in mediating the existential anxieties which death was seen as representing to the individual and to the social order (Ariès 1981, Gorer 1965). Set against the wider British context of social uncertainty about the appropriateness of death-related rituals and mourning (Walter *et al.* 1995), such perceptions can lead to unfounded assumptions about the therapeutic benefits of rituals for Black and ethnic minority people:

> 'one of the most traumatic things for me was watching a ... young woman dying of HIV and her mother going absolutely bananas and spare, you know with the grief and although I felt very frightened and felt out of control, I remember thinking "I expect she gets this out of her system better than we do."'
>
> (Focus-group participant)

The issue here is that although mourning rituals can be more public and expressive within some communities, there can also be a tendency to project and confuse private feelings with public behaviour (Kellehear 1984), leading to oversimplified assumptions about the relationships between ritual behaviour, social support and subjective grief. As anthropological studies have suggested, ritual can actually invoke anxiety rather than alleviate it (Radcliffe-Brown 1922). However, when subjectivity is smothered by cultural reductionism, the space to address such complexities is actively restricted. In such instances responsibility for emotional accompaniment can again be readily abandoned, in this case through the imbuing of cultural and religious practices with spurious emotional, self-servicing roles. The underlying ambivalence of these romanticised perceptions, while holding professionals both repelled and awe-inspired, can also create spectacular dilemmas for staff by overturning established practice ideals.

The intensity of such professional dilemmas can be further influenced by multi-cultural discourses and by the implications of individual cases for levels of professional support and/or challenge. For example, multi-culturalism is grounded in enabling unqualified respect and support for a diversity of cultural practices. When taken together with reductionist perceptions, real difficulties can be constructed for and by professionals in reconciling and responding to affirming behaviours and to more ambivalent or restrictive practices. The two following cases, related by focus-group participants, indicate how such issues can become particularly acute when individual choice appears to go against mobilisations of cultural prescription. The cases related to individuals returning to their countries of origin, to die in the first case, and for burial in the second:

> 'he was a young man who wanted to die in the hospice . . . and the friends he had said he should go home to die. . . . And I would always go with patient choice, but I mean, it was partly difficult because sometimes he wasn't conscious to say it. But also feeling . . . that it was quite hard to disagree with these people who perceived themselves as being extremely helpful and knowing something that I didn't know. . . .'

> 'A young African woman . . . And she'd specifically said "I do not want my body to be returned because I want what little money there is to stay here with my kids." But the culture says that her body must go back and so there's a huge wrangle going on within the family now, and the men will win because the men in the family always get their say. Um, but I was thinking how it touches me as a worker. . . . And I was thinking that's often a conflict . . . you know, is it that I only respect . . . other cultures' attitudes so . . . long as it doesn't impinge on my own values, which are that, you know, that the kids are more important and they should benefit. . . .'

Because factfile resources are constructed around the benign description of cultural and religious practices, they overwhelmingly neglect to address such ambivalences and power relations which criss-cross and continually destabilise cultural practices. In particular, the exaggeration of cultural prescription gives little recognition to Black and ethnic minority people as active subjects whose subjective and materially influenced performances can re-affirm, modify and challenge cultural scripts. As Taylor (1992) has suggested, individuals are not simply puppets of social practices, but against a context of 'inescapable horizons' of moral, social and political significance, struggle towards subjective authenticity. What the preceding two cases illustrate is that for Black and ethnic minority people, such subjective explorations can also involve the challenging of cultural and religious practices.

A very real concern is that blanket multi-culturalism and the prevalence of reductionist perceptions can actually make it more difficult for professionals to support the choices of individual Black and ethnic minority users:

> 'your own desire to be sensitive ... somehow overrides your normal, I mean, it certainly does with me, my normal and total commitment to individual patient right. And, um, it, it does become more, more confusing and more difficult, you know, out of hopefully the right sort of desire to be sensitive and um, anti-discriminatory, but ... perhaps sometimes it actually leads to ... reverse racism. ...'
>
> (Focus-group participant)

POWER RELATIONS

As I have argued throughout this chapter, factfile resources, as part of a professional discourse on multi-culturalism, use conceptualisations of cultural and religious practices which can legitimate mechanisms of discrimination. However, the dangerousness of resources lies not just in their promulgation of crude caricatures of social practices within Black and ethnic minority populations. A fundamental limitation of nearly all the resources is that they remain scandalously silent about racism and its effects on professional–user relationships and on experiences of death and dying. As Ahmad has argued in relation to culturalist approaches in health-care:

In this perspective, racialised inequalities in both health and access to health-care are explained as resulting from cultural differences and deficits. Integration on the part of the minority communities and cultural understanding and ethnic sensitivity on the part of the health professional, then become the obvious solution; personal and institutional racism and racial discrimination have no part in this equation.

(1993: 2)

Similarly, factfiles offer cultural and religious knowledge as the solution to professional and institutional difficulties in meeting the needs of Black and ethnic minority users. Yet as Ferguson (1991) has suggested, it is the culture of the health-care system, as well as that of the users, which needs to be examined in interaction. In fact, in considering the specific area of accommodation of multi-cultural practices within palliative care, it is possible to see deep stresses and tensions arising from challenges to the disciplinary power of medicine. Thus even within the limited cultural and religious arenas defined by factfiles, it is apparent that multi-cultural knowledge *per se*, cannot always enable the accommodation, let alone the empowerment, of difference.

Tensions and resistance to accommodating perceived cultural needs are not however constant and uniform. As Rattansi (1994) has highlighted, institutional racism is often constituted by a set of contradictory and uneven processes, which are themselves caught up with 'the specificity of modern disciplinary institutions', embodying radicalised, gendered and class-specific standards of order and control. It is the extent to which behaviours by Black and ethnic minority people threaten such standards, which can also determine the extent of accommodation or resistance to particular behaviours. For example, although hospice staff were in unanimous agreement about the need for multi-cultural food and for multi-faith support, there was a greater reticence towards public mourning rituals within hospice wards. Wider romanticised beliefs about the therapeutic benefits of rituals became suspended or subsumed by the overriding need for control of the physical and emotional environment:

'I remember ... the ward was in complete chaos ... a young woman had died ... [from] ... a Northern African family ... and there were about twenty people in the side room ... and the majority of them were wailing. ... And ... it was very difficult for the staff on the ward and also other patients really, to hear that sort of wailing. And that level of sort of emotional demonstration on the ward was very stressful. . . .'

'I remember a Greek man dying . . . and his family were . . . clutching his body and screaming and lying on the floor and, you know, were . . . just expressing their grief very, very rawly, which we tend not to do . . . and in the context of a bay that's quite shocking for other patients and other families. . . . I mean there's no denying it, it's not easy for us to contend with . . . because . . . anybody who expresses their grief really rawly, makes huge demands of our attention.'

Behaviours which overtly threaten the disciplinary codes of health service organisations thus inevitably involve real struggles of interest between users and health professionals and also between different groups of service users. Yet the multi-cultural narratives of factfiles ignore these conflicts of interest and obfuscate the nature of organisational and political barriers to meeting the needs of Black and ethnic minority people. I would argue that this role plays a central part in the reassuring, though highly ambivalent, functions of factfiles. On the one hand, reified and reductionist conceptualisations of need can function to reassure professionals that it is only increased multi-cultural knowledge and task-oriented changes in practice that are required to meet needs. On the other hand, the non-recognition of conflicts of interest can also offer reassurances that multi-culturalism can be practised within a framework in which individual and structural power relations remain intact. The underlying contradiction of these reassurances is that the distance between the 'safe' and manageable multi-cultural territory of factfiles, and the reality of power-based and emotionally charged multi-culturalism in practice, can leave professionals stranded without guidance or reference points. In examining professional responses to public mourning rituals further, it becomes clear that 'challenging' behaviours by Black and ethnic minority users can trigger deep emotional sequences of distress and fear which can also destabilise professional roles. As a hospice nurse disclosed:

'I think the fact that it was so raw [mourning]. So . . ., um, it felt very frightening because I felt it was on the edge and I guess that feeling is often there, but we're often spared from it because people culturally determine a way to behave and these people are saying, "No. This is how we want to behave. This is how we would behave. This is how we are behaving." And that is very frightening if it's different from what, what you perceive as normal.'

Several issues emerge in examining the detail of such power struggles. In the context of the disciplinary standards of health service organisations, a key site of struggle can be located in the racialising of public space. With regard to multi-culturalism, professionals can find themselves engaged in intensive projects of emotional labour around the policing of spatial boundaries, involving both self-management and the management of racism towards Black and ethnic minority people. For example, participants in all the focus groups pointed to racism from white service users as a significant and common difficulty for multi-cultural practice. The following case, narrated by a hospice nurse, relates to a situation where a white man was placed in a bay with three Afro-Caribbean men. The white man's wife had made repeated racist comments and expressed open hostility at having to the share the bay with Black people:

'I felt really, really, dreadful about it and this woman was making loud comments about how "These Black people come in all loud, during the day and night, and they're noisy and they bring in smelly food." … We had a big debate about whether this white bloke should be moved in to a side room, and I felt that I didn't want my other patients to be exposed to his wife, but I also felt that was giving his wife exactly what she wanted. So in the end I spoke with the chap [one of the Afro-Caribbean users] … and just used him. … And he said "No", he felt that that man should stay there and they would cope with it and the other … blokes were really supportive. And I think I learned a lot about that, and it made me feel less frightened of actually discussing racism with, with people who aren't white because I think I've always been too embarrassed to … because I felt so shameful, so responsible for it.'

What the two preceding cases illustrate is that, far from being passive victims, Black and ethnic minority people are frequently and successfully able to stand their ground within racialised territories. However, it is also the case that professional multi-cultural discourses appear wholly inadequate in addressing the significant emotional constituency of multi-cultural practice. In part, this down-playing of professional emotion is a by-product of the depoliticising themes of multi-culturalism which ignore power relations and racism. For example, although hospice staff expressed some concern about a lack of knowledge of death-related cultural and religious practices, they were also confident about how to access such knowledge. Thus, consulting carers, community organisations and their own chaplaincy department were all readily cited as working examples of strategies to gain appropriate guidance. Yet staff expressed considerably greater anxiety in having to manage inter-personal issues which held implications for individual and institutional racism. In this respect, fear was repeatedly identified as having the most limiting effect on multi-cultural practice. Key issues were seen as: fear of causing offence, fear of confronting one's own racism, fear of confronting racism in others, fear of being identified as racist and fear of triggering the 'rage and fury' of Black and ethnic minority people.

In terms of factfiles, the irony is that the impetus for their development was partly based in the recognition of professional feelings of anxiety in multi-cultural contexts. However, having acknowledged emotion, factfiles proceed to distort the 'signal-function' (Hochschild 1983) of such emotions, mystifying both the nature of subjective threat and the psycho-social influence of power relations. Although knowledge of cultural and religious practices can undoubtedly reduce levels of professional threat, it only scratches the surface of professional anxieties. What factfiles lack is a radical framework for understanding the complex and sometimes contradictory ways in which power relations can frame the nature of threat and also experiences of discrimination.

In considering factfiles in the light of power relations, it is important to recognise the implications of what they articulate and also what they remain silent about. In broad terms, the construction of the need for knowledge in multi-cultural practice is based upon fundamental judgements about the meaning and dimensions of multi-culturalism. These judgements can be seen as choices which reflect, but which in turn also come to influence, social and political agendas. Thus, factfiles are inextricably tied up with the bureaucratic need for the management of difference, reflecting organisational, rather than user-oriented interests. Moreover, by staying silent about racism, they also serve to negate the influence of structural and inter-personal power relations. Far from being innocuous, this silence can actively 'speak' about and define the legitimate limits of multi-cultural competencies. As Lyotard has argued:

> The negative phrase that the silence implies could be formulated respectively: This case does not fall within your competence, This case does not exist, It cannot be signified, It does not fall within my competence.

(1988: 13)

CONCLUSION

The preceding discussion has sought to examine critically factfile resources, through the interweaving of conceptual explorations with empirical data on professional experiences of multi-cultural practice. The critique suggests that many factfiles mobilise highly ambivalent conceptualisations of culture and identity, which can be deployed both to facilitate multi-culturalism and to legitimate discrimination.

It would be premature to dismiss the value of factfiles altogether, particularly since they appear to act as an informative 'comfort blanket' for particular aspects of professional practice. However, if they are to be more effective in addressing the concerns of professionals and service users, then there is a need for a radical reworking of their aims and content. Such developments, although limited, have already occurred, with some resources attempting to combine cultural information with an explicit recognition and examination of racism (Henley 1987, Mares et al. 1985). Unfortunately, these have been isolated developments and the more recent spate of factfiles has overwhelmingly neglected the implications of racism for multi-cultural practice.

Without a dynamic and politicised conceptual framework, factfiles will continue to run the risk both of constraining professional practice with Black and ethnic minority users and carers and of confirming discriminatory processes. Their use will thus inevitably become part of a management, rather than a radical empowerment process.

ACKNOWLEDGEMENT

The study upon which this chapter draws was funded by the Economic and Social Research Council.

REFERENCES

Ahmad, W. (1993) 'Making black people sick: "race", ideology and health research', in W. Ahmad (ed.) *'Race' and Health in Contemporary Britain*, Buckingham: Open University Press, pp. 11–33.

Ariès, P. (1981) *The Hour of Our Death*, London: Allen Lane.

Bal, P. and Bal, G. (1995) *Health Care Needs of a Multi-Racial Society: A Practical Guide for Health Professionals*, London: Hawkar Publications.

Bhabha, H. (1983) 'The other question: the stereotype and colonial discourse', *Screen* 24 (6): 18–36.

Dodge, J. (1969) *The Fieldworker in Immigrant Health*, London: Staple Press.

Elias, N. (1985) *The Loneliness of Dying*, Oxford: Blackwell.

Ellis, C. and Flaherty, M. (1992) 'An agenda for the interpretation of lived experience', in C. Ellis and M. Flaherty (eds) *Investigating Subjectivity: Research on Lived Experience*, Newbury Park: Sage, pp.1–13.

Ferguson, B. (1991) 'Concepts, models and theories for immigrant health care', in B. Ferguson and E. Browne (eds) *Health Care and Immigrants: A Guide for the Helping Professions*, Sydney: Maclennan & Petty, pp. 20–41.

Firth, S. (1993) 'Approaches to death in Hindu and Sikh communities in Britain', in D. Dickenson and M. Johnson (eds) *Death, Dying and Bereavement*, London: Sage, pp. 26–32.

Gilroy, P. (1987) *There Ain't No Black in the Union Jack: The Cultural Politics of Race and Racism*, London: Hutchinson.

Gorer, G. (1965) *Death, Grief and Mourning in Contemporary Britain*, London: Cresset.

Green, J. (1991) *Death with Dignity: Meeting the Spiritual Needs of Patients in a Multi-Cultural Society*, vol. 1, London: Macmillan Magazines.

—— (1992) *Death with Dignity: Meeting the Spiritual Needs of Patients in a Multi-Cultural Society*, vol. 2, London: Macmillan Magazines.

Harper, B. (1995) 'Report from the National Task Force on access to hospice care by minority groups', *The Hospice Journal* 10 (2): 1–9.

Henley, A. (1979) *Asian Patients in Hospital and Home*, London: King's Fund.

—— (1982) *Caring for Muslims and their Familes*, London: DHSS/King's Fund.

—— (1983a) *Caring for Sikhs and their Families*, London: DHSS/King's Fund.

—— (1983b) *Caring for Hindus and their Families*, London: DHSS/King's Fund.

—— (1987) *Caring in a Multiracial Society*, London: Bloomsbury Health Authority.

Hill, D. and Penso, D. (1995) *Opening Doors: Improving Access to*

Hospice and Specialist Care Services by Members of Black and Ethnic Minority Communities, London: National Council for Hospice and Specialist Palliative Care Services, Occasional Paper 7.

Hochschild, A. (1983) *The Managed Heart: Commercialisation of Human Feeling*, Berkeley: University of California Press.

Hunt, M. (1991) 'Being friendly and informal: reflected in nurses', terminally ill patients' and relatives' conversations at home', *Journal of Advanced Nursing* 16: 929–38.

Hutnik, N. (1991) *Ethnic Minority Identity: A Social Psychological Perspective*, Oxford: Clarendon Press.

Irish, D., Lundquist, K. F. and Nelson, V. J. (eds) (1993) *Ethnic Variations in Dying, Death and Grief: Diversity in Universality*, Washington, DC: Taylor & Francis.

Johnson, M. (1993) 'Equal opportunities in service delivery: responses to a changing population?', in W. Ahmad (ed.) *'Race' and Health in Contemporary Britain*, Buckingham: Open University Press, pp. 182–98.

Karmi, G. (1992) *The Ethnic Factfile*, London: The Health and Ethnicity Programme, North East and North West Thames Regional Health Authorities.

—— (ed.) (1996) *The Ethnic Health Fact File: A Fact File for Health Care Professionals*, Oxford: Blackwell.

Kellehear, A. (1984) 'Are we a "death-denying" society? A sociological review', *Social Science and Medicine* 18: 713–23.

Lyotard, J. (1988) *The Differend: Phrases in Dispute*, Manchester: Manchester University Press.

Mares, P., Henley, A. and Baxter, C. (1985) *Health Care in Multiracial Britain*, Cambridge: Health Education Council/National Extension College.

Neuberger, J. (1987) *Caring for Dying People of Different Faiths*, London: Austen Cornish and Lisa Sainsbury Foundations.

Noggle, B. (1995) 'Identifying and meeting needs of ethnic minority patients', *The Hospice Journal*, 10: 85–92.

Pearson, M. (1986) 'Racist notions of ethnicity and culture in health education', in S. Rodmell and A. Watt (eds) *The Politics of Health Education*, London: Tavistock, pp. 38–56.

Radcliffe-Brown, A. R. [1922] (1964) *The Andaman Islanders*, New York: Free Press.

Rattansi, A. (1994) '"Western" racisms, ethnicities and identities in a "postmodern" frame', in A. Rattansi and S. Westwood (eds) *Racism, Modernity and Identity*, Cambridge: Polity Press, pp. 15–86.

Seale, C. (1995) 'Heroic death', *Sociology* 29 (4): 597–613.

Solomos, J. and Back, L. (1995) 'Marxism, racism and ethnicity', *American Behavioral Scientist* 38: 407–20.

Taylor, C. (1992) *The Ethics of Authenticity*, London: Harvard University Press.

Walter, T., Littlewood, J. and Pickering, M. (1995) 'Death in the news: the public invigilation of private emotion', *Sociology* 29: 579–96.

Williams, R. (1989) *A Protestant Legacy: Attitudes to Death and Illness Among Older Aberdonians*, Oxford: Clarendon Press.

Chapter 10

Death, gender and memory
Remembering loss and burial as a migrant

Gerdien Jonker

INTRODUCTION

In his classic text 'The Stranger', Alfred Schutz describes the problems which an individual faces in seeking entrance into a new group (Schutz 1964). One can learn the language, he says, as one might also learn how to behave in order to become accepted. But the one thing 'The Stranger' will never be able to share in his new country is the other's experience of the past. As Schutz puts it, 'from the viewpoint of the group he approaches, he is a man without history'. To Schutz, crossing the border implies bidding a farewell to all those images and actions which binds one to one's own past. The possibility of shared memory is left behind, or in Schutz' own words: 'graves and memories can neither be transferred nor conquered'. His 'stranger' is thus predestined to remain 'a marginal man' exactly because of the problematic character of things past: his own past becomes invisible and therefore non-existent in the eyes of the dominant group, while the other's past remains inaccessible.

This chapter raises the question of the use of memory under circumstances of migration. More precisely, it looks at the ways in which memory structures responses to loss and burial in a foreign environment. It is equally a fact for residents and immigrants alike that when someone dies, a train of memories is set into motion. The deceased person's life is remembered and gradually stitched into a shared past by those who survive him or her (Jonker 1995, 1996b). Also, memories of other losses and burials are activated and searched for instruction, in order to be able to handle this particular loss. Under circumstances of migration especially, this praxis becomes an urgent one, because a result is badly needed in order to shape the collapsing present. How this is done will be a central issue of this chapter.

THE SOCIAL CHARACTER OF MEMORY

What Schutz did not refer to is the social character of memory. Raising memories is necessarily a group affair. Ever since the work of Maurice Halbwachs on collective memory we know that memory needs people and places in order to come into existence and that it uses objects to take substance (Halbwachs 1980). Memory needs to be shared, but it also needs tools to reactivate particular events from the past. According to Halbwachs, the obvious way to make this happen is to go back to the place where it happened or to contact the group with whom one shared the events. Houses, streets and memorials, but also family, friends and religious communities hold on to segments of the desired past. Together, they might be able to conjure up a picture of the past which suits the present and enables the actors to shape the event.

But what happens if one has left one's place of origin, what if the family has become fragmented because of migration, and if friends have not shared the same experiences? As Schutz rightly remarked, the receiving country can be of no use here since it is not able to offer shared stories or a material reality with whose help memory could be obtained. Thus in the absence of a shared space and a shared past, many migrants turn to the one public institution which is able to recall both: the religious community.

In 1994–5, I conducted research in Berlin on the way migrant Greek and Turkish communities respond to dying, death and burial.[1] The two communities adhere to different faiths which organise their lives in different ways. However, when it comes to responses to loss and burial they have much in common. It seemed worthwhile to regard their answers not as a particularly Muslim or Orthodox Christian response to death, but as a common rural Mediterranean way of reacting to loss. The responses described here are in fact shared by many people who have migrated from all over the rural Mediterranean to northern Europe. However, Greeks and Turks do not share these experiences with one other. Greeks remember the way death was handled back home as involving typically Greek cultural values, while Turks identify with the same images and actions which they now consider

'Turkish' and 'Muslim'. Remembering is a selective action which tells us more about the present than about what the past really was like.

Here, as elsewhere in the world, it so happens that whenever people talk about death, memory of their childhood experiences plays a major part in shaping the story. I was confronted with many reminiscences of how things had been done back home. People pondered over all those details which had been common enough in their youth but had now turned into precious goods: the consolation of togetherness, the singing for the dead, the exact timing, the care for the grave and the days of remembrance. And in this regard Greek and Turkish memories appeared to be very much alike.

Also, in both religious groups men and women related to loss and burial in different ways. Naturally enough, they both told me the details of the parts they had attended themselves and minimised or neglected other parts which they had not. This often accounted for there being two different stories of the same event. While other reasons are more difficult to discern, there is one obvious reason for this, namely that there was an established division of roles between men and women in both Turkey and Greece. While women expressed loss, men took care of the burial. Memories are shaped accordingly. It is less obvious that although both sexes are generally aware of the activities of the other, women know more about the men's role in the burial than vice versa. This seems to be connected with the present roles of men and women within their migrant communities. Most of the men I talked to presented themselves in word and action as the protectors of traditional cultural values in their new surrounding. In contrast to this, some of the women seemed to function as self-appointed transmitters of cultural knowledge. These different functions shaped the form in which the two parties presented their stories and the way each valued the past as a means of shaping the present. Male and female memory thus appeared to be tied to the different functions that structure their present communities.

STRUCTURAL DOMAINS

When somebody dies, the home of the bereaved is the first place where the survivors meet (Örnek 1971, Alexiou 1974, Auerbach 1987, Spohr-Rassidiakis 1990). The prayer hall (church, mosque), community centre and graveyard offer further possibilities to perform the necessary steps and to remember the deceased. Back home, Greek and Turkish women in rural areas traditionally took care of the body and the remembrance of the dead person. As they now remember it, this part of the farewell ceremony was performed at home and in the graveyard. Both domains functioned as public spaces where they performed their duties for all to see and to participate in. It was the women's responsibility to wash and clothe the corpse, to organise the private farewell by holding a wake and singing dirges, to cook special food on special days and to take care of the grave. While going through these ceremonial steps, women organised the memory of the deceased into a coherent and commonly shared whole. In doing so, they also instructed the younger generation on how to improvise a dirge and to prepare food in memory of the dead (Örnek 1971, Alexiou 1974, Zarmas 1975, Danforth 1982).

But because 90 per cent of Turks and 70 per cent of Greeks who die in Berlin are flown back home to be buried there, this part of their duty hardly counts in migration: consequently, the possibilities a graveyard might offer to cope with loss are almost non-existent. People do come to the house to sit awhile with the bereaved and shed tears together (Tan 1995: 248–314). But there is no body to say goodbye to, which gives this getting together a certain awkwardness, especially where the communal singing of dirges is concerned (Tan 1996; Karakasoğlu 1996). A woman from Thessalonica, an experienced *mirologísta* (singer of dirges), whom I will call Mrs Zersopoulos,[2] expressed it thus:

> Sure we want to sing. But well, you know, after a while you fail to do so. You feel you are being ridiculed. You need to cry but you cannot give vent to your feelings and sing for your dead. You hold yourself back.

Another problem is the fact that most apartments are too small to allow a large gathering. Moreover, the walls may be thin, and there is a general fear that the neighbours might take offence. As a consequence, gatherings which used to take place at home are now held in the community centre:

> In Greece – I don't know what they do in the cities nowadays, but in the village people gather in the house of the deceased to eat and drink. There is no place in Berlin for that. You are

forced to go to the church. But there [you eat and drink] with those who happen to be around. It is definitely better in your own home. Your whole family, your friends and your very best colleagues are sure to be there. Such a pity, these little apartments in Germany!

(Mrs Bethava)

In contrast to this development, both the Islamic and Orthodox Christian prayer halls, with their attached community centres, offer important possibilities to those who wish to remember the dead collectively. In order to experience togetherness and consolation women meet in the community centre, men in the prayer hall. Here they can pray for the soul of the deceased and sit afterwards to talk. The Orthodox liturgy contains songs for the dead which are sung as soon as the usual liturgy is finished. These songs are performed not only for the newly dead, but also mark the remembrance days which used to be the sole responsibility of the household concerned. The priest will read the names of those who are to be remembered and sweets in memory of the deceased are brought before the altar, where they receive a blessing before being eaten by all those present.

This collective remembering of members of the community was originally brought from Greece, but in migration it has absorbed other forms of remembering, and its symbolic value has increased accordingly. In a similar way, although without food and songs, the dead are remembered in the Islamic Friday service. After the communal prayer and the preacher's sermon, the Imam will say a special prayer for those who have died during the previous week. The prayer also functions as an announcement and is carefully listened to.

Within the domain of the prayer hall, actions which formerly took place in homes and in burial grounds are now often scrutinised and either rejected or fitted into the theological framework. This too is a new development and its influence is considerable. It is met with opposing reactions. Mr Akbulut from eastern Anatolia, while reminiscing about the beauty and consolation of shedding tears together, commented bitterly on present attempts by the mosque to discourage this custom:

Our religion says: 'Don't cry. Life is an improvised stretch and only complete when one has gone to God': at least, this is what the men, especially the older ones, keep on telling us here. But on the other hand, crying is a duty. That's how it is. At the very least one should show a sad face.

Community life in migration has brought about severe restrictions for all those manners and customs which used to be linked to religious practices but really did not belong to religion. For Mr Akbulut, a former Koran reciter, this is a reason to stay away from the mosque, 'to give our children a chance'. Others have come to the opposite conclusion and turned into faithful believers. Another Greek lady, Mrs Nikolais, who had acquired an active role in community life herself, phrased this dilemma in the following way:

> They called me because their father had died. They said: 'What shall we do, what shall we do?' I have told them how things stand. I said: 'It is like this, one should attend church now and then.'

The three domains which originally structured the responses of men and women – home, burial ground and prayer hall – have all been subjected to considerable changes, due to the changed circumstances of living in migration. Some ceremonies of remembering have acquired a high value because of their concentration in the cult. Other ceremonial ways of taking leave from the dead, which formerly were not considered as belonging to the religious sphere, have not become the subject of theological scrutiny. Handling death has become concentrated in the space occupied by religion. It is here that both men and women have traced out the territories in which they do their duty whenever somebody dies. Within these limits, they also imagine a future place for themselves.

MEN

Greek and Turkish men are both traditionally responsible for the burial. A consequence of this is that they now organise the transport of the body home and deal with institutions outside the community. They are present at the religious ceremony, which they feel to be their responsibility. They also consider the possibility of acquiring a burial ground for future use. Those men who were prepared to talk to me about death were almost all professionals, bearers of responsibility. They occupied socially recognised positions within the community, such as religious leaders, under-takers, heads of cultural organisations and social workers. To this group of men was attached a small group of professional women, mostly social workers and employees of the community centre. What this group of people had in common was a feeling of respon-sibility for 'their' community, which they translated into actions of representation and interaction with the outside world.

When these men (and women) talked about death, they imag-ined their own future death. Accordingly, the question of where they themselves were going to be buried loomed large. The Orthodox Turkish Imam Guksal told me that he had only obtained German citizenship and taken measures to be buried in Berlin to set an example to his community. The Turkish undertaker also spoke of his wish to be buried in Berlin. He had already told his two young daughters to take an active part in his burial if he died and even to participate in the Koran reading. He said he wanted to give them what he himself had missed most while living in Berlin, giving a proper farewell to his parents and the possibility of visiting their graves.

The head of the Greek cultural centre, Mr Psychopedis, spoke of a 'corruption of morals', because, in his view, the next gener-ation would no longer know how to bury their parents. Therefore he was heading a 'burial ground committee' to secure a proper Orthodox burial place for his community:

> These people come from every possible region and every social class. When it comes to performing a proper burial, they all act a bit differently. Nothing is clear any more. What I feel is that our morals are being corrupted. That is why I want a grave-yard of our own. In this way, the next generation can be taught our custom. They will learn easier.

When asked about personal experiences, these men preferred to cite expert knowledge. Whenever they spoke about tradition, it was in terms of others, mostly the elderly and women, whom they wished to protect. It was to these women that they delegated the performance of traditional knowledge. Most of them did not show any interest in the details. Whenever they talked about death, it was in terms of the future, where they discerned a role for themselves in protecting the past, the tradition and those who transmitted it. As the head of the Greek cultural centre said: 'What happens at home is private. I do not go there. At least in

Berlin I have never witnessed it. I only go to the procession: that is the important part.'

To his knowledge, women still performed the same actions he had seen as a little boy. They would hold a wake, prepare sweets and shed tears. When asked whether they still sang songs for the dead, he answered irritably: 'Do they sing? Of course they sing!' It was a striking feature of his own narrative about death that he often used the future tense in combination with the third person 'they'. It was as if he imagined the future as a deputy acting for other persons. Other men also spoke in the future tense. A Greek social worker spoke of older women who, when they died, 'will want to stay near the children'. The Turkish undertaker said that his own children 'will want to give their own father a proper burial' where they live.

Both Greek and Turkish men occupy the central space in the prayer hall. In most mosques, women actually sit in another room and follow the communal prayer on a monitor. In the Orthodox church, they stand on the left side or upstairs on the balcony. At the few rare burials I witnessed in Berlin, Turkish men do the carrying and say the prayer.

WOMEN

Greek women in Berlin who wanted to talk to me about death mostly belonged to the older generation. They are aware of possessing a precious good, one that has become rare in migration: the cultural knowledge considered necessary to keep the group together. The majority of them are situated low in the social scale and occupy the status of housewife or low-paid employee. The knowledge they possess they acquired as a child or young woman back home. In migration they now feel responsible for its proper performance. They also worry about transmitting it to the younger generation. Through the performance of these actions, this group of older women has a structuring function within their community. Although I spoke to more Greek than Turkish women, I had the impression that the latter basically held the same view. Both Greek and Turkish women were accompanied by a small group of older men who had little education and were shaped by their ritual upbringing. These too worried about transmitting 'their' cultural values to the younger generation.

When talking about death, these women (and men) invariably talked about the deaths of others. When recounting particular burials, the details were often shaped against an inner blueprint of 'how it should be'. As a consequence, their form of narrative often used the present tense. For them, every single experience was part of their cultural inheritance, and, as a narrative, was situated in timeless tradition. The time they spoke of was an accumulated, 'timeless' past containing their own experience and the sum of experiences of past generations. It was never 'now'. This past seemed to be connected with an ideal image of 'home'. Thus not only was the time never 'now', the place in which they situated their story was hardly ever 'here', as may be seen from the following account:

> I am from Athens and my husband comes from the Peloponnese. Last year, my mother-in-law died in our home. I did not know what to do. I looked at what others had done and then did exactly the same. In the cities, one does not keep one's dead at home any longer. They are taken to the mortuary. But in the village we keep our dead at home. When somebody dies during the day, the body is laid out and kept at home overnight. I was very impressed – my mother-in-law had many sisters who all came – how we sat round her body and cried for her.
>
> (Mrs Bethava)

Many of these women contemplate being buried in their home village. They say they fear the thought of not receiving a proper farewell and abhor the rationality of German institutions.

> I used to want to be buried here. But then I saw [the burial of] my brother. An excavator! My God, they used an excavator to take the earth out! It's so cold, everything is cold here.
>
> (Mrs Zersopoulos)

She had heard about the plans of the burial ground committee and said this of course would change everything. A Greek place, where one could set up Greek graves and take care of the dead in the proper way, with a light and a photograph, she considered ideal, even if the community had to share it with Serbs and Russians. But as long as these plans were not realised, not even her children could convince her to stay:

> My elder daughter said to me: 'when the time has come, we want you to be here. We live here and want to visit your grave

and light a candle for you.' But I said: 'You are not lighting any candles for me right now, why do you want to do it when I am dead?'

(Mrs Zersopoulos)

Mrs Nikolaos, whom I had often seen busy in church, taking care of the communion bread and helping the family to give out *kólliva* (sweets in memory of the dead), was especially worried about the next generation, whom she accused of knowing 'next to nothing'. She described to me a situation in which the deceased had been brought to the church for the final procession. The account sheds light on her role in the proceedings:

> Someone from Katerini died. Many people came, all from Katerini. Men and women, nice clothes, well trimmed. And then? They had no idea what should be done. We laid out the table, we took care of the cross and the candlestick. We lit up the large cross. They all kept standing in the forecourt. They had brought candles, four or five each, but they kept standing there. I went up to them and said: 'Those of you who have been invited to the service for the deceased should enter and stand before the bishop's throne.' Nothing happened. The moment arrived where the Evangelist was read. We bowed. Nothing happened. You would have thought that they had been forced to come, that it was a service for my dead, not theirs.

The place these women occupy during the weekly service is the back of the church. Every action the believers perform themselves, and these are almost all actions connected with the dead, falls within their responsibility. They lead the bereaved family to the altar when it is time for the blessing and tell them where to stand. They hand a paper to the priest containing the names of the dead who are to be remembered that day. They keep an eye on the church warden and tell him to move the cross or carry the blessed food away. They set up tables in the entrance and help spoon out the *kólliva*.

Turkish women certainly occupy a less visible place in the prayer hall. But they too are responsible for the mourning and the days of remembrance. Turkish women will generally come to the procession, although many men say that women should not be present at the burial. They mourn in different ways (Jonker

1996a, 1996b). Turkish women also organise the fortieth day or *mevlut*, on which the men go to the mosque to pray while the women prepare sweets, *halvà*, for the memory of the deceased. Then the story of the birth of the prophet is read and all present shed tears (Tapper and Tapper 1987, Abu-Zahra 1991). This is considered the most important moment to pardon the deceased for his sins, and some will say afterwards that he has been seen standing behind the door listening.

MEMORY DOMAINS

Whenever people meet far from home and talk, whether at community gatherings or in shops, after a service, at burials or political meetings, a continuous narration of the common past is being transmitted. In circumstance of migration people will refer to the past to reminisce, to express their homesickness, to underline deficiencies in the present or to formulate the steps that must be taken. The past is an ever-present reality which is continually being produced. However, men and women add in different ways to this production.

Where death is concerned, the domain of memory is constituted by two realities which oppose yet need one another. At the one end, there is the experience of death. At different stages in their lives people have witnessed loss and been present at burials. These experiences have now turned into the past. This past used to be structured by a clear sexual division of labour. Women did the mourning, a responsibility which was closely linked to the production of memory for the deceased. Men took care of the burial, an act connected with representation. Within this framework people made choices, as different rural practices existed alongside each other and inhabitants of large cities adapted their burials to different ways of living.

At the other end looms the reality of the present, of what is here, the presence of life in migration. This presence has witnessed an avalanche. The several domains which sustained the sexual division of labour and enabled religious and non-religious ceremonies have been shrunk into one single space. This is the domain of the prayer hall, of religious life and theological reasoning. The choice people can make in migration is therefore not one between different rural customs; it is a choice between the religious community or staying on one's own.

In between these realities are the actors, men and women, who remember this or that, whatever they shared with one another or see fit to communicate to the present. Of course both parties will stress what they themselves have seen and heard, which, given the sexual division of labour, might result in two different pictures of the same event. However, it turns out that women know more about the men's world than the reverse. It has been suggested in these pages that this asymmetry is linked with the present roles men and women occupy within the community.

Basically we identified two different roles, those of protector and transmitter. It was shown that more men than women adopted the role of protector of cultural values, whereas women both were considered and saw themselves as transmitters of these same values. These roles define a gendered discourse on the past and result in a gendered memory. In closing this section I will offer some examples of this discourse.

Protectors of cultural values do not pay much attention to details. Their discourse is a normative discourse. They judge from afar the actions which the transmitters of cultural values perform. The sentence 'Now I am speaking from a religious/theoretical viewpoint' was repeatedly used by both Greeks and Turks who occupied such positions. The position they speak from oscillates between support and denial of rural custom. To underline their position, protectors often use proverbs. The Orthodox Turkish Imam Guksal said: 'When people do not live with death, they turn cold.' This proverb closely resembles a Greek saying which one of the social workers recited to me: 'He who cannot communicate with the dead cannot communicate with the living' (Mr Vichos). Other protectors opted for the position expressed by Mr Psychopedis, the head of the Greek cultural centre, who feared that morals were being corrupted. The Turkish leader of a religious fundamentalist community stated that 'one should get rid of all these practices'. And his colleague underlined this with a saying from the tradition of which the new normative order speaks loud and clear: 'There is Koran. There is Allah. The dead are dead. We must only remove them' (Imam Dural).

Protectors weave these proverbs and other normative expressions into their daily speech whenever they are reminded of life's finality, and both the Muslim and Orthodox Christian religious leaders were said to preach regularly about the meaning of death.

Transmitters of cultural values tell stories which mix past and present and are used as a means of ensuring the necessary knowledge of performance. Many examples present themselves. To quote but two:

> Three days after death one prepares *kólliva* from wheat, raisins, flour, nuts, sesame, sugar and a couple of cloves. Then one goes to the grave and scatters a plateful of it. This way one wards off the disaster from happening again. Then time is divided into nine, forty, etc., days after death.
>
> (Mrs Bethava)

This account represents the pragmatic approach: it offers a recipe and recounts the calendar for the days of remembrance. But these accounts have a strong narrative side too, in which the past is summoned to appear:

> A gifted woman starts to sing and she sings, sings and sings, just like that, without [printed] text or example, just wonderful. Or a little boy of 10 years old: everybody cries because the father has died, but he just sits there and starts singing by himself. Twenty, forty, fifty, a hundred couplets did that boy sing. He thought them up in a jiffy, music and text, just like that.
>
> (Mr Akbulut)

Such stories are only told when people are confronted with death. But questions must be posed to set them into motion: 'They have to ask questions. To neighbours, aunts, anybody! As long as they ask' (Mrs Zersopoulos).

Transmitters of cultural values await questions and fear that the younger generation will stop posing them. They have lost their old domains: home and burial ground, where they used to transmit their knowledge while acting. The collective wakes and long preparations in the kitchen provided them with both the time and the opportunity to recount the old stories and instruct the young. Living in circumstances of migration has forced them to find other places. It has been shown that these were retraced in the religious domain.

CONCLUSION

Hearing these proverbs and stories, I realised that the memories men and women produce service first and foremost their own present needs. There is a large difference between those of protectors and those of transmitters. Protectors do not dwell on details because they do not need them. Their discourse is about, and for the benefit of, others. Their main concern is to establish a clear position marking the borders of their community, which is obtained through frequent recourse to normative theological viewpoints. In contrast, transmitters depend on details. They listen carefully to the stories others have to tell and often contradict them. From these stories they abstract rules of conduct with which to handle situations and instruct others, especially the younger generation. It is a narrative and truly pragmatic approach.

Remembering is an action performed by immigrants and residents alike. However, when one has left one's place of origin, memory of earlier losses and burials becomes a necessity. With its help a train of new dynamics is set in motion. Alfred Schutz, himself an immigrant from Austria before the war, experienced what it meant to be a 'man without a history' in the US and came to the conclusion that 'graves and memories can neither be transferred nor conquered'. Schutz stayed on his own and consequently did not have the help of a community who shared memories of their lost world. Migrants who came to Europe in the 1970s adopted their new world collectively. The new circumstances they had to come to terms with also changed the three domains which structured responses to death; home, burial ground and prayer hall were now restructured in an all-encompassing religious domain. This again restructured the established division of roles between men and women. Both sexes remember death in a different way, but their choice of roles while living in migration is one between protector and transmitter of cultural values. It was stated that more men opted for the role of protector than did women. Although elements of class and learning add to this decision, it is shaped by memory more than anything else.

NOTES

1 This research was made possible by a two-year grant from the Berliner Senatsverwaltung für Arbeit und Frauen.
2 The original names have all been changed.

REFERENCES

Abu-Zahra, Nadia (1991) 'The Comparative Study of Muslim Societies and Islamic Rituals', in *Arab Historical Review for Ottoman Studies*, Zagwan, 3 (4): 7–38.

Alexiou, Margaret (1974) *The Ritual Lament in Greek Tradition*, Cambridge: Cambridge University Press.

Auerbach, Susan (1987) 'From singing to lamenting: women's musical role in a Greek village', in Ellen Koskoff (ed.) *Women and Music in Cross-Cultural Perspective*, Westport, CT: Greenwood Press, pp. 112–42.

Danforth, Loring M. (1982) *The Death Rituals of Rural Greece*, Princeton: Princeton University Press.

Halbwachs, Maurice (1980) *The Collective Memory*, Introduction by Mary Douglas, Cambridge: Cambridge University Press.

Höpp, Gerhard and Jonker, Gerdien (eds) (1996) *Sterben in der Fremde, Islamische Bestattung in Deutschland*, Berlin: Arbeitshefte Moderner Orient.

Jonker, Gerdien (1995) *The Topography of Remembrance: The Dead, Traditions and Collective Memory in Mesopotamia*, Leyden: E. J. Brill.

—— (1996a) 'The knife's edge: Muslim burial in the diaspora', *Mortality* 1 (1): 27–43.

—— (1996b) 'Die Totenklage in der Migration: interkonfessionelle Bewertungen einer traditionsreichen Praxis', in Höpp and Jonker (1996), pp. 131–47.

Karakasoğlu, Yasemin (1996) 'Probleme, Einstellungen und Praxis hinsichtlich der Beerdigung türkischer Muslime in Deutschland', in Höpp and Jonker (1996), pp. 83–107.

Örnek, Sedat Veyis (1971) *Anadolu Folklorunda Ölüm* (Death in Anatolian Folklore), Ankara: Dil ve Tarih-Cografya Fakultesi Basimevi.

Schutz, Alfred (1964) *Collected Papers II: Studies in Social Theory*, pp. 91–106. The Hague: Martinus Nijhoff.

Spohr-Rassidiakis, Agni (1990) *Fünf Totenklagenmelodien aus der Gegend des Assterùsia-Gebirge auf Kreta*, Göttingen: Editon Re.

Tapper, Nancy and Tapper, Richard (1987) 'The birth of the prophet: ritual and gender in Turkish Islam', in *Man*, London: pp. 69–92.

Tan, Dursun (1995) *Sterben in der Fremde. Sterben, Tod und Trauer unter Migratiuonsbedingungen – am Beispiel einer Einwanderungsminderheit in Deutschland*, unpublished PhD thesis for the University of Hanover.

—— (1996) 'Wandlung der Trauerritualen in der Migration', in Höpp and Jonker (1996), pp. 107–31.

Zarmas, Pieris (1975) *Studien zur Volksmusik Zyperns*, Baden-Baden: Nomos.

Chapter 11

Death and difference

Neil Small

INTRODUCTION

Contributors to this book have explored differences in the way death is experienced not only in various cultures but also by men and women. Something of the variety of experience that exists between different ethnic groups is presented in chapters by Smaje and Field and by Gunaratnam. Jonker looks at how these experiences are shaped by the overall cultural and social context within which a particular minority group lives. Social context is explored via the public representation of death and dying and the reactions to it in Littlewood, Pickering and Walter's chapter. They critique press reports in terms of gender portrayals and in so doing link with those other contributors who underline the need to recognise differences between genders. Here, as in the chapters by Hockey, Hallam and Thompson, the approach is to emphasise specific aspects of death and dying and look at these in the context of gender. Chapters by Lovell and by Riches and Dawson offer a further variable, that is the characteristics, particularly the age, of the person who dies.

We are not all the same in the end. As we asserted at the beginning of this book, death is not the great leveller. In this chapter I will build on the diversity described in previous chapters by considering the way social theory has looked at, or has avoided looking at, death. Underlying the detail of the argument I will present is a concern to recognise that we must engage with the challenges of postmodernism. Even if we do not want to take on the whole 'postist' discourse we must consider how far we have space to pick and choose from modernisms. The driving force of modernity, from the mid-to-late eighteenth century, was the belief that both personal and social wellbeing would be enhanced by the application of reason, science and technology. Dying, death and the dead would always occupy positions of challenge to epistemes of control, improvement and certainty. But they also pose challenges for postmodernism in that they intrude the mortal body into a rhetorical approach to the reflexive verisimilitude of the lived world.

This chapter will live within the space between 'old certainties and rhetorical postist discourses' (Jenkins 1995: 7). It will consider the way that death has been manifest in ritual, how it has been examined via models that rely on identifying stages of development, be they historical or psychological, and how it has been considered within social theory. Here there will be a concentration on questions concerning the body. Consistent with the overall theme of this book the chapter will be concerned with death and difference throughout. Difference here will be explored, in part, through deconstructing the overall category 'death'. The chapter will, further, be concerned with how far death is a process rather than an event and at the way the dead remain a part of both the referential and symbolic systems of the living.

THEORY AND DIFFERENCE

Sociology, anthropology and social theory offer a critical understanding of the nature of cultural production and increasingly recognise the need to pose, even within apparently well established hegemonic constructions, a variety of experience and approach. For example if we look at death in different cultural contexts we have to accommodate, on the one hand, the way that the westernised gaze seeks to make exotic, to anthropologise, non-western practices. On the other hand, we need to recognise the west's attempts to seek to restructure the world in its own image either through the aggressive promotion of a particular approach or through the misrepresentation of the cultural codes and meanings of non-westerners (see Airhihenbuwa 1995, Hockey 1996, Walter 1995).

If the agenda of the west in its interactions with other cultures is contradictory, it is equally evident that the recipients of these attentions do not experience them passively. Further, in seeking to exercise influence there is a concomitant impact on the west. Said describes the:

enormously systematic discipline by which European culture was able to manage – and even produce – the Orient politically, sociologically, militarily, ideologically, scientifically and imaginatively during the post-Enlightenment period. ... that European culture itself gained in strength and identity by setting itself off against the Orient as a sort of surrogate and even underground self.

(1978: 3)

If these macro relations between cultures and societies are complex, it appears equally evident that at the micro level of the individual we have to recognise the diverse, shifting and reflexive. This is the postmodern habitat. In effect we live within a broad-ranging paradox of, on the one hand, a fast developing globalisation and, on the other, the development of a mosaic of sites of individual choice. Further, as individuals our lives are lived in a social context that 'thoroughly privatises responsibility for the business of life; it stoutly refuses all pre-ordained assignment to life-models, and instead construes life as a process of self-constitution' (Bauman 1992: 21).

Sites of practice and of choice have, then, to be problematised. Generalisations are not much help. But we also need to look more closely at the subject area under consideration. Death is too big. We need to accept that death, the dead and the dying have to be considered separately. Within modernist, albeit late modernist, discourse we find that

Death remains the great extrinsic factor of human existence; it cannot as such be brought within the internally referential systems of modernity. However, all types of event leading up to and involved with the process of dying can be so incorporated.

(Giddens 1991: 162)

Death and the dead do not fit into modernity; they are sequestrated (Mellor 1993). Dying is different. There are ways in which it can and has been critiqued. For example one can look at its medicalisation or its privatisation. As such it is present in medical sociology, anthropology and history.

We can also ask if the postmodern habitat ends with the last heartbeat? Is postmodernism only about 'life'? How is being dead different? Bauman sees the ultimate incongruity as being 'between the freedom of the symbol-making and symbol-using subject and its fatal dependence on natural body' (Bauman 1992: 1). Post-modernism revels in difference, the question here being whether death is a difference too far. As this chapter progresses some of the approaches postmodernists have taken – Derrida on death and meaning and Baudrillard on the symbolic, for example – will be introduced and it will be argued that, as with modernism, we have only a partially developed approach to the overall complex of death, dying and the dead.

To illustrate, we can consider the picture Walter has offered us of a postmodern death. He presents this as an ideal type, an attempt to progress beyond the modern way of death. Dying is controlled by the dying person; after death the postmodern funeral celebrates the unique life of the deceased; and this is followed by a period in which those who grieve are able to express and talk about how they feel (Walter 1996: 194; see also Walter 1994).

Walter's postmodern ideal type (which in itself is something of a contradiction) asserts the authority of the postmodern consumer and the primacy of everyone involved to write their own script. But it has not, as yet, been developed beyond a concern with consumption and choice to engage that part of the postmodernist view which is concerned with reflexivity and irony. The symbol-making and symbol-using person, introduced by Bauman above, is likely to engage with dying, death and the dead in such a way that challenges not just established procedures but also the status of the significant and, through that, the nature of its construction and its positionings.

DEATH AND THE WORLD OF THE LIVING

Death remains the great outsider. But it is an outsider which does not stay where it is put. Death and the dead keep coming back into the world of the living. One way that the world of the living and the state of the dead are linked is through ritual. Anthropologists have recorded many varied and in some cases enduring rituals. Vintage photographs in the collection of the Pitt Rivers Museum, University of Oxford, depict highly personalised grave houses and celebratory funeral rituals observed in New Guinea in the early years of the twentieth century. The photographs appear to express an understanding of the inevitability of death and of its place, and the place of the dead, in the everyday life of the living in these societies. But they also show how western observers sought to impose their own constructions of narrative progression on the events they were witnessing (Edwards 1995).

Other death rituals are recorded as far back as we can study. Ancient Egyptians built an entire civilisation around their concepts of death and the afterlife in which temporal existence was a prelude to the afterworld. The place of the dead was also a place of physical reality. Material resources were dedicated to providing suitable conditions for the next life. Here the distinction between embodied life and disembodied death is not recognised, and hence neither is the end of the process of symbol making and using, or of self-constitution.

The trilogy of novels written by Pat Barker between 1991 and 1995, *Regeneration, The Eye of the Door*, and *The Ghost Road*, juxtapose the anthropological studies of W. H. R. Rivers in Melanesia and his work with invalided soldiers in World War One. In *The Ghost Road* the place of the dead and the community of the dying in the death huts of the Pacific and in the trenches and battlefields of the Western Front are explored via the themes of intimacy and exclusion. These novels offer a route into under-standing the complex way that, in the west in the twentieth century, we can sequestrate death, but also how those who see themselves as near to death, in this case soldiers about to 'go over the top' in World War One, seek the authenticity of that commu-nity who are living near death. Social exclusion is both imposed and sought. (Similar themes are explored in Frank McGuiness's 1985 play, *Observe the Sons of Ulster Marching to the Somme*.)

In the late twentieth century we still see ritual, of course, but these in the main accentuate the private tragedy rather than the social event of death. Littlewood (1993) argues that although death-related rituals are still widely performed, outside certain specific and relatively rare circumstances they have been removed from the community and relocated in the private world of the individuals who have been bereaved. A newspaper report in October 1995 offers an intriguing glimpse into a possible future where the remains of the dead are most profoundly expelled from the world of the living. A firm in the USA was offering to send a person's ashes into space, their advertising copy suggesting that science fiction writers and scientists might be likely customers (*Guardian*, 9 October 1995). Indeed the ashes of Gene Rodenberry, creator of *Star Trek*, and Timothy Leary, psychologist and guru of psychedelia, are booked on to a rocket (*Guardian*, 1 June 1996).

THE VISIBILITY OF DEATH IN SCHOLARSHIP

By 1981 historians were able, with some confidence, to argue that the history of death in the Anglo-Saxon world during the modern period was well established, at least in outline (Whaley 1981). That outline, in some notable works, identified a series of historical stages. For Illich (1995) the last 500 years has seen six different ways in which death has been conceptualised, each with its distinct iconographic expression. The fifteenth century saw a shift from death being a decision of god to a recognition that death had become something human, an inevitable and intrinsic part of life. This was followed by a shift whereby death changed from being a lifelong encounter to the event of a moment. By the mid-eighteenth century the relative egalitarianism evident in death up until then was replaced by a social hierarchy. There were now those who could afford to pay to keep death away. Health became the bourgeois privilege of waiting for timely death.

> We have seen death turn from God's call into a 'natural' event and later into a 'force of nature'; in a further mutation it had turned into an 'untimely' event when it came to those who were not both healthy and old. Now it had become the outcome of specific diseases certified by the doctor. Death had paled into a metaphorical figure, and killer diseases had taken his place. The general force of nature that had been celebrated as 'death' had turned into a host of specific causations of clinical demise. Many 'deaths' now roamed the world.
>
> (Illich 1995: 199)

In a further metaphorical twist these many deaths became the enemy that twentieth-century social organisation wages war against (see Sontag 1977, who describes how the military metaphor in medicine first came into widespread use in the 1880s).

This identification of epochs of death represents an influential way that historiography has contributed to the scholarship of death and dying. Perhaps the best known exponent of such an approach is Ariès (1974 and 1981). He presented a chronology, a periodisation, of attitudes to death. But it was not a straightforward chronology. He accepts that mental attitudes change over time, such that new attitudes overlap existing ones. The oldest, longest held and most common attitude towards death was of a familiar resignation to the collective destiny of the species. Ariès summarised it by the phrase, 'and we shall all die'. It was followed, from around the twelfth century, by an increasing concern with the self and one's own existence. The phrase, 'one's own death' summarised this new attitude. Beginning with the eighteenth century, western societies moved towards exalting and dramatising death. There was now less concern with one's own death and more with 'the death of the other person'. As the most recent change, he describes a shift from this romantic welcome for death and a concern with the surviving family to a stage of 'forbidden death', the suppression of ideas of death and dying (Ariès 1974).

In style Ariès' approach has been summed up as 'broad pattern weaving' and as a move to join the 'chorus of thanatologues' who had become vocal in the 1960s (McManners 1981: 129 and 117; see Feifel 1959, and for a direct influence on Ariès, Gorer 1965). Ariès' ambition carries dangers but also potentialities:

> refusing to bother about the problem of how many examples are needed to prove a trend or justify a general assertion, and dipping recklessly into the mass of disparate evidence thrown up by liturgies, art and literature, he has glimpsed, vividly, some sharply contrasting patterns of human reactions.
>
> (McManners 1981: 118)

Ariès' methodology, his results and his emotional involvement in the subject have been much criticised. One critic called his 'not a work of scholarship but a piece of nostalgic devotional literature' (see Whaley 1981: 8).

The approaches of Illich and Ariès are rich in their historical detail. They explore the symbolic domain in examining representations of death and see in imagery a way into understanding both the antecedents and the impact of particular constructions of death on broader society. They are, appropriately, concerned with many layers of significance. But while meeting that symbol-making agenda of postmodernity, they do so within the modernist structure of stages, epochs even, of the idea of historical time as progressing through largely discrete and identifiable stages. The remit of such scholarship is that of adding order to the past and explanation to the present. It is the wish to control the subject through containing it. Death is the apotheosis of this grand dream of control and of the belief in the power of the ordered and, as such, death scholarship that claims too much of the domain of rationality seems to miss the mark.

There are other examples of this same modernist episteme. Glaser and Strauss (1965) present a trajectory theory which had widespread impact on understanding and practice. Kubler-Ross (1970) offers a picture of five, generally progressive, emotional stages in one's response to the diagnosis of terminal illness; denial is followed by anger, bargaining, depression and finally acceptance. The developing practice of hospice and palliative care involves attempts to synthesise, to varying extents, symptom control, nursing care, spirituality and the holism of seeing the patient as both an integrated whole and part of a family and community network (see Saunders 1967).

But where do we go if we resist the broad sweep of historical stages, or any other modernist construction of referential systems? For example, what alternative might there be to a belief that there is a life cycle or a trajectory? Frankenberg (1987) is critical of the pervasive idea of 'life cycle', reminding us that human life does not go on for ever, in circles. At some point it ends. He is also critical of the Strauss concept of trajectory to describe the 'lifedeath' progression (see Strauss *et al.* 1985). Frankenberg is not really a geometrician; he does not like circles or arcs. They do not allow for the role of the individual; they are too deterministic. He prefers the idea of 'lifedeath as pilgrimage' as a way of overcoming 'the bogey of sociological over determinism' which catches both structuralists and interactionalists. Pilgrimage needs to incorporate both 'long periods of more or less accepted structure (marriage, work, school, family) with phased dramatic crises that are partly structured to produce antistructure' (Frankenberg 1987: 133). A person's life and death are influenced

> not only by the history of their own past and the antecedent biographies of the actors, but also by the conscious and unconscious foreshadowing of the shape of things to come – Sartrean protentions in contrast to retentions (Sartre 1956: 109, n.) – then men and women can still be seen as making their own biography within the framework of past and future mortality.
>
> (ibid.)

If there is danger in too easy generalisation and in the imposition of overarching structures, be they in evolutionary historical stages or individual trajectories, there is also a danger in not recognising the inherent complexity of our subject. Consistent with the overall content of this book we must stress not only the need to recognise differences between and within countries, but differences within the overall subject classification. Cannadine concludes his essay on war, death, grief and mourning in modern Britain thus:

> even in countries as superficially similar as Britain, France and the United States, there are fundamental differences in chronology, in technical developments and in general attitudes. ... the history of dying, of death, of grief, of mourning, of bereavement, of funerals and of cemeteries are all distinct subjects, the relationship between which is at best complex and at worst obscure. ... any attempt to trace the evolution over time of an emotion like grief, or even to generalize about such an emotion at a given time in a given society, is an extraordinarily difficult, if not impossible task. ... the history of death is at least as complicated as the history of life.
>
> (1981: 242)

We might go further. The approach to death in scholarship might be even more flawed. McManners put this well:

> La Rochefoucauld's famous observation: that it is impossible to look directly at the sun or at death applies, in a different sense to its original meaning, to the historian, who when he writes about death always turns out to be writing about something else.
>
> (1981: 130)

Artist Damien Hirst titled his most famous work, a dead shark displayed in a large tank of formaldehyde, 'The Physical Impossibility of Death in the Mind of Someone Living'. While he, and his supporters, claim a continuity between this work and 'the long tradition of art which deals with the issues of life and death' and in so doing challenge what Hirst sees as 'the paranoiac denial of death that permeates our culture' (Stallabrass 1996: 153), it is his title that shows us one way forward. We have to consider the language we use and the way that we cognitively comprehend death. We also have to consider the visceral, the body – Hirst's work at least is unambiguous in engaging with this dimension.

THE PARADOX OF THE LANGUAGE OF DEATH

The debates as to the nature of interpretive inquiry in the social sciences have included much on the nature of language. Without seeking an acceptable explication of the relation between language, action and history we risk seeing the shortcomings of system building and the intrinsic difficulty of focusing on the subject, as described above, condemning us into either inactivity or a retreat to relativism, into compiling lists and engaging in scenic tours through the exotica of different sites of practice.

If writers about death seem to be talking of something else it might be because language is something that 'mediates between the finite historical nature of humankind and the world' (Held 1980: 311; see also Gadamer 1975). As such it is inherently limited. Jacques Derrida argues that cultural life involves texts we produce and that intersect with other texts in such a way that any influence is hard to unravel. Neither our own nor others' texts are settled or stable (Lyon 1994: 13). Not only are things unsettled and unstable but they are characterised by paradoxes and aporias.

In *The Gift of Death* (1995) Derrida seeks to show how the event of death always exceeds our attempts to master its meaning. This is a step further than La Rochefoucauld's observation that we cannot look directly at death. Indeed, to seek to establish some linear connection, such as that we die as a necessary step into eternal life, is to enact the death of mystery in the very endeavour of seeking to engage with the mystery of death. The gift of death contains both promise and danger. It is always excessive and undecidable. It does not place a closure on the meaning of what is given to human thought and experience; rather it remains a secret and a mystery (Derrida 1995).

That secret and mystery may, in part, lie in what Freud identified as the duality of life and death. He saw this as an instinctual ambivalence, in itself a species-specific characteristic and an integral feature of human ideology and culture. From such a view it follows that 'Man [*sic*] is the animal which has separated into conflicting opposites the biological unity of life and death, and has then subjected the conflicting opposites to repression' (Brown 1968: 97). Repression of death occurs both in the individual and in society. In effect our language and our cultural expression act against the reintegration of these parts of the biological unity (Bauman 1992: 8). The consequence is an impoverishment of modern civilisation via the detachment of the death instinct from its necessary interaction with libidinal energy (Giddens 1992: 167).

Freud brings us back into the sphere of modernist system building. It is not that, as with Derrida, we make a mistake in seeking to question mystery using the linear constructs of language – rather it is that the answer to mystery simply lies hidden. One either seeks to live within constraints or to utilise the insights of Freud, as for example Marcuse (1969) has done, to fuse life and death instincts in such a way that allows us to move from repression and denial to a human and social creativity which allows instinctual gratification.

Marcuse went further in that he argued for the necessity of a carefully differentiated analysis of the social totality that goes beyond simply seeking to answer questions about, for example, existence, in terms of 'existence itself'. For Marcuse the division of society into classes was *ipso facto* sufficient justification for this further analysis. We might add, in the context of this book, that gender, ethnic, religious and national differences also impinge on the potential of a simple identification of being in the world (Marcuse 1969).

If the language we use to approach an understanding of death is crucial, so too is a recognition of these objective contexts of social reality. Habermas seeks an acceptable explication of the relation between language, action and history. A plausible critical social theory requires a critique of the truth content of tradition and the nature of how meaning is created and renewed. But it also needs to be located in the practice of the lived world (see Held 1980: 311). Here critical theory is building on the argument developed by Heidegger (1927) that 'being' as opposed to 'truth' was the most appropriate ground for the concerns of philosophers. Further, it is not only in the lived world that social theory has to operate; it is also in the context of the embodied life.

THE BODY AND DIFFERENCE

The body is everywhere today. In popular culture, avant garde art and the social sciences, the human body appears in a variety of forms. In sociology the body is reproducing itself – so to speak – in analyses of consumer culture, gender, sexuality and, of course, health and illness.

(Bury 1995: 36)

The body in such a context is not, of course, a fixed construct. Indeed the volatility of consumer culture can mean that the approved-of body changes rapidly. People are left insecure about their embodied selves (Featherstone 1987). What does not change, though, is that high status is attached to the living, acting, body. Old age brings, for most, a decline in the symbolic value of the body and the dying and dead body is largely hidden.

Featherstone (1991) develops an analysis of the body in consumer culture:

> With appearance being taken as a reflex of the self the penalties of bodily neglect are a lowering of one's acceptability as a person, as well as an indication of laziness, low self-esteem and even moral failure.
>
> (1991: 186)

It is no surprise to find therefore that pain, suffering and death are seen as unwelcome intrusions in the midst of a happy life (Ariès 1974). Indeed there is a detachment of the biological from the social in the body (Elias 1985). Amongst images of comfort, fulfilment and cleanliness, the unpleasant odours and sights surrounding death become intolerable. 'The dirty death' has to be hidden away (Ariès 1981: 568).

That is not to say that the 'body gone wrong' does not occupy a pivotal position. Modernism is, according to Cunningham, haunted by 'vile' bodies. 'The body will not 'simply stay in place as a zone of comfort and joy, of *jouissance'*:

> we are concerned above all with bodies gone wrong, bad bodies, sick bodies, bodies harmed, messed about, disempowered, tortured, mutilated, done to death and otherwise estranged from normal pursuits and happy purposes.
>
> (1996: 15)

In part, in sociology at least, some of this concern draws on the impact of Foucault's narratives of repression which depict the history of western European societies since the seventeenth century as a period in which a series of prohibitions were brought to bear on individuals and their bodies (Smart 1985: 95). But it is also linked with three major themes in modernity. First, if one rejects transcendence, then all there is left to rely on is the body, 'our meaning, our text, our final signifier, our place of ultimate signification.' Second, 'body theory is sustained by, as it endorses, that pronounced body narcissism and solipsism that so mark our modernity' (Cunningham 1996: 15). The third theme is the argument that we are increasingly associated with our bodies because of the sweeping away of those traditional certainties that gave people a stable sense of self-identity (Giddens 1991).

But aren't people different? The problem with much writing about the body and about the mind is that it is not sufficiently grounded in either history or anthropology. Nor does it allow for an explanation of the way that different people, ostensibly within the same cultural space, experience death (and life) in such different ways. Shilling directs us to Bourdieu, and his identification of 'habitus', as a route to explain variations between 'similar' people. Habitus is a set of dispositions, created and reformulated through the conjuncture of objective structures and personal history and knowledge. Shilling hypothesises that:

> For example, we might expect the prospect of bodily demise and death to vary for people as a consequence of the time and effort they have invested in their bodies as a source of symbolic capital.
>
> (1993: 187)

It is also likely that people will differ according to both the extent and the way in which they cognitively comprehend death. Most clearly age is a factor. Much work has been done to identify stages of death comprehension in children (Nagy 1959) and, although there is not a corresponding developmental theory, there is some work on changes in adult constructions of death (Kastenbaum 1992). It is also evident that different cultures structure the cognitive conceptualisation of death in varied ways. Kastenbaum offers a salutary warning to those who might contemplate their own view as the most mature:

> There are as many kinds of 'mature' constructions of death as there are ethnophilosophical orientations towards life. Then again we might just decide that 'maturity' is a term to be used with great caution when applied to a topic that so challenges the limits of human thought and knowledge. Do we really know death so well that we can say that somebody else's construction is 'immature'.
>
> (1992: 115)

While we must engage with these differences of habitus and comprehension there is also a need to deconstruct a too-easy juxtaposition of death, dying and the dead. Consider an influential argument present in the social theory of high or late modernity that a privatisation of life is replicated in death: 'Progress has to exclude death by relegating it to the private sphere of the individual' (Redner 1982: 34). There is a recognition, of course, that one cannot escape death but that one can seek to escape particular causes of death. 'Death as such is inevitable, but each instance of death is contingent. Death is omnipotent and invincible, but none of the specific cases of death is' (Bauman 1992: 5).

Each death is 'from something' and, by inference, that something could be delayed or avoided. Given this, we enter what Canetti (1973) called a 'survival mode'. In this we do not live through our own death but through the death of others. It is a sinister scenario. The death of others gives meaning to our own success; we are still alive. The desire for a long life really means wanting to outlive one's contemporaries. 'Survival needs constant reassurance; and the only convincing reassurance is the death of others; not me' (see Bauman 1992: 11).

We have, therefore, a separation of dying and death. It is dying that is to be avoided. I will seek to avoid, either practically or conceptually, dying of one or another thing. For example, I may believe that if I exercise I will not have a heart attack, or I may believe that people like me don't have AIDS. These approaches are ways of making death contingent. Within such a scenario death is, indeed, privatised but dying is both privatised and drawn into a professionalised paradigm occupied by the medical profession. Doctors do not fight mortality but mortal diseases. 'A death that has not been prevented does not undermine the authority of the medical profession. At worst it may stain the reputation of an individual doctor' (Bauman 1992: 6).

The dead are a further category. They are kept at a distance in what Baudrillard called the first ghettos, the archetypal ghetto and the pattern for all ghettos to come – the cemetery (Baudrillard 1993). It might be that we seek to keep the dead at a distance and in so doing negate the threat they offer, but the site of exclusion is not very secure; 'haunted lives testify to the porousness of cemetery walls' (Bauman 1992: 2).

But perhaps the cemetery is no longer a ghetto; the ghetto has taken over the modern world.

The cemetery no longer exists because modern cities have entirely taken over their function; they are ghost towns, cities of death. If the great operational metropolis is the final form of an entire culture, then, quite simply, ours is a culture of death.

(Baudrillard 1993: 127)

Baudrillard is engaged in a debate with the founding figures of sociology as he seeks to assert the superiority of the symbolic over the semiotic, the obligation of the gift over the cash nexus, while witnessing the apparent destruction of the former by the latter. In writing about death he identifies the destruction of the original unities of life and death and the rituals which integrated the relations between generations in traditional society.

There is an irreversible evolution from savage societies to our own; little by little, the dead cease to exist. They are thrown out of the group's symbolic circulation ... we no longer know what to do with them, since, today, it is not normal to be dead, and this is new ... Death is a delinquency.

(ibid.: 126)

Death only ends active involvement in the life of the living, and death, albeit social death, can occur when a person is still alive. Perhaps 'death is a process not an event'. This expression was used in a recent TV programme by the Chaplain of St Christopher's Hospice, London, who spoke of how he sees a time both before and after death in the hospice when the person exists in a different way (*Everyman*, BBC TV, 11 February 1996).

When a condemned person moves from the cells to the execution chamber in a US prison, a guard shouts out 'dead man walking' and all on the route turn away. The 1995 Tim Robbins film, *Dead Man Walking*, based on Helen Prejean's book, offers in its depiction of the events surrounding this occurrence a particularly striking example of the phenomenon of social death (Prejean 1995). The fictional story 'Things to do in Denver when you are dead' (directed by Gary Fleder, 1995) has as a central location a business that records the words of the dying on video to play back to their children when they need guidance in their lives. The film's protagonists are a group of criminals condemned to death by another criminal and its narrative concerns the way they come to terms with their self-perceived and other-perceived social death (to borrow Kalish's 1985 distinction).

Social death has been explored since Glaser and Strauss (1965) described how a 'hopelessly comatose' hospital patient was treated as 'merely a body'. In such situations it can be argued that people cease to exist socially before they are biologically dead (see Sudnow 1967). Perhaps sometimes such changes are best described as interactional, sought as well as imposed. Kalish (1985) offered a distinction between self-perceived and other-perceived social death. It may also be that after a person has died they still play a part in the social world of the living. Mulkay (1993: 33) cites an example of distraught parents regularly visiting the grave of a dead child where they talk of their previous life together and the reunion to come. An involvement by the biological dead in the life of the living is surely not restricted to the dramatic and distraught. Many of us might 'converse' with the assumed views of the dead as we contemplate the trials and triumphs of life.

A further area of complexity arises if we consider those who die but whose bodies are not found, or are not found for some time after death. This is a phenomenon characteristic of many deaths in war; 'missing in action' and the 'tomb of the unknown soldier' are two expressive ways in which the experience has been framed. But it is not something exclusive to war. Marian Partington has written a poignant account of her sister Lucy who disappeared in 1973, then aged 21. For many years Lucy's family and friends, as well as the authorities, searched for her. No trace of Lucy was found and twenty years after her disappearance the family met together to plant a tree in her memory. In 1994 it became clear that Lucy had been murdered and her body buried by multi-murderers Fred and Rosemary West early in 1974. Marian tells us:

> My sister was murdered; she was one of the Wests' victims. It makes my throat ache. It was easier to say, 'My sister disappeared', but more difficult to live with that sense of unresolved loss.
>
> (Partington 1996)

Death and the dead, indeed death and the body, cannot too easily be assumed as synonymous.

Marian Partington's story reminds us that the avoidance of death characteristic of much of contemporary life is challenged by the specifics of individual experiences. Perhaps the place death has in anyone's life resembles having children, or being burgled: you don't pay too much attention to it and then when it happens to you it seems to be happening to everybody you know. Blake Morrison describes how, after the death of his father, everything he seemed to come across offered some parallel to his recent consuming experiences. 'It makes me feel I've been caught up in a *Zeitgeist* of morbidity, a sickly *fin-de-siècle* where death is the only theme ever discussed' (1993: 210).

CONCLUSION: FROM THE SOCIOLOGICAL TO THE ONTOLOGICAL

We have then a culture of death, but a symbolic existence that excludes the dead. Further, as we have seen above, in a society dominated by a survival mode we have decided that dying is what other people do. Neither the mortality of the body nor the psychic need to engage with death has overcome that observed historical trend to suppress death, dying and the dead. But I have also argued that scholarship which identifies a grand scheme of things is flawed for three fundamental reasons. First, because it does not recognise the diversity that has been so identified in other parts of this book. Second, it does not, in terms of Habermas's schema for what makes an adequate social theory, engage with a critique of the truth content of tradition and the nature of how meaning is created and renewed. Third, in its modernist rationality it does not allow us to explore, or cross over, the epistemological break that the end of embodied life entails. It is not just the limitation of language and the modernist concern with truth as opposed to being, but it is the reluctance to go as far as Derrida or Baudrillard would take us – that is, into an aporetic and paradoxical discourse of death and life.

Death and difference is both social and individual. Bourdieu helps here with 'habitus', an invaluable concept when it comes to locating differences between individuals in apparently similar social situations (see Robbins 1991). But we need something a little more visceral. If it is not normal to be dead when we consider social discourse or individual self-perception, we have to live in a world where everyone dies. We have to incorporate a concern with *being* embodied and *becoming* dead. There is a point where the sociological succumbs to the ontological but an ontological which has been changed, at postmodernism's insistence, to identify meaning in what is missing (Bourke 1996). Many writers have sought to underline how death, the dying and the dead are missing. What is also missing is grand narrative. We are now concerned with perspectives and positionings and with the deconstruction of categories. As contributors to this book have illustrated, we must engage with death and difference. This final chapter has sought to illustrate how it is different being dead not only in terms of social practice but also in social theory.

REFERENCES

Airhihenbuwa, C.O. (1995) *Health and Culture: Beyond the Western Paradigm*, London: Sage.

Ariès, P. (1974) *Western Attitudes Towards Death*, Baltimore: Johns Hopkins University Press.

—— (1981) *The Hour of Our Death*, New York: Knopf.

Baudrillard, J. (1993) *Symbolic Exchange and Death*, London: Sage.

Bauman, Z. (1992) 'Survival as a social construct', in M. Featherstone (ed.) *Cultural Theory and Cultural Change*, London: Sage, pp. 1–36.

Bourke, J. (1996) *Dismembering the Male: Men's Bodies, Britain and the Great War*, London: Reaktion Books.

Brown, N. O. (1968) *Life Against Death*, London: Sphere Books.

Bury, M. (1995) 'The body in question', *Medical Sociology News* 25 (1): 36–48.

Canetti, E. (1973) *Crowds and Power*, Harmondsworth: Penguin.

Cannadine, D. (1981) 'War and death, grief and mourning in modern Britain', in J. Whaley (ed.) *Mirrors of Mortality. Studies in the Social History of Death*, London: Europa Publications Ltd, pp. 187–242.

Cunningham, V. (1996) 'Vile bodies', *Times Higher Education Supplement* 8 March: 15.

Derrida, J. (1995) *The Gift of Death*, Chicago: University of Chicago Press.

Edwards, E. (1995) 'Seeing how "others die", in V. Williams and G. Hobson, *The Dead*, Bradford: National Museum of Photography, Film and Television, pp. 28–35.

Elias, N. (1985) *The Loneliness of Dying*, Oxford: Basil Blackwell.

Featherstone, M. (1987) 'Leisure, symbolic power and the life course', in J. Horne, D. Jary and A. Tomlinson (eds) *Sport, Leisure and Social Relations*, London: Routledge & Kegan Paul.

—— (1991) 'The body in consumer culture', in M. Featherstone, M. Hepworth and B. S. Turner (eds) *The Body*, London: Sage, pp. 170–96.

Feifel, H. (ed.) (1959) *The Meaning of Death*, New York: McGraw Hill.

Frankenberg, R. (1987) 'Life: cycle, trajectory or pilgrimage? A social production approach to Marxism, metaphor and mortality', in A. Bryman, B. Bytheway, P. Allatt and T. Keil (eds) *Rethinking the Life Cycle*, London: Macmillan, pp. 122–380.

Gadamer, H.-G. (1975) *Truth and Method*, London: Sheed & Ward.

Giddens, A. (1991) *Modernity and Self-Identity*, Cambridge: Polity Press.
—— (1992) *The Transformation of Intimacy*, Cambridge: Polity Press.
Glaser, B. G. and Strauss, A. L. (1965) *Awareness of Dying*, Chicago: Aldine.
Gorer, P. (1965) *Death, Grief and Mourning in Contemporary Britain*, London: Cresset.
Heidegger, M. (1927) *Being and Time*, New York: Harper & Row.
Held, D. (1980) *Introduction to Critical Theory*, London: Hutchinson.
Hockey, J. (1996) 'The view from the west: reading the anthropology of non-western death ritual', in G. Howarth and P. C. Jupp (eds) *Contemporary Issues in the Sociology of Death, Dying and Disposal*, Basingstoke: Macmillan, pp. 3–16.
Illich, I. (1995) *Limits to Medicine*, Harmondsworth: Penguin.
Jenkins, K. (1995) *On 'What is History?'*, London: Routledge.
Kalish, R. A. (1985) *Death, Grief and Caring Relationships*, Monterey, CA: Brooks Cole.
Kastenbaum, R. (1992) *The Psychology of Death* (2nd edn), New York: Springer Publishing Co.
Kubler-Ross, E. (1970) *On Death and Dying*, London: Tavistock.
Littlewood, J. (1993) 'The denial of death and rites of passage in contemporary societies', in D. Clark (ed.) *The Sociology of Death*, Oxford: Blackwell, pp. 69–84.
Lyon, D. (1994) *Postmodernism*, Buckingham: Open University Press.
McManners, J. (1981) 'Death and the French historians', in J. Whaley (ed.) *Mirrors of Mortality*, London: Europa, pp. 106–30.
Marcuse, H. (1969) 'Contributions to a phenomenology of historical materialism', *Telos* 4: 64–76.
Mellor, P. (1993) 'Death in high modernity: the contemporary presence and absence of death', in D. Clark (ed.) *The Sociology of Death*, Oxford: Blackwell, pp. 11–30.
Morrison, B. (1993) *'And when did you last see your father?'* London: Granta Books.
Mulkay, M. (1993) 'Social death in Britain', in D. Clark (ed.) *The Sociology of Death*, Oxford: Blackwell.
Nagy, M. (1959) 'The child's view of death', in H. Feifel (ed.) *The Meaning of Death*, New York: McGraw Hill, pp. 79–98.
Partington, M. (1996) 'Salvaging the Sacred', *The Guardian Weekend*, 18 May: 14–23.
Prejean, H. (1995) *Dead Man Walking*, London: Fount.
Redner, H. (1982) *In the Beginning was the Deed: Reflections on the Passage of Faust*, Berkeley: University of California Press.
Robbins, D. (1991) *The Work of Pierre Bourdieu*, Milton Keynes: Open University Press.
Said, E. (1978) *Orientalism*, London: Routledge & Kegan Paul.
Sartre, J.-P. (1956) *Being and Nothingness*, New York: Philosophical Library.
Saunders, C. (1967) *The Management of Terminal Illness*, London: Hospital Medicine Publications.
Shilling, C. (1993) *The Body and Social Theory*, London: Sage.

Smart, B. (1985) *Michel Foucault*, London: Tavistock.

Sontag, S. (1977) *Illness as Metaphor*, Harmondsworth: Penguin.

Stallabrass, J. (1996) 'In and out of love with Damien Hirst', *New Left Review* 216: 153–60.

Strauss, A., Fagerhaugh, S., Suczek, B. and Weiner, C. (1985) *Social Organisation of Medical Work*, Chicago: University of Chicago Press.

Sudnow, D. (1967) *Passing On: the Social Organisation of Dying*, Englewood Cliffs, NJ: Prentice Hall.

Walter, T. (1994) *The Revival of Death*, London: Routledge.

—— (1995) 'Natural death and the noble savage', *Omega*, 30 (4): 237–48.

—— (1996) 'Facing death without tradition', in G. Howarth and P. C. Jupp (eds) *Contemporary Issues in the Sociology of Death, Dying and Disposal*, Basingstoke: Macmillan.

Whaley, J. (ed.) (1981) *Mirrors of Mortality. Studies in the Social History of Death*, London: Europa Publications Ltd.

Index